# NINETEENTH-CENTURY COLONIALISM AND THE GREAT INDIAN REVOLT

This book examines the ruptured characteristics of colonialism in nineteenth-century India. It connects the British East India Company's efforts at the bourgeoization of India with the Revolt of 1857. The volume shows how the mutiny of Indian sepoys in the British Indian Army became a popular uprising of peasants, artisans and discontented aristocrats against the British. Tracing the rationale and consequences of this conflict, the monograph highlights how newly introduced political, economic and agrarian policies, as part of industrial Britain's colonial policy, wreaked havoc, resulting in high land revenue assessment and its harsh mode of collection, rural indebtedness, steady immiseration of peasants, widespread land alienation, destitution and suicide.

Using rare archival sources, this book will be an important intervention in the study of nineteenth-century India, and will deeply interest scholars and researchers of modern Indian history and politics.

**Amit Kumar Gupta** is Research Consultant at the Indian Council of Historical Research (ICHR), New Delhi, India.

# NINETEENTH-CENTURY COLONIALISM AND THE GREAT INDIAN REVOLT

*Amit Kumar Gupta*

NEW DELHI  LONDON  NEW YORK

First published 2016
by Routledge
2 Park Square, Milton Park, Abingdon, Oxon OX14 4RN

and by Routledge
711 Third Avenue, New York, NY 10017

*Routledge is an imprint of the Taylor & Francis Group, an informa business*

© 2016 Amit Kumar Gupta

The right of Amit Kumar Gupta to be identified as author of this work has been asserted by him in accordance with sections 77 and 78 of the Copyright, Designs and Patents Act 1988.

All rights reserved. No part of this book may be reprinted or reproduced or utilised in any form or by any electronic, mechanical, or other means, now known or hereafter invented, including photocopying and recording, or in any information storage or retrieval system, without permission in writing from the publishers.

*Trademark notice*: Product or corporate names may be trademarks or registered trademarks, and are used only for identification and explanation without intent to infringe.

*British Library Cataloguing-in-Publication Data*
A catalogue record for this book is available from the British Library

*Library of Congress Cataloging-in-Publication Data*
A catalog record has been requested for this book

ISBN: 978-1-138-93544-0 (hbk)
ISBN: 978-1-315-67694-4 (ebk)

Typeset in Sabon
by Apex CoVantage, LLC

In
memory of
my mother.

# CONTENTS

|   |   |   |
|---|---|---|
| *Acknowledgements* | | ix |
| *List of abbreviations* | | xi |
| | Antescript | 1 |
| 1 | For bourgeoization | 7 |
| 2 | Against feudalism | 46 |
| 3 | For Rent Theory | 73 |
| 4 | Against peasantry | 95 |
| 5 | For confrontation | 117 |
| 6 | Against qualitative change | 140 |
| | Postscript | 167 |
| | *Glossary* | 175 |
| | *Bibliography* | 181 |
| | *Index* | 191 |

# ACKNOWLEDGEMENTS

I am grateful to Professor Mushirul Husan, ex–Vice Chancellor of Jamia Millia Islamia, New Delhi, for offering me a Visiting Professorship (2009–10), and thus enabling me to undertake the research for this book. I am also thankful to the then Director, Professor Shakti Kak, and other colleagues at the Centre for Jawaharlal Nehru Studies, Noam Chomsky Complex, Jamia Millia Islamia, where I had been placed as Visiting Professor, for allowing me to do full-time research on the book for two years without any encumbrance.

I am much obliged to Professor Suman Gupta of the British Open University, the United Kingdom, for going through the typescript of this book, making useful observations and suggesting improvements; as well as to Dr Maya Gupta, formerly of the Nehru Trust Fund and the Nehru Memorial Museum and Library, New Delhi, for helping me to get over a few of my confusions and doubts during the time of its drafting. I am beholden indeed, to the Indian Council of Historical Research, New Delhi, for awarding me a Foreign Travel Grant to facilitate my consultation of some of the valuable sources for this study in Britain. My thanks are due to the authorities and staff of the India Office Records, British Library, and the University of Roehampton Library, London; the National Archives of India, the Nehru Memorial Museum and Library and the Indian Council of Historical Research Library, New Delhi; and the National Library and the Asiatic Society Library, Kolkata. I must also thank my fellow young researchers in the Dictionary of Martyrs project, Indian

## ACKNOWLEDGEMENTS

Council of Historical Research — Rajesh Kumar, Ashfaque Ali, Mod. Naushad Ali, Shakeeb Athar and Md. Niyas A. — for keeping me intellectually energized and running errands to take care of the slightest of my needs. I should by no means fail to express here my gratitude to Devendra Singh Bisht for his efficient typing and clerical assistance.

I must also record here how gratified I am to Routledge India, New Delhi, for the methodical and smooth way they have gone about producing this distinctive publication.

# ABBREVIATIONS

| | |
|---|---|
| Br. | Branch |
| Cons. | Consultation |
| Dept. | Department |
| Gov. Gen. | Governor General |
| IO/BL | India Office/British Library |
| Lt. Gov. | Lieutenant Governor |
| NAI | National Archives of India |
| NWP | North-Western Provinces |
| PP | Parliamentary Papers |
| Proc. | Proceedings |
| Rev. Br. | Revenue Branch |
| Secy. | Secretary |

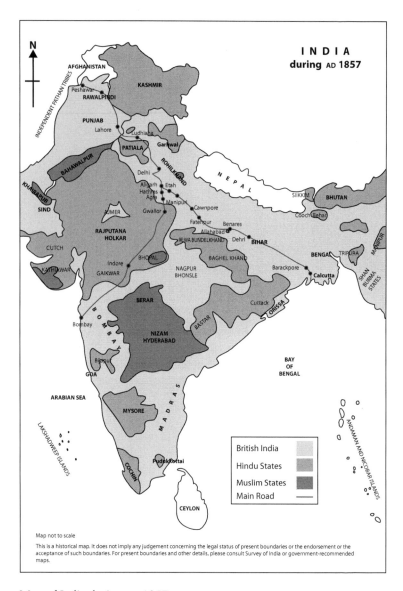

Map of India during AD 1857

# ANTESCRIPT

As one who has tried, over a considerable period, to understand some of the 20th-century developments in India, especially between the 1910s and the 1960s, the author of this study has often felt perplexed at the contrarieties and cross-currents this field presents, and the manner in which contradictions tend to become neutralized therein. In socio-economic and political terms, India did make, under British rule, considerable progress from the mid-18th century onwards, and at the end of the 19th century seemed poised — even as a colony — to become a modern state of substance and energy. Curiously enough, however, by the beginning of the 20th century, India was found to be suffering from debilitating incongruities: it had entered into the modern age, but could not break from medieval shackles; it had been brought into a technological era, but depended mainly on the cultivation of land (some degree of industrialization had been initiated, but India remained agro-economic in the main); it had stepped on to the path of bourgeois progress, but remained largely a source of raw materials and a market for British manufacturers. India was encouraged to continue with counterpoising conflicting modes of economic production: the domineering capitalist one that industrial Britain prompted, and the declining feudal one that imperial Britain thought it prudent to retain and protect. This curious coexistence of the capitalist and the feudal systems in the economy of India had in effect subjected its people to exploitation by both metropolitan capitalists and indigenous aristocratic and landlordist elements.

Generally, the appropriation of social surplus by native feudal forces was directly through their rack-renting of land, exaction of irregular levies and tolls, and extraction of forced labour (*corvée*), as well as the compounding of interest which creditors (money-lenders in the main, but also landlords) charged on indebted peasants, resulting in large-scale alienation of their lands and in their being engaged primarily in subsistence agriculture. Unlike such straightforward feudal means, the capitalist mode of social appropriation was a roundabout one. Capitalist Britain ruled by operating an unequal trading arrangement whereby India was made to export raw materials and foodstuffs, and import British-manufactured goods, and that too on terms favourable to manufacturers in Britain and expatriate investors (in plantations and mines, for example) in India.[1] The heavy bias in exports of raw materials and imports of manufactured goods thus meant that, through the instrumentality of foreign trade, India was being subjected to an unequal division of labour — between Britain and India — where manufactures generated high productivity (because of the use of machinery) and high payment for less labour, while agricultural produce showed low productivity (because of the use of poor technology) and low payment for more labour. Besides, foreign trade was run internationally in the 19th century by traders abroad cornering profits directly through trading practices, as well as indirectly through their control of the mechanism of trade, i.e., shipping, banking, insurance and internal transportation. Moreover, the basics of Indian export trade, such as tea, coffee, indigo, jute, textiles and minerals, were the products of the application of foreign capital, and therefore, most of the profits from their manufacture and export were pocketed by foreign capitalists, leaving little for Indians. At the same time, India was compelled to maintain a constantly rising export surplus from foodstuffs and raw materials, without much of a return, to cope with the exportation of profits of British merchants and capitalists and the savings and pensions of British civil servants (the Government of India's 'Home Charges' amounting in the early 1880s to 4.14 per cent of the Indian national income).[2]

The working of the imperio-capitalist system, on the one hand, and the continuance of the feudal-landlordist arrangement on the other, had a very adverse effect on the prospects of the Indian economy and on the well-being of the Indian people. For Indians, it was hard enough to cope with imperio-capitalist modes of exploitation, and their hardship more than doubled when they had to simultaneously endure feudal exploitative operations.

However, this mode of double exploitation, and the enormity of the difficulties it brought about, was by no stretch of imagination an Indian imperative or the logical outcome of the country's social history. Historically, feudalism had not only been found to be a backward economic process compared to industrial capitalism, but also an inferior productive mechanism which was undermined and supplanted by the capitalization or bourgeoization of society — including its metropolitan variety — to ensure growth and dynamism. A full-fledged capitalist society, therefore, would hardly co-exist with the continuation of feudal practices, except in their moribund state till their unhurried absorption in or drastic replacement by capitalism. None of these situations seems to have prevailed in 19th-century India, leaving both the growing forces of capitalism and the unrelenting clutches of feudalism to persist and work side by side rather than against each other, leading to a certain hybrid, perverse and disjointed socio-economic configuration. Such tolerant and peaceful complementarity of the two discordant and antithetical exploitative methods — one medieval and another modern — seems utterly incomprehensible if one considers the British industrial capitalists' natural tendency for monopolizing the extraction of social surpluses from their vast and resourceful colony, and not sharing it with anybody else, and certainly not with the parasitical native feudal elements living on unearned income.

The natural tendency of the British bourgeoisie seems to have been evidenced in India in the first half of the 19th century. Their main agency in the colony (the Companyraj) had evinced an

# ANTESCRIPT

antagonistic design on Indian princes, chiefs and the ruling families, as was apparent from its flouting of their treaty rights and jurisdictions, interfering with their successions and functioning, foisting British armies upon their kingdoms, and forcibly annexing their territories on some pretext or the other. The Companyraj's anti-feudal proclivity was discernible from the manner in which it treated the landlords, questioning the legality of their authority over vast stretches of lands, enjoyment of freedom from tax on a substantial amount of holdings, exercise of magisterial and police powers, imposition of certain dues and levies over and above squeezing rent out of the tenants, and failure to carry out agricultural improvements and increase in outputs. It was not in the interest of the British or imperial capitalists to see India suffer under feudalism or be stultified by it; instead they wanted India to be turned into 'a reproductive country',[3] producing its own sustenance, readying its bounties to be gathered by the metropolitans in the main. India's productivity in raw material had to be boosted infrastructurally by unfolding the country's natural resources, providing irrigational facilities, improving means of conveyance and reinforcing the exchange of the produce. At the same time, India had to be developed to a necessary extent so as to be able to perform as an increasingly vast market for finished products — almost without competition. Such 'opening up' of India (for its own good, and of course, immensely more so for industrialized Britain) had to occur concurrently with the bourgeoization (or modernization or Westernization) of a medievalistic, status-quoist feudal society. The imperialist capitalists from Britain had to perform a double mission in India: 'one destructive, the other regenerating'[4] — the dismemberment of its traditional social fabric, and laying the foundation of a modern one in its stead.

Despite their steady loss of strength, and though placed at a disadvantage, the nobility and landed magnates tried hard to resist the imperial bourgeoisie's mounting pressure. They waged political and legal battles in defence of their ever-deteriorating position, sympathized with the sepoys in their mutiny against the Companyraj, took up arms on the rebel side, and fought and led the fighting in the civil war of 1857–58. The Indian feudal elements and the British bourgeoisie were thus placed so antagonistically against each other in the subcontinent by the middle of the 19th century that any rapprochement between the two seemed impossible. And the whole issue, it appeared at that juncture, could only be settled with the uprooting of feudalism in India, paving the way for the country's advancement on bourgeois entrepreneurial lines. The demise of feudalism and the rise of capitalism from its deathbed presented themselves to be so axiomatic that nobody could dream of the slightest alteration of any kind in the situation. And yet, to the amazement of all, a dramatic change was brought about through the enactment of an *entente* between the forces of capitalist development and those of feudal underdevelopment. By the 1860s, the Indian people were subjected suddenly to the dual control of metropolitan capitalism and indigenous feudalism — a joint venture of both the external and the internal exploiters, the senior and the junior partners, to take scrupulous care of each other's interest and well-being.

It is not unusual in history for an imperialist power to lean upon certain influential categories of people in a subject country to facilitate its domination over the multifarious and multitudinous rest. But such an alignment has generally been put into practice for a short period, primarily to tide over the difficulties at a certain phase, and not for a long duration or in permanence as a part and parcel of the imperialist strategy. The author of the present study was, therefore, much exercised by the evidence of a long and unbelievably durable partnership between imperialist Britain and feudal India, which persisted for about a century (ninety years to be precise) or till the end of British rule in India. It withstood several ups and downs, the offensive (more against the imperialists than the feudal elements) of the educated, articulate middle classes, the resentment and resistance of the early nationalists of both 'moderate' and 'extremist' varieties, and the challenges of the flamboyant militants among them. More significantly, the *entente* survived the huge, uproarious waves of Gandhian mass movements, and succeeded in dealing with the liberal opposition in legislative assemblies and with the agitations of the *praja mandal*s in the Indian states,[5] and was able largely to frustrate the massive mobilizations of the *kisan*s, *majdoor*s, youths and students.

At every point, the collaborative senior and junior partners worked in unison and offered a helping hand to one another. The aristocrats and landlords, for example, were the forerunners of the Indian loyalists who stood behind the British war efforts in the two World Wars, discouraged participation of the people generally in nationalist agitations against the British Raj, backed up all its legislative and administrative measures regardless of merits, and competed among themselves to curry favour and earn the title of 'Rai Bahadur' and 'Khan Bahadur'. The Raj, illustratively on its part, did not hesitate to send British armed contingents to quell popular unrest within the Indian states, to undertake severe repression to counter peasant struggles against the landlords, and to turn a blind eye to the landed magnates' extraction of *begar*, enforcement of *salami*, collection of *nazrana* and imposition of *abwab*.

Considering the very long duration of the *entente* between imperial and feudal forces, and its effects on the socio-economic and political fortunes of the Indian people, the author of this present study felt compelled to try — despite doubts and fumblings — to find out how had it been formed, why, and under what circumstances.

## Notes

1 For elucidation of this and other issues, see Bipan Chandra, *Essays on Colonialism*, Orient Blackswan, New Delhi, 2009.
2 Irfan Habib, *Essays in Indian History: Towards a Marxist Perception*, Tulika, New Delhi, 1995, p. 279.
3 Iqbal Husain, Irfan Habib and Prabhat Patnaik, *Karl Marx on India*, Tulika, New Delhi, 2006, p. 47.
4 *Ibid.*, p. 46.
5 For definitions of all non-English terms used in this work, please see the Glossary at the end of the book.

# 1
# FOR BOURGEOIZATION

India's initiation into the modern world of the West drew upon a long process of bourgeoization in Britain. The process occupied more than a century of British history (from the middle of the 17th century and through the 18th), and marked, on the one hand, the collapse of the old relations of production, and the emergence, on the other, of new industrial capitalism. Industrial capitalism in Britain was the result of the British bourgeoisie's steady rise in prosperity through a spurt of their export manufactures, showing an increase of 76 per cent between 1700 and 1750, and 80 per cent between 1750 and 1770.[1] To cope with such phenomenal increase, industrial entrepreneurs had to go all out to capture foreign markets with the help of an aggressive Government under their influence, and use the means of war and colonization to control the export market of a large part of the world. The rate at which Britain was able to expand its elaborate export market rendered the creation of a centralized, large-scale production system not only a matter of entrepreneurial convenience, but also one of sheer survival.

It was the Industrial Revolution that came to Britain's rescue, and together with transforming the country's economic structure, it marked the remarkable British success in the latter half of the 18th century in dealing with the challenge of growth (according to the idiom of the time, 'either you grow or you go down') and making a spectacular breakthrough. The breakthrough coincided with the domination of mineral energy over fuel, and it was catapulted by ingenious technological inventions (from the flying shuttle in 1738, the spinning jenny, 1764, and spinning rollers in 1769; to the spinning mule, 1799, and the power loom, 1785; culminating in James Watt's steam engine in 1785) used thoughtfully in the leading sector of the British economy — cotton textiles. The cotton mill was the precursor of an industrial age characterized soon by factories and chimneys, smelting plants and blast furnaces, the man/woman and the machine. Coupled with the beginnings of the chemical (gas lighting and chlorine bleaching) and engineering (capital goods manufacturing) industries, the Industrial Revolution brought into play a new method of mass production in Britain that successfully warded off the threat posed by an unprecedented growth of population in the entire continent — the haunting spectre of the Malthusian generation. According to the Census Report of 1851, about ten million people were added to the British population in the previous fifty years,[2] and the population grew in England by 280 per cent between 1550 and 1820.[3] Such a high rate of increase in population could have pressurized the country's available resources and jeopardized the prevailing standard of living of its people. That it did not do so was primarily because of the impact of the Industrial Revolution, resulting in a steady rise of real incomes per head, and in the growth of Britain's gross national product at the fastest and the highest rate in Europe.[4] The Industrial Revolution also introduced a new economic relationship within the British society, showing the way the machine could obediently serve the spirit of humankind, dwarf the standing of ordinary mortals, and signal the triumph of capital over labour.

Almost as profoundly as within Great Britain (Britain indeed was fast becoming 'great' by then), the Industrial Revolution and its chief promoters and beneficiaries — the bourgeoisie and the 'middling elements' — shaped British interactions with other European and non-European countries, with the colonized world, and with India in particular. Together they succeeded in overriding the bounds of the mercantilist system, especially such of its fundamentals as Britain's accumulation of bullion by incentivizing export and restricting import, by discouraging manufacturing in a colony, and by holding all commerce with the colony as the metropolitan country's exclusive preserve. The newly dominant industrial and financial capitalists in Britain — those who started harnessing the forces of the Industrial Revolution — did not find the manner in which India was being ruled up to 1820 (signifying British mastery over the country at the fall of the Marathas) to be satisfactory either for the Indians or even for themselves. The East India Company's rule over India so far had been based on monopoly trade with the colony (vis-à-vis other European companies and Indian traders and producers), as well as the collection of revenue from the subjugated people. Gains from the earnings and the profiteering were used for waging wars, maintaining trading posts and purchasing colonial products (India did not import many British goods then), and paying merchants, Company shareholders and the British exchequer. Since the appropriation of social surplus through the purchase of Indian handicrafts and agricultural products (under buyers' monopoly) and through the control of revenue had been rather uncomplicated, there was little need for effecting basic socio-economic and administrative changes in the country. Except in the army and in land administration, where changes were needed for the advancement of the military machine and to optimize the squeezing out of revenue, respectively, the British had not undertaken any significant or far-reaching reform. Consequently, they had had no reason up to this stage to quarrel with the prevailing feudal system: the then mode of production and the state of society and polity. It was in effect a myopic one-way traffic — a relentless drawing upon India's resources and produce without heed for its productivity, a continuous draining of the country without allowing it opportunities for recuperation. It was too short-sighted an approach to make use of a subjugated India for British imperial purpose, too predatory to let the country be plundered, bled and 'undersold'.[5]

The newly dominant bourgeoisie in Britain had started about this time to realize the advantage of protecting their long-term interests in India by allowing it to survive, to replenish and turn itself into 'a reproductive country',[6] so as to preserve the proverbial goose for laying golden eggs. They wanted colonial India to reproduce for its own welfare, but more importantly to contribute to the sustenance

FOR BOURGEOIZATION

of capitalist Britain: for upholding its economy, and working in concert with it within an emerging world capitalist set-up. India must, therefore, be opened up for absorption of its bounties by British capital — to serve as an ongoing supplier of raw materials for British industries, as well as an outlet for their finished products. They desired India to be bourgeoized by the supersession of the feudal mode of production with the capitalist order, and simultaneously modernized by the supplantation of the medieval outlook with a rationalized world view.

I

Among those bourgeois ideologues who were concerned about the British-Indian possessions and took a keen interest in these, the most prominent were radical theoreticians such as Jeremy Bentham and James Mill, and aggressive religionists like Charles Grant and William Wilberforce. In the first half of the 19th century, Bentham in particular influenced a significant number of fine intellects, like Francis Burdell, John Cartwright, John Bowring, Perronet Thompson, Thomas Malthus and David Ricardo, and, most importantly, James Mill. Together they propelled a Benthamite intellectual movement (Utilitarianism) whose watchwords — i.e., the attainment of 'the greatest happiness for the greatest number' in the society — dominated the juridical, politico-economic and administrative discourses in Britain. Both the founder (Bentham) and the high priest (Mill) of the denomination committed themselves to the reformation of India on the lines of bourgeois development and in support of industrial Britain. Their urgency for reforming India to match British expectations was based on the understanding that the country was in a pre-modern stage, geared to a feudal social structure (euphemistically termed 'oriental despotism'), and stuck within a medieval state of society — much worse than in Europe's darkest feudal age. Indian society was built upon 'tormenting superstition' and kept 'harassed and degraded' under a vast political and religious tyranny.[7] The Utilitarian diagnosis of India's ills was somewhat similar to what the Evangelicals of the Clapham sect, in alliance with manufacturing and commercial interests,[8] had detected: i.e., the 'despotic' nature of society and state in India and the unrestrained domination of the 'crafty and imperious priesthood'.[9] But the similarity did not go beyond these findings, and the Evangelicals and the Utilitarians differed widely in their approaches towards the solution of the Indian problem. Evangelicals saw India's salvation through evangelization — a kind of European Christian Reformation — which could free an ignorant, 'lamentably degenerate' society from the clutches of the priestly exploiters.[10] Since the blessings of Christianity were not only spiritual upliftment but also material progress, the advances of the Christian West needed to be assiduously followed up in India, and the Western mind had to be implanted in the Indian soil. For achieving all this, and in preparing Indians for the inculcation of true Christian values, to get rid of their superstitions and untruths, it was imperative to 'educate' them, i.e., to introduce them to Western education. The spread of English education, therefore, became a priority for Evangelical activism in India — a missionary cause less objectionable to the authorities in India, but more useful for converting natives to Christianity.

Education was promoted by the Utilitarians in India for cultivating individuals, not merely through formal education, but also through domestic and social education — not merely in English, but also in the vernaculars. However, educating Indians, in English or otherwise, would, in the opinion of the Benthamites, be a painfully slow process for modernizing or Westernizing India, the main aim that the British bourgeoisie should set for itself. And for the achievement of this fundamental object, it was essential for them to depend primarily on the forces of law, governance and taxation based on Western experiences, and also secondarily on the Western system of education, rather than on the strength of Christianity, the Gospel and Divine Justice. Neither Bentham nor Mill was a follower of the Christian faith, and both had long abandoned their earlier religious views. Despite their disbelief in Christianity, they nevertheless observed a studied reticence about it in their writings, perhaps because the Evangelicals enjoyed the favour of financial and industrial capital, and also because of the missionaries' zeal — like their own — for changing the medieval face of India. The basic change, according to the Utilitarians, that needed to be effected in India must take place in the functioning of the Government and the formulation of laws for administering justice — 'the primary sources of good and evil'[11] — before any other betterment was attempted. Without the force of law, even while education was being promoted, neither could the people's misery be tackled nor their 'happiness' be ensured. Efficient governance and strengthening the instrument of law should proceed hand in hand for the introduction of qualitative improvement in society, as well as for the protection of individual person and property. To be effective, laws should be scientifically devised and simplistically stated in the codes, or what Bentham termed as 'parmonium'. Similarly, the Government machine should be smooth and unobtruded, to be run with speed, efficiency and impartiality.

Governance, after all, was a matter of science and skill, not of passion and good wishes, and it had to be based, in Bentham's view, upon cohesion, discipline and subordination — almost like that of a military body.[12] Since the Government's normal function was the exercise of authority, it had a tendency to be authoritarian unless restrained and guided by the system of representative democracy. Once the popular mandate was expressed through this system (in the case of India, by the British Parliament), the Government or the executive should be free from judicial and legislative interferences. Bentham and Mill together opted for a uniform, centralized state under a strong, self-confident executive exercising absolute authority. It should in effect be a kind of Hobbesean Leviathan, or an absolutism committed to public good ('happiness'), without any diversion or distraction. Absolutism had to be practised, in their opinion, autocratically and single-mindedly by the executive head at the centre (in the case of India, by the Governor General in Council). The task of 'redeem[ing] a people sunk in darkness and rais[ing] them in the scale of civilisation',[13] therefore, depended largely on the enlightenment, benevolence and dictatorial drive of the Governor General.

Both Bentham and Mill found, or imagined they found, their knight errant for rescuing India in the personality of Lord William Bentinck, their much sought-after enlightened or benevolent despot. Bentinck's ability to fight the early setback in his career, his penchant for doing public good in India's southern peninsula,[14] and his military role in Italy during the Napoleonic Wars, especially his commitment to the Sicilian cause,[15] rendered him the most suitable for the governor generalship of a starkly deficient India in the eyes of the Utilitarians. They might also have found, had they been alive, another person to be worthy of their choice — the Marquis of Dalhousie. Between Bentinck, by no means a wholehearted Utilitarian himself but a favourite of the Utilitarian masters, and Dalhousie, not so closely known to them but a thoroughbred Utilitarian to his contemporaries, there were three more Governors General, apart from an acting one (Sir Metcalf), i.e., Lord Auckland (1836–42), Lord Ellenborough (1842–44) and Lord Hardinge (1844–48), who contributed usefully to the furtherance of the Companyraj. However, none of them could match the Utilitarian reformist standard that Bentinck and Dalhousie attained. With Bentinck as the Governor General, Bentham felt overjoyed, 'as if the golden ages of British India were lying before me', and asked his follower in an Agency House in Calcutta, James Young, to explain the details of Benthamite principles to the new Governor General.[16] Whether Mill had similarly been rapturous about Bentinck or not, the newly appointed Governor General was certainly so about Mill: 'I am going to British India, but I shall not be the Governor General. It is you that will be the Governor General.'[17] Authoritarian by birth, training and instinct, Dalhousie described himself 'a curious compound of despot and radical ... a despot for many radical changes'.[18] His contemporaries took him to be the symbol of 'alliance between the scientific Benthamite administrator and the authoritative Tory gentleman'.[19] Dalhousie clearly belonged to the Utilitarian school: 'the strong authoritarian reformer, the enlightened despot, which Bentham and Mill thought the ideal type for the government of India'.[20]

## II

For freeing India from medieval entanglements, and paving the way for its bourgeoization, the Companyraj's enlightened despots were required by the Utilitarian standard to carry out far-reaching reforms: first, by reorganizing the laws of the country, and second, by reorienting its system of education. These two kinds of reforms were taken up under the patronage of Bentinck, the proconsul who wished 'the modern improvements of Europe' to be brought into India,[21] and whose latter-day successor Dalhousie, a fellow modernizer, followed his example twenty years later by pursuing the second more energetically than the first. It goes, however, to the credit of Bentinck's advisor, T. B. Macaulay, the intellectually gifted first Law Member of the Governor General's Council, for taking up both reforms simultaneously. Macaulay was confident from the outset of his being able to give suitable expression to Bentinck's desire for instilling into Indian society the essential Western notion of the rule of law, or governance based on 'universal science and philosophy of law'.[22] He was equally hopeful in foreseeing that 'a great people sunk in the lower depths of slavery and superstition' would become 'desirous and capable of all the privileges of citizens' through European instruction. He wished to turn India into 'the imperishable empire of our arts and morals, our literature and our laws'.[23]

It was Macaulay who largely succeeded in systematizing the legal processes in India through a uniform codification of its multifarious laws. The concept of legal codes, though given a concrete shape by Macaulay, actually owed its inspiration to Bentinck. During his Sicilian experience (long before his governor generalship in India), Bentinck became well versed in the pursuit not only of a uniform code of laws, but also in a rational functioning of the courts.[24] For rationalizing judicature, especially at the lower and middle levels,[25] Bentinck did away with the expensive and time-consuming special Provincial Courts of Appeal and Circuit, gave magisterial powers to the collectors of revenue, and enlarged the numbers, as well the jurisdiction, of modestly paid Indian judges (who earned a fourth of the salary of European judges). Apart from ensuring economy, these measures of the Governor General relieved the accumulating pressure on the courts, and rose above the race barrier that had hitherto squeezed out, at the instance of Lord Cornwallis in particular, qualified Indians from all high offices. Bentinck appears to have anticipated Macaulay, who conferred on Indian judges civil jurisdiction over the racially privileged Europeans through his 'Black Act' of 1836, much to the resentment of Europeans. Almost in a similar vein, it seems, Bentinck foreshadowed Macaulay's course of action with regard to the codes in India — the work of 'digesting a vast and artificial system of unwritten jurisprudence'.[26] He had expressed his Government's anxiety to solve the problem of competing systems of law, and recommended the remedy of one uniform body of laws for the entire British-Indian territories.[27] Bentinck and a few of his judicial advisors — like Edward Ryan, Alexander Ross and James Young — laid the ground for a Law Commission to be set up under the Charter Act of 1833, to be chaired by Macaulay, the Law Member, for undertaking the task of codification. Macaulay, who had no doubt that India 'stands more in need of a code than any other country in the world',[28] started his momentous work a couple of months after Bentinck left India in March 1835.

In June 1835, Macaulay planned for his Law Commission to codify laws expeditiously in three stages: a Penal Code to be made ready by the end of 1836, a Code of Criminal Procedure by the end of 1837, and a Code of Civil Procedure during 1838.[29] Considering the complexity and enormity of the work involved in a country of wide diversities, Macaulay's time frame for the whole assignment was too tight, indeed, almost impracticable. Compounded by the prolonged illnesses of the other members of the commission (J. Macleod, E. Anderson and C. Hay Cameron), Macaulay's schedule fell far short of its overall target, despite his being able single-handedly to complete the first phase of the three-phased programme of work, namely, the Penal Code.

Influenced by the Napoleonic Code Penale, and the Benthamite doctrine of jurisprudence, Macaulay divided offences in four categories: offences against the public, offences against the person (human body), offences against property, and offences against condition and reputation.[30] Since he did not approve of the stereotyped 'Statement of Objects and Reasons', he appended 'Notes' to the code instead, clarifying the grounds of various provisions.[31] Following Bentham's dictum of 'brevity', 'simplicity' and 'completeness', Macaulay imparted the essence of European philosophical tradition into Indian legislation in ordinary language and through precise definition of terms. The speciality of his code was, however, the employment of 'illustrative examples' to demonstrate the law in full operation, and to show what its effect could be on the occurrences of common life. Another distinctive feature in the code was Macaulay's attempt at analysing the psychology of crime — an examination of the ingredients of crime, or the motive, intention and consciousness behind 'voluntary culpable homicide'. Punishment in his code consequently was designed to be commensurable, variable, and equable to the offence — exemplary, reformative and remissible.[32]

The Penal Code that Macaulay prepared through Herculean efforts by 1837, and which enshrined his name in the annals of Indian legal history, was not passed, intriguingly, in the succeeding twenty years. Even the strong-willed Governor General Dalhousie, who wanted to uphold Macaulay's Penal Code but could not agree to its disfigurement at the hands of his anti-Benthamite Law Member, Drinkwater Bethune, declined to clinch the issue, and referred it to the home authorities for a final decision.[33] It was eventually enacted in 1860 as the General Criminal Law of India Act XLV,[34] more than two years after the great Revolt, without having thereby much impact on the pre-1857 public mind in India. Despite its being based on bourgeois modernism, Macaulay's Penal Code remained in suspended animation for the Indian people at large, who had neither the comfort nor the discomfort of experiencing it for decades.

Such was, however, not the case with Macaulay's other notable venture, namely, his decisive role in the reorientation of the education system in India with immediate as well as far-reaching consequences. He was geared up for this role very soon after his arrival in Calcutta in September 1834, when the Government appointed him the President of the General Committee of Public Instruction. As President, the newly appointed Law Member was required to decide upon an ongoing controversy within the committee between two schools of thought among its members, namely, the Orientalists, or those who were in favour of spreading classical knowledge in the country through Arabic and Sanskrit, and the Occidentalists or Anglicists, those who wanted to disseminate Western literary and scientific knowledge in India through the English medium. Their difference of opinions eventually boiled down to a debate over the utilization of a fixed Government fund for the promotion of education in India — whether primarily through Arabic and Sanskrit, or through English in the main.

## III

The Government fund had its origin in 1813 when the East India Company's Charter was renewed in Parliament. The Charter asked the Governor General of India, under Clause 43, to set apart each year £10,000 or Rs. 1 lakh — after defraying all costs of governance and defence — and apply it 'to the revival and improvement of literature and the encouragement of learned natives of India, and for the introduction and promotion of knowledge of the sciences among the inhabitants of the British territories in India'.[35] The Government appointed the General Committee of Public Instruction in 1823 to give effect to the avowed object, and placed Rs. 1 lakh at its disposal for use in the cause of Indian education. With the amount, the committee of ten (the majority of whom were Orientalists led by H. H. Wilson and H. T. Prinsep) reorganized the Calcutta Madrassa and the Sanskrit College, established oriental institutions in Calcutta, Agra and Delhi, gave grants to the oriental schools, and published books in Arabic and Sanskrit. Meanwhile, all through the 1820s, privately financed (by the Indian rich as well as the not-so-rich) institutions for English education in Calcutta, such as the Hindu College and the General Assembly's College, had been opening up the exciting new vista of Western knowledge, and causing a commotion in the public mind, especially those of the middle classes. Even the committee, with its increased number of younger Anglicist elements, could not but notice by 1831 the growing Indian interest in the English language, and its teaching in private schools by Hindu College students. It had to take such steps for meeting the increasing public demand for English as to arrange for its lessons in the oriental institutions, and establish English schools in Delhi and Benares.

Apparently, both the Orientalists and the Anglicists were aware of the significance of imparting Eastern and Western learning in India. However, they differed over the medium of instruction and the degree of importance to be attached to it. While the Orientalists interpreted the term 'literature' in Clause 43 of the Charter Act of 1813 to signify Arabic and Sanskrit literature, and a 'learned native' to mean an Indian scholar of repute in either of the two languages, the Anglicists wanted to include English in the category of 'literature', and the English-proficient among those considered 'learned natives'. The English versus Arabic and Sanskrit debate heightened considerably at the time of further renewal of the Company's Charter, when the Charter Act of 1833 increased the educational grant from £10,000 to £100,000 or Rs. 10 lakh. The two warring groups in the committee insisted on laying claim upon a lion's share of the grant either in favour of Arabic and Sanskrit, or in support of English. Both submitted in January 1835 their respective views to the Government in two separate representations, and Macaulay, the recently appointed President of the committee, was called upon to decide whether the grant in question was to be utilized exclusively for the promotion of oriental learning, or also for the encouragement of Western education. He gave his decision on the subject through his famous minute of 2 February 1835, in which he argued that 'literature' in the disputed clause did not stand wholly for Arabic and Sanskrit, and that it included English as well. Similarly, the phrase 'learned natives' in the clause was applicable not only to the *maulavi*s and *pandit*s of India but also to Indian scholars familiar with the poetry of Milton or the metaphysics of Locke. The Government, he asserted, was not fettered by any pledge, expressed or implied, and it should be free to employ the fund as it chose.

Macaulay then discussed the vital question of the medium of instruction, and examined the rival claims of the mother tongues, the classical languages and English. He rejected the claim of mother tongues on the ground that the Indian languages were too poor and crude to be made vehicles of serious thought and expression, and therefore were unfit for the pursuance of higher education through them. (Macaulay had, however, little doubt that the mother tongues could be developed and enriched in due course with the help of classical languages and English.) Between the claims of Arabic and Sanskrit, and that of English, Macaulay preferred English, and considered it superior to either of the classical languages. He forcefully argued that English — the key to modern knowledge — was more useful than Arabic and Sanskrit due to its status as the language of the rulers of India, its emergence as the language of commerce in the East, as well as its dominant position among the Western languages. Macaulay believed that English could bring about a renaissance in India as Greek and Latin had done in England, or as the languages of Western Europe had done in Russia. He felt that the natives of India were desirous of learning through English, and not through Arabic and Sanskrit, and that these two had needlessly been kept up by 'bounty money'. It was possible, he felt, to turn the natives of India into thoroughly good English scholars, and 'to that end our efforts ought to be directed'. Of course, Macaulay did not expect the body of the people to be English-educated forthwith, but he certainly hoped to bring about, through English education, 'a class of persons Indian in blood and colour, but English in tastes, in opinions, in morals and intellect', and expected modern education to filter down from them to the masses.[36]

Expected to be on the same wavelength as his Law Member, Governor General Bentinck gave his 'entire concurrence to the sentiments expressed' in the Anglicist minute of Macaulay, despite the protestation of the Orientalists. Bentinck brushed aside their objections that English education had the support of only a small Hindu minority, and the vast majority and the Muslims were opposed to

FOR BOURGEOIZATION

it, and also that it would be unpopular to regard classicism as useless, and to withdraw endowments for its promotion.[37] Instead, he ardently took the spreading of Western knowledge among Indians to be the prime objective of the British rule in India, and decided to commit his Government to its realization. He was, however, not opposed to the continuance of the existing institutions of oriental learning, but firmly ruled in his Resolution of 7 March 1835 that all educational funds in the main 'be henceforth employed in imparting to the native population a knowledge of English literature and sciences through the medium of English language'.[38] Bentinck's successor, Auckland, also trod the beaten Macaulaian track. In 1837, he replaced Persian as the court language by English and other Indian languages. Auckland upheld Macaulay's concept of filtering English down from the more educated to the less educated (the so-called Filtration Theory), and passing on the wealth of Western knowledge through English to the 'greatest number of students who may be ready to accept it at our hands'.[39] He started English colleges and schools at various urban centres and district headquarters. Meanwhile, English education was being steadily connected with the career prospects of Indians: through widening their scope for joining the judiciary, increasing their suitability for employment in the private and public sectors, and, finally, by Lord Hardinge's Resolution of 10 October 1844 declaring that in all Government appointments, preference would be given to persons with a knowledge of English.[40]

It is apparent from the overview of the Companyraj between the 1830s and the 1850s that Macaulay — with his strident insistence on setting up an Anglicist system of education — was the central figure who charted out the academic directions for the bourgeoizing process in India. Despite his intellectual arrogance,[41] and his expedient authoritarianism,[42] Macaulay does not seem to have primarily been motivated (as dubbed later on, and even today, by Indian anti-imperialist observers of all hues) by the great need of producing subordinate clerks and *babu*s to cope with the increasing workload of expanding Government offices and European business houses. Rather, one comes across in Macaulay a passion for

## FOR BOURGEOIZATION

Westernizing and modernizing India for the good of the British and of the Indians under Britain's imperial rule, even in contravention of imperialism itself. In Macaulay's own words:

> It may be that the public mind in India may expand under our system, that by good government we may educate our subjects into a capacity for better government, that having become instructed in European knowledge, they may in some future age demand European institutions. Whether such a day will ever come I know not. But never will I attempt to avert or retard it. Whenever it comes, it will be the proudest day in English history.[43]

The Companyraj's policy of educating India evidently did not stop, and could not have stopped, with Macaulay and Bentinck or those who immediately followed them. It was soon taken up by Dalhousie and his lieutenant in the North-Western Provinces (NWP), James Thomason (whose land revenue initiatives will be discussed in the following chapters), and culminated in an educational blueprint for India as drawn up by Sir Charles Wood.

To begin with, Dalhousie did not seriously think about educational developments in India till he came to know of Thomason's pioneering attempts at vernacular education in the NWP Struck by the virtual lack of education among the cultivators, Thomason thought it necessary for his provincial Government to try to spread vernacular education in the countryside, so that tenants and landholders were able to check what was shown against their names in the registered titles and settlement records, as well as calculate the amount of revenue to be paid by them. Thomason detailed a scheme for setting up a model school in every revenue district (*tehsil*) in addition to village schools, and planned to monitor and support them with the help of the official visitors (inspectors). Much impressed, Dalhousie upheld the scheme before the home authorities, and, while it was being successfully experimented within the NWP, he adopted it for Punjab, Bengal and Bihar in 1853–54 at a moderate cost (about Rs. 4 lakh). He also favoured the teaching of English in these schools, provided there was a demand for it. But he did not extend the scheme either to Bombay, where a mixed English–vernacular school system had already come into existence, or to Madras, where the educational condition was not ready yet for its reception.[44] At the level of Anglo-vernacular education in Calcutta, Dalhousie thought of starting branch schools of the Hindu College and the Calcutta Madrassa for all sections of people, and reserving the Sanskrit College and the Calcutta Madrassa essentially for the purpose of classical learning. He also decided to take over the running of the Hindu College (which at that point had been facing the problem of dual management by non-officials and officials), and to create in its place the 'Presidency College', as distinct from other local and private institutions, a college open 'to all youths of every caste, class or creed'.[45]

Dalhousie was firmly in the saddle when the Companyraj's Charter came up again for renewal in the British Parliament in 1853. Sir Charles Wood, President of the Board of Control, was called upon to present a detailed policy statement on Indian education. This he very ably did in his memorable Despatch of 19 July 1854 that laid the foundation of a modern and comprehensive system of education for the whole of the vast country. Being the man on the spot, and in charge of the Indian administration, Dalhousie could not but have played some important supportive role in the making of the Despatch, howsoever much Wood himself failed to acknowledge it, or his appreciators later tried to play it down.[46] The Governor General and his able counsellors (including Dr Mouat, C. Beaton, J.D. Bethune, F.J. Halliday and J.P. Grant) were known to have forwarded reports, made proposals and analysed ground realities. If they had not sent home to the Court of Directors the necessary inputs, and if Wood had not had full access to these, it would simply have not been possible to make a preliminary draft of the Despatch.[47] However, despite the contributions of all others in India and Britain — usefully, or not so usefully — Wood's Despatch was primarily his own, and he was responsible for it, as well as for its profound impact.

In his scheme, Wood planned for a co-ordinated system of education for India, from the lowest to the highest stage, based on an adequate number of efficient teaching institutions such as the primary schools and colleges, each leading to the next higher step. The scheme planned to integrate all private institutions with the proposed Government system of education, and provided for Government grants for their running. The entire arrangement had to be managed by special Departments of Education in each province, having a sufficient number of inspectors under them for overseeing higher education. A university was to be established in each of the Presidency towns, and it would function mainly as an examining body on the model of London University. Higher teaching would be imparted chiefly through the colleges, but universities might institute professorships in law, civil engineering, the vernaculars and the classical languages. The scheme laid stress on mass education, female education, and the training of teachers. It aimed at reinforcing and improving the vernaculars, and anticipated that European knowledge would percolate down to the common man and woman through these languages. As regards religious instruction in the Government schools, the Despatch emphasized the fact that these were founded for the whole population of India, and not for any of its sections, and 'that education conveyed in them should be exclusively secular'.[48]

## IV

The avowed ideal of secularism, and the Government commitment to secular education, was the grand bourgeois liberal objective that the Companyraj had set for itself in the pre-1857 days. Steering clear of the religiosity of any community in India, especially that of its rulers' representatives, and in the face of an Evangelical challenge at home, and on such an issue as the civilizing and educating of Indians, was an immense task. The immensity could be gauged to an extent if one remembers that those who were to work out the tasks in the colony did not come from any specific coterie of religious non-conformists — who might not have been particularly devout, but were not heretics either. Although Bentham and Mill kept themselves strictly away from their initial loyalties to Christianity, the British-Indian practitioners of the precepts they preached were all sympathetic members of various Christian persuasions. If Bentinck consoled an Evangelical President of the Board of Control that 'it is Christianity, the whole of Christian Church whose cause in this heathen country [India] we are to cherish',[49] Macaulay assured his Evangelical father (Zachary Macaulay) that, following the imparting of English education in India, 'there would not be a single idolator among the responsible classes of Bengal thirty years hence, that this would be effected without any effort to proselytize'.[50] And Dalhousie was reluctant to ignore 'so completely as we do the agency of Ministers of our own True Faith'.[51] Likewise, Thomason, son of a chaplain in Calcutta (Rev. Thomas Thomason) and a devout Christian like many of his counterparts in the services, was known for encouraging the Church in Agra by making large gifts from time to time.[52] Canning, Dalhousie's successor and the first Viceroy of India, was reportedly committed to the Christian cause, and subscribed to every missionary society that had for its object 'the conversion of the natives'.[53] Consequently, these architects of the Companyraj's lofty imperialism in India could not have been disagreeable to any Evangelical initiative that had the authorization of as high an authority as the British Parliament. This was exactly what had happened in 1813 in an early liberal Britain under the web of expansionist Christian fervour.

The Charter Act of 1813 decided to grant permission to Christian missionaries for imparting 'useful knowledge' and effecting 'religious improvements' among the inhabitants of British dominions in India. Simultaneously, it provided for setting up at the Government expense one Church of England bishopric for the whole of India, and three archdeacons, one for each Presidency.[54] The next Charter Act of 1833 went further by authorizing the Governor General in Council to grant in favour of the Christian missions 'such sums of money as may be expedient for the purpose of instruction or for the purpose of places of worship'.[55] By the terms 'useful knowledge' and 'instruction', the home authorities meant the promotion of missionary activities in the field of education, by setting up schools and colleges with English either as a medium of instruction or at least (in the countryside) as one of the main subjects of study. True to this advice, the Companyraj offered the missionaries all material help in setting up their educational institutions, which nevertheless was also the prime Evangelical aim in India from the start — the most non-controversial vehicle for Christianizing India. And from 1854, when Dalhousie introduced (on the English model) grants-in-aid for financially supporting non-governmental schooling in India, liberal grants were also offered by the Government to the missionary institutions. The importation of Western knowledge into India had always been, in the missionary view, a very useful means of achieving the one and singular end, namely, the conversion of 'the sinners of God' to His righteous ways. Traditional Indians soon came to realize that a missionary did not confine his efforts to the enlightenment of the student's mind alone, but strove for what was of far greater importance: the reclamation of the youthful souls. Conversion, or what the Charter Act signified as 'religious improvement' and 'places of worship' (churches), seemed to the common man and woman in India the inevitable corollary of Western education,[56] apart from, of course, another effective proselytizing method, i.e., missionary preachings.

Since preaching in chapels, accompanied by music and the singing of hymns, did not prove to be very successful in effecting conversions, the missionaries resorted to preaching in public places like *bazaar*s and *hat*s, and also to village perambulations or survey marches through villages. Despite having a ready crowd of listeners, such preaching apparently was very unpopular due to the preachers' tendency to run down the indigenous faiths while extolling their own, and led often to unruly remonstrances, and even to acts of violence. Consequently, the missionaries in the *bazaar*s and villages needed protection by peons and guards,[57] and very frequently the intervention of local magistrates was sought.[58] The Government also had to protect the civil rights of Indian converts by changing the inheritance and property laws that afflicted them, much to the disgruntlement of the vast number of non-Christians.[59]

But to be fair to the Government, one must concede that such safeguarding of the converts' interests was not so much for according them a privileged status, but for treating them as equals with other religionists. Thus, the authorities tried their best to show off, as well as to live up to, an official policy of religious neutrality. In a country overwhelmingly of non-Christians with very large followings of several faiths, the Companyraj simply could not afford to be partial to its Christian subjects, or to promote Christian interests at the expense of those of other creeds. They did not show any perceptible keenness in employing Indian converts in their services, and declined to make the study of the Bible a part of the curriculum in the Government-run schools. Even when Dalhousie was willing to give grants-in-aid to the missionary educational institutions, he wanted the money to be spent by them on 'the extension of sound secular education throughout the masses of the population in India'.[60] Wood's Despatch further confirmed the Companyraj's intention to maintain the secularity of India's education.

Education in India at this juncture was not only secular, somewhat non-elitist and village-oriented, but also gender-friendly, and the cause of educating women was attracting some public and private attention. The missionaries were the first to take initiative in this direction, and established girls' schools under the London and Church Missionary Societies. They were followed by philanthropic bodies like the British and Foreign Schools Society, which opened a school for female children in Calcutta in 1821. In 1826, the Society had thirty schools and 600 students under its charge, and these were put together in 1828 into a central school under the management of the Ladies' Society for Native Female Education. The voice for women's education in the 1830s and 1840s was feeble on account of the traditional Indian society's male chauvinist hostility against it. Dalhousie's Government, however, was in favour of its open encouragement; his Council Member, J.E.D. Bethune, in his capacity as the President of the Council of Education, had taken up the cause of women's education by founding a girls' school in Calcutta in 1849 much against local obstruction, and by obtaining Government support for running it. Despite intimidations,

Bethune's school made good progress in a year's time, and the number of its students increased from eleven to thirty in 1850, and then to fifty in 1856.[61] The official patronage and a certain non-official drive resulted in the founding of girls' schools in Uttarpara, Jessore and Barasat, as well as six more schools in Calcutta.

It was at this point that Pandit Ishwar Chandra Vidyasagar, the outstanding exponent of Indo-Western intellectual fusion (or the 'Indian awakening'), came forward in support of Bethune's school against conservative public opinion. It was Vidyasagar who established in 1854 about twenty girls' schools in the rural areas of Hooghly, Midnapore, Burdwan and Nadia during his tenure as the Government inspector of schools, over and above his functioning as the Principal of the Sanskrit College. A delayed Government grant did not discourage him, and he ran the schools on his own, apart from setting up in 1855 a Normal School for training their teachers. By 1858, the schools founded by Vidyasagar were reported to be educating more than 1,300 female students.[62] Soon, Indian educational enterprise was found to be bearing fruit: Maghuabhai Karramchand contributed richly to the foundation of two girls' schools in Ahmedabad; three such schools were known to have been set up in Poona and one at Dharwar; and a few received Government grants-in-aid at Dacca and Howrah, apart from Agra, Mathura and Mainpuri. At one such girls' school in Mainpuri, there was an attendance of '32 Mahomedan girls of respectable parentage'. Women's education seemed to have made good progress in all parts of Punjab, according to its Board of Administration.[63] The situation was also encouraging in the Deccan Division, and Captain Lester, Acting Educational Inspector, felt by 1859 that 'the prejudices against female education were fast disappearing'.[64]

V

Infinitely more damaging than their palpable disadvantage in education, Indian women suffered social brutalities and inhumanities in the first half of the 19th century. The worst, and the most discussed by posterity, among these inhumanities was *sati* (or *suttee*) —

the heinous practice of burning widows on the funeral pyres of their husbands. *Sati* was apparently the remnant of a Scythean practice of burning the wife of a chief 'along with the remains of her husband' during the 3rd and 4th centuries B.C.[65] It was adopted in India and prescribed by some Hindu scriptural accretion as the only course for a virtuous wife, namely, her self-immolation on the cremation pyre of the dead husband. Not only would such a woman enjoy eternal peace with her husband, but also expiate the sins of three generations of their families. To this blinding faith was added the male relations' greed for the dead couple's properties and inheritances, and they invariably persuaded, drugged and physically forced the victim to die on the pyre amidst the deafening noise of drums, bells, conch shells and wild shouting. Successive Governments of the Company under Cornwallis (1786–93) to Wellesley (1798–1805) and Minto (1807–13) to Amherst (1823–28) did think about stopping or restricting the ghastly practice, but could not make any real progress in apprehension of a strong Hindu backlash. They took refuge conveniently in the specious plea of religious non-interference, despite a growing and increasingly assertive anti-*sati* movement among Indian intellectuals and social reformers led by the liberal Raja Ram Mohan Roy.

It took a Utilitarian despot, committed to Western moral law and good governance (for the greatest number of people), like Bentinck to decide to ban *sati* throughout the country. He made up his mind with characteristic military promptitude within a year of his arrival in India as the Governor General, and declared on 4 December 1829 that the practice of *sati* would be illegal and punishable under Regulation XVII. Obviously, Bentinck did this against the wishes of advisors and well-wishers in India who anticipated widespread resentment among the Hindus, and even against Ram Mohan's advice to go slow. By taking this dangerous decision, he acted immensely courageously for a person who had previously been accused of tampering with the religious faiths of the sepoys in 1806 as the youngest Governor of the Madras Presidency. Bentinck had suffered the ignominy of a recall on being held responsible for the Vellore mutiny, and had fought furiously against the injustice of the recall.

As it happened, this turned out to be a case of fortune smiling on the brave, and nothing untoward happened outwardly, except the numerously signed petitions of remonstrance by orthodox Hindu leaders to the Governor General as well as to the authorities in England. Ram Mohan countered by sending a congratulatory and supportive letter to the Governor General, signed by 300 Calcutta notables. In one bold stroke, Bentinck seemed to have lastingly embossed his name in the annals of British-Indian history:

> Bentinck! 'Twas thine the bloodless crown to win
> Proud victor over deeds of death and sin!
> Spirit of England's fame, no longer dim
> A voice of thunder, thou didst speak in him.[66]

Banning *sati* hardly meant its extermination, and all of Bentinck's successors had to remain vigilant against the heinous practice. They showed no indulgence to the perpetrators of *sati* within the British territories, and dealt with them as severely as possible. Dalhousie, however, found it rather problematic to enforce the ban in the Indian States, and he had to remonstrate strongly with the *durbar*s under whose jurisdiction the evil persisted. He was known to have censured the States of Alwar, Bikaner and Udaipur, and in Dungarpore (under British management) he suitably punished the ruler and his son for participating in a *sati*.[67] Apart from dealing occasionally with the death of widows by burning, Dalhousie had to encounter the more numerous killings of newly born daughters in secret. Such female infanticide was an age-old practice widely prevalent in the north-western, central and western parts of India, and since these acts were committed within the household and behind the purdah, often in forced connivance with the victims' mothers, the British authorities had found it practically impossible to counter them. Despite the registration of births, secret enquiries, rewards and criminal proceedings ever since the close of the 18th century, they were not able to control infanticide to any considerable extent.

Since the threat of force (charging the killers of female babies of murder), and the actual use of force (convicting them as murderers, and in case of suspicion, forfeiture of the family pensions and other benefits), had not produced the desired result, Dalhousie was persuaded by Thomason and Charles Raikes, the Lieutenant Governor and a civilian, respectively, in the NWP, to make some governmental effort at correcting the social behaviour and custom. In concert they found the main cause of infanticide to be two fold: 'pride of birth and pride of purse; that is parents murder their infant daughters, either because they cannot afford the marriage expenses which must one day be incurred on their account, or because they foresee difficulty in marrying them suitably' (within the proper caste hierarchy and status structure).[68] Together, it boiled down to the huge expenditure in marrying off a daughter, including the high dowry to be paid to the bridegroom's family belonging to a comparable caste and socio-economic position; not to be able to do so was regarded as worse than death. Having the reduction of marriage expenses in mind, with the help of the Lawrence administration in the Punjab (a region notorious for infanticide),[69] Dalhousie's Government convened, during Diwali at Amritsar in 1853, 'a great meeting of the representatives of all tribes' — members of the nobility, as well as Muslim *nawab*s and Hindu *zamindar*s, the *maulavi*s, plus the high civil and judicial British officials. The congregation promulgated certain rules, 'the observance of which would effectually secure that no man should feel any real difficulty in providing for his daughter in marriage, and should consequently have no motive for the commission of infanticide'.[70] Even if female infanticide did not recede dramatically thereafter, and the public mind still remained largely unstirred, the Amritsar meeting of 1853 should be considered very significant indeed, as the starting point of an anti-infanticide movement in India.

Though conventionally considered a blessing, the institution of marriage seems to have been the greatest bane for Hindu women in the 19th century. Some were burnt alive when widowed, and a significant number were killed immediately after birth because of their families' anxiety about the costs of marrying them off. Many were given in marriage soon after they started walking and long before puberty. The Brahmins, especially in the Bengal Presidency, were keen to marry their daughters to the *kulin*s, or the highest stratum among them, so as to move up the social and pietistical ladder. The *kulin*s on their part would take — ostensibly as an act of service to society and religion — as many such wives as they could during their lifetime. (Since these wives stayed mostly in their parental homes, they were free from the liability of maintaining them.) On their deaths, the *kulin*s would leave a large number of young and child widows. The ranks of child widows were further inflated on account of the popular craze for child marriage, and also occasionally due to the death of child husbands. Hindu widows were (and sometimes continue to be) subjected to disdain, utter neglect and ill-treatment for the remainder of their days, presumably because of being held fatalistically responsible for their husbands' deaths.

The only reasonable way out of the young and the child widows' plight appeared to be their remarriage, which was conventionally forbidden. Enlightened Hindu opinion in India was favourably disposed towards the issue of widow remarriage in the Presidencies of Bengal and Bombay: the Brahmo Samaj in Calcutta and the press in and outside the city were advocating it from the 1830s. The issue was referred in Calcutta to such religious bodies as the Dharma Sabha and the Tattva Bodhini Sabha, but the matter did not make much progress till it was taken up by Ishwar Chandra Vidyasagar. It was Vidyasagar who led a movement of progressive Hindus in favour of widow remarriage, justified it on the basis of the *Parashara Samhita* (a classical Sanskrit text), published a book on the subject (*Vidhava Vivaha*), and debated the issue furiously in public.[71] Vidyasagar's endeavour, however, had little prospect of success against the strong current of traditional opinion in the country, and it depended on the sympathy and support of the ruling circles. Dalhousie's Council at this point came forward to provide Vidyasagar with the necessary support. Its members, some of whom were familiar with the eminence of the Sanskrit College Principal, encouraged him to submit a petition to the Legislative Council of the Government in favour of widow remarriage, signed by nearly a thousand public men and endorsing a draft Bill for its consideration. The Bill was moved in the Council in November 1855, inviting sharp reactions both in its favour and against. The opponents submitted, under the leadership of Raja Radhakanta Deb, a counter-petition of nearly 4,000 people. With a supportive Governor General at its back, the Bill was destined to succeed against the formidable opposition, and the Hindu Widows Remarriage Act, which was finalized by Dalhousie himself before his departure from India, was duly passed under Canning's governor generalship on 25 July 1856.[72]

Other sorts of inhumanity arising from superstition and religiosity were also evidenced at the time. Two such deeply pricked the Companyraj's conscience: the murderous cult of the *thuggee*s, who combined robbery with ritual; and the terrifying tribal rite of Meriah sacrifice. The *thuggee*s — Hindu and Muslim followers of the cult of Kali — would, at the end of the cultivating season, undertake journeys through the long trading routes. They moved about in groups, befriended the travelling pilgrims and merchants on the way, and strangled them in their sleep as acts of human sacrifice to content the goddess. They would hurriedly dig graves to hide the dead bodies, loot the belongings of their victims, and take to the roads again in search of fresh prey. The *thuggee*s, operating mainly in central India, started spreading their criminal nets in other parts of the country, and forced Bentinck's Government to take urgent stern steps against them in 1830. Colonel William Sleeman, who was made in-charge of the anti-*thuggee* campaign, achieved remarkable success by using the intelligence from a captured *thuggee* leader (Feringhea), and by ceaselessly storming the *thuggee*-infested villages. It was reported that between 1831 and 1837, more than 3,000 *thuggee*s were captured and convicted.

The other practice, namely, the Meriah rite, was prevalent among the inhabitants of the hills and jungles in Orissa (belonging predominantly to the Khond group of tribes). The rite involved the sacrifice of 'young human victims for the propitiation of the especial divinity who presided over the fertility of the earth'.[73] Measures for the suppression of the ghastly rite had been taken before the arrival of Dalhousie by his predecessor, Hardinge, but these were pursued more vigorously only after 1848, resulting in the rescue of multitudes of victims and the abandonment of the practice by most tribesmen.[74] While both the *thuggee* and the Meriah rite had by and large received the attention of the Companyraj's chroniclers, the continuance of slavery of both men and women in the 19th century as the worst form of human exploitation and suffering seems somehow to have been largely sidelined. However, the Companyraj on its part could not ignore the existence of millions of slaves at the height of an emotionally surcharged anti-slavery movement in Britain. Under its profound impact, the predecessor of Dalhousie, Lord Ellenborough, decided to abolish slavery in India, and did so by passing Act V of 1843.

## VI

If education and legal reforms were devices for spreading bourgeois values and standards among the colonized, the measures against *sati*, female infanticide, *thuggee* and the Meriah rite, and in favour of widow remarriage, were attempts at extricating them from the medieval stranglehold. All these steps were thought to be necessary for paving the way for an advanced industrial society of the future — for building a political-economic system that would ensure British dominance over the world capitalist system. Fitting India into world capitalism, in supplementation and in subordination to Great Britain, necessitated exploration into its potentialities — primarily as a supplier of raw material for British industries and as a consumer of their industrial products, and secondarily as a growing collaborationist industrial nation in itself. For achieving these goals, it was incumbent on Britain to concentrate on infrastructural developments: to accelerate communication, speed up transportation and link up the markets and the outlets (ports) with as many nooks and corners of the land as possible. During the thirty years of the Companyraj from 1828 to 1858, and between two of its benevolent despots, Bentinck and Dalhousie, India marched infrastructurally into the modern world of steam, arterial roadways, posts and telegraphs, and the railways.

Transport being fundamental to the opening up of India as much in British as in Indian interests, Bentinck took special care in spreading arterial roads across the Indian subcontinent and in utilizing the marvel of steam power for both internal and external navigation. Ever since his first personal experience of a steamer journey in 1822, he often thought of using steamboat services more for developmental purposes than for industrial progress. On his arrival in India in 1828, Bentinck took over the semblance of the steamer transport that existed in Calcutta, revamped the ramshackle vessels, and re-routed them (freeing them from their confinement in Assam) up the Ganges towards the strategic and throbbing north — to Benares, Allahabad, Kanpur and beyond. With his procurement of technologically superior steamers from England, a regular three-weekly service on the Ganges started running by the end of 1836. The service was wholly under Government control, since Bentinck did not expect private capital in India to come forward at that point, though he anticipated that 'the merchants of England in the trade to China and India' would get interested in it.[75] Sea-borne steam navigation had also caught Bentinck's imagination, and from 1830 he was apparently possessed with the idea of an oceanic steamer service to England from Calcutta, over and above Bombay, via Suez. Though eminently viable, the Suez Canal project was still under serious European planning only; but that did not discourage Bentinck from approaching the Court of Directors for spending money on a steamer service from Calcutta to the Suez. A steamer in fact reached Suez from Calcutta in 1834–35[76] to explore transportation through a 100-mile Mesopotamian corridor to the Mediterranean. Even after leaving India, Bentinck had not stopped contemplating the blessings that steam and steamships could shower on India, bringing Europeans and Indians closer to each other and enhancing India's material and 'moral improvement'.[77]

Though less romanticized than steam navigation, Bentinck's emphasis on transportation through a network of roadways found suitable expression in his rebuilding of the great Grand Trunk Road. Routing the road along a higher level in Burdwan, instead of the readily inundated Bankura during the rains, he vastly improved the stretch between Calcutta and Benares. More importantly, however, Bentinck succeeded in laying the road afresh from Allahabad to Delhi, and then turning it into the gorgeous northern Indian plains. Dalhousie seems to have been more enthusiastic about road reconstruction than the other successors of Bentinck. He was responsible for the prolongation of the Grand Trunk Road through Punjab via Lahore, Wazirabad, Rawalpindi and Attock to Peshawar. He also took an interest in the roadways between Patna and Gaya, Cuttack and Sambalpur, Calcutta and Dacca, as well as the roads in Hyderabad, Nagpur and Sind, and in the Bombay and Madras Presidencies. Like Bentinck, Dalhousie also felt keenly about steam navigation, though he confined his efforts to the furtherance of internal steamer services through the Indus between Karachi and Multan, through the Narbada and the Godavari, and by using the great Ganga canal, the Bari Doab canal, and the canals between the Adyar and the Palir in South Arcot, and extending to Coimbatore.[78] However, Dalhousie's, as well as the Companyraj's and British capital's, greatest contribution to India and its people was their revolutionizing the transport system through the introduction of the railways.

The so-called railway mania in Britain in the course of the Industrial Revolution was bound sooner than later to bring the resourceful Indian territories under its spell. The spell was cast in the 1830s when a railway system for India was often thought of and discussed, and it took a concrete shape in 1843, or the year Rowland Stephenson, a British engineer, proposed to the Government of India a plan for giving the British capitalists a chance to build railways in a country of multifarious vastness. Negotiations soon started between the Companyraj and the investors in Britain on the line of 'guarantees', i.e., the Government guaranteeing the railway constructing companies against risk of loss at the rate of 5 per cent per annum. After construction through 'private' enterprise at 'public' risk, the companies would run the railways for ninety-nine years, under the watchful eyes of the Companyraj of course, before turning them over to the Government. In 1849, the Government of India entered into a contract with the East India Railway Company to undertake work in the eastern and northern parts of the country from

Calcutta. Similarly, two more companies, the Great India Peninsula Railway Company and the Bombay–Baroda and Central India Railway Company, started work from Bombay in the western part, and the Madras Railway Company did the same in the southern part from Madras.[79] Dalhousie, who had experience of the railways as former Chairman of the Railway Board in England, got on the job as soon as he arrived in India by setting up a central Railway Department.

Surveys started in all parts of the country in 1851, and in the spring of 1853 the Government of India submitted to the Court of Directors the plan of a system of trunk lines, connecting the interior of each Presidency with its principal ports, and linking all the Presidencies with each other. In Bengal in 1854–55, the line from Burdwan to Agra via Allahabad, Kanpur, Mathura and Delhi was planned and approved. Alternative lines from Delhi to Lahore, Mirzapur to Jubbalpore, and from Mirzapur to Agra and Kanpur were also thought of. The line from Calcutta to Raniganj — a distance of 120 miles — was opened on 3 February 1855. However, the first line of railway employed for public traffic in India had already been opened between Bombay and Thana on 16 April 1853. In 1855, the line from Bombay to Khandesh by way of the Thall Ghat was sanctioned with an extension to Nagpur. Surveys were also conducted from Khandesh to the iron and coal districts on the Narbada and as far as Mirzapur. While a line was being planned from Bombay to Baroda and Ahmedabad, and over the Ghats to Indore, it was decided in the following year to run a track from Bombay by the Bhare Ghat to Poona as the first section of the trunk line from Bombay to Madras. The city and port of Madras, Dalhousie felt, needed to be approached from the north, bringing down the rich produce of the Ceded Districts and the country by Cuddapah. The other approach was to come from the west and the south by way of Arcot, Vellore, Variembaddy, Salem towards Coimbatore to Poonay on the Malabar coast. A branch line from Variembaddy to Bangalore was under contemplation, with a proposal to extend it to Bellary and reach the Krishna for uniting the Presidencies of Madras and Bombay.[80] By the time Dalhousie left

## FOR BOURGEOIZATION

India in 1856, he had succeeded in his plan of binding India in iron chains, bringing the interior of the country to its exterior, linking it strongly to the ports for exports. The railways had the effect of unifying India, bringing travellers from diverse places and cultures, the elite and the lowly, the rich and the poor to journey together, to know each other. It contributed to India's unity, its blossoming into a nation with a national consciousness.

Like the systems of transportation, the lines of communication constituted a crucial means for developing 19th-century India into an advanced economy with accompanying socio-cultural fallouts. For achieving this, information had to travel fast within the British-Indian territories, from place to place and person to person, reliably, and of course cheaply, at a uniform cost. Dalhousie contributed richly to the dramatic improvements in communications by reorganizing and reactivating the postal arrangement, simultaneously with the introduction of the electric telegraph. Telegraph, being in use in Europe and America since the 1830s, was initially considered for use in India in 1839 by Dr O'Shaughnessy, an Assistant Surgeon, and Colonel H. Forbes, an engineering enthusiast. O'Shaughnessy advocated the laying of underground telegraph lines, while Forbes was in favour of having them aerially. Dalhousie decided to try both. Experimentally, telegraphy was attempted in 1851–52 between Calcutta and Burdwan, as well as between Calcutta and Diamond Harbour. In October 1853, the Court of Directors sanctioned Dalhousie's proposal for constructing telegraph lines in India, beginning from Calcutta to Benares through Barrackpore, and along the Grand Trunk Road. From Benares it was to run, parallel to the Grand Trunk Road again, to Peshawar via Mirzapur, Agra and Meerut. Instead of connecting it to Calcutta by a direct line, Madras was included in a Bombay-centred system through Arcot, Vellore, Bangalore, Bellary, Dharwar, Belgaum, Kolhapur, Satara, Poona and Bombay. The line from Bombay was to join the Calcutta–Peshawar line in Agra through Thana, Nasik, Dhulia, Mhow and Gwalior. Calcutta was also planned to be linked up with Assam and eastern Bengal through a separate branch line. An adequately staffed Telegraph Department was set up centrally under

O'Shaughnessy, and the construction of telegraph lines began in 1853. The work made satisfactory progress, and the first telegraphic message between Calcutta and Agra was sent on 24 March 1854. When Dalhousie was about to retire from India, he had the satisfaction of seeing the completion of an almost comprehensive telegraphic network in India, touching most major towns and places of commercial, military and political interest. Between November 1853 and February 1856, approximately 4,000 miles of electric telegraph had been laid in India, overcoming many topographical and engineering problems, braving hills and jungles and crossing some seventy principal rivers. The expenditure remained fairly moderate, not exceeding Rs. 21 lakh, costing about Rs. 500 a mile.[81]

Noticing the inferiority of the postal services in India, and the unsatisfactory manner in which postal departments functioned in every Presidency — in comparison, of course, with the Western countries — Dalhousie's Government appointed in 1854 a commission to examine the post office system and suggest improvements. The commission, having representatives from all the Presidencies, along with other high officials and experts, duly submitted its recommendations. With the approval of the Court of Directors, Dalhousie's Government decided to put these suggestions into practice. By the Post Office Act of 1 October 1854, the postal services were centralized throughout India as a Government of India department, superintended by a Director General (Mr Burton Beanet) over four Post Masters General (NWP, Bengal, Bombay and Madras). The Act also provided for the establishment of a uniform single rate of postage of half an *anna* (3/4 d.) and of an *anna* (1½ d.) for newspapers and journals, irrespective of the distance. The rate for the postage of letters between England and India was fixed at 6 d. per half ounce. The cash payment for the postage was substituted by postage stamps, and severely restricted the privilege of official 'franking' (the enjoyment of postage-free services).

The centralization of the services, the uniformity of postage, and the introduction of postage stamps so qualitatively improved postal communications in India that as early as 1856, the Government found a 25 per cent increase in the volume of postal correspondence. The magnitude of the changes and their dramatic social effects were recorded by Dalhousie himself with the help of illustration and contrast. He pointed out that a single letter was conveyed to any part of the British Isles for 1 d.; in India it was to be conveyed over distances 'immeasurably greater' — from Peshawar on the border of Afghanistan to the southernmost village of Cape Comorin, or from Dibrugarh in Upper Assam to Karachi at the mouth of the Indus — for no more than 3/4 d. 'The postage chargeable on the same letter three years ago in India would not have been less than 1 s., or 16 times the present charge.' Again, with the uniform rate of postage between England and India, a Scottish recruit who joined his regiment at Peshawar could write to his mother at the farthest corner of Scotland for 6 d. 'Three years ago', Dalhousie observed, 'the same sum would not have carried his letter beyond Lahore'.[82]

Dalhousie took immense pride in his infrastructural achievements, in the introduction for the first time into India of 'three engines of social improvement, which the society and science of recent times had previously given the Western nations — Railways, uniform Postage and the Electric Telegraph'.[83] He not only effected a gigantic technological leap in the British-Indian territories, but also was mindful of the need for safeguarding its effects. Thus Dalhousie established under the central Government the Public Works Department (in place hitherto of the military) to cater to the increasing demand for governmental constructions. Dalhousie was also alive to the need for obtaining professional services and for nurturing engineering skills within the country. Following the example of a College of Engineering that Thomason had set up in 1847 at Roorkee, he founded in 1854–55 the Civil Engineering Colleges in Calcutta, Bombay and Madras, and arranged for engineering teaching in Lahore and Poona. One may recall in this connection his predecessor Bentinck's concern for spreading Western medical learning in India, and establishing in 1835 the Calcutta Medical College — the first of its kind in the East.

FOR BOURGEOIZATION

During their Indian tenures, Bentinck and Dalhousie, and also those who succeeded and preceded them, did live up to the expectations of their mentors and ideologues, Mill and Bentham, respectively. Utilitarianism, the school of thought that Bentham created and Mill upheld, remarkably represented industrialized Britain's bourgeois aspirations and intentions, and was admirably suited for application in the underdeveloped political economy of colonial India. The grand British design for elevating and bourgeoizing India — to suit its own interests more than India's — seemed to be paying good, if not rich, dividends. India, by the bourgeois liberal standard, was put on the right course of progress: shorn of some of its cruel superstitious practices, bestowed with a rationalized system of law, treated with increasing doses of Western education, touched by a humane and scientific world view, and provided with dramatic infrastructural innovations. All these were certain to help immeasurably in the process of India's bourgeoization, but still not enough to bring it about from within. To bourgeoize India, a battle had to be waged against Indian feudalism, for freeing most Indians from the grip of an exploitative and oppressive feudal system. Centred on the utilization of land and its administration and the social relations based on it, feudalism reigned supreme in rural India where the overwhelming number of Indians lived and struggled for life. Unless this feudal dominance was challenged and its perpetrators cornered, the process of bourgeoization in India hardly had any rosy prospect. It was in the countryside, and in an anti-feudal contest, that the fortunes of the British bourgeois experimentation in India fatefully depended.

## Notes

1 E. J. Hobsbawm, *Industry and Empire: An Economic History of Britain since 1750*, Weidenfield and Nicolson, London, 1968, p. 32.
2 J. T. Ward (ed.), *Popular Movements, c. 1830–1850*, Macmillan, London, 1970, p. 5.
3 Population, marriage age and wages being interdependent, it was noticed that whenever wages rose, the marriage age fell and population

tended to rise, and vice versa, i.e., fall in wages resulted in the rise of marriage age and fall in population. This process of rise and fall was occurring in Britain all the time (as observed by the population experts), depending upon the fluctuation of food prices and productivity. On the whole, however, population seems to have continued to increase in Britain at a modest pace over the centuries up to the 19th century, since the rate of deaths is found mostly to be lower than births. Population increased rapidly with the onset of the Industrial Revolution in the latter half of the 18th century that opened up the chances of larger supply of raw industrial material from abroad, more employment opportunities, and some lessening of food prices.

4 M. J. Daunton, *Progress and Poverty: An Economic and Social History of Britain, 1700–1850*, Oxford University Press, Oxford, 1995, p. 135.
5 Husain et al., *Karl Marx on India*, p. 47. British mill-owners were known to have left no stone unturned in buying Indian goods at the cheapest.
6 *Ibid.*
7 James Mill, *The History of British India*, 2nd edn., Vol. 2, London, 1820, pp. 166–67, cited in Eric Stokes, *The English Utilitarians and India*, Clarendon Press, Oxford, 1959, p. 54.
8 The alliance between the missionaries and the merchants was built upon the Evangelical concern that India should overcome its civilizational backlog and attain material prosperity, and on the Lancashire manufacturers' eagerness to uphold both these precious causes. After all, the British manufacturing interests had so far had a very limited market in India on account of — by their own reckoning — Indian consumers' lacking in affluence, as well as failing in living standards.
9 Charles Grant, *Observations on the State of Society among the Asiatic Subjects of Great Britain, Particularly with Respect to Morals; and on the Means of Improving It*, London, 1797, pp. 73–74 and 8, cited in Stokes, *The English Utilitarians and India*, pp. 31–32.
10 *Ibid.*, p. 31.
11 Stokes, *The English Utilitarians and India*, p. 56.
12 Bentham's views as discussed in *ibid.*, p. 309.
13 *Ibid.*, p. 302.
14 Bentinck had been the Governor of Madras Presidency from 1803 to 1807, and was recalled for his failure to prevent the mutiny of the sepoys at Vellore in July 1806. On his return to England, a disgraced Bentinck passionately fought the recall, and managed to extract the

Court of Directors' admission of its harshness on him. Bentinck's public image also improved when his governorship was believed to have been innovative in the financial, judicial and land administration of the Presidency, and in tune with 'the good of the governed'. See Maya Gupta, *Lord William Bentinck in Madras and the Vellore Mutiny, 1803–7*, Capital Publishers, New Delhi, 1986, p. 245. His complete vindication, however, came in 1828 when he was appointed by the authorities as the head of the Government of India.

15 Bentinck served from 1811 to 1815 as the Military Governor of Sicily — a virtual British protectorate during the Napoleonic Wars — and as his country's military advisor on Italian affairs. He played a significant role in Italy's nation building in general, and in strengthening the political and civil liberties in Sicily in particular. See John Rosselli, *Lord William Bentinck: The Making of a Liberal Imperialist, 1774–1839*, Thomson Press, New Delhi, 1974, part III, sections 4 and 5.

16 Stokes, *The English Utilitarians and India*, p. 51.

17 *Ibid.*

18 Suresh Chandra Ghosh, *Dalhousie in India, 1848–1856*, Munshiram Manoharlal, New Delhi, 1975, p. 139.

19 *Ibid.*, p. 127.

20 Stokes, *The English Utilitarians and India*, p. 249.

21 Rosselli, *Lord William Bentinck*, p. 249.

22 *Ibid.*

23 Macaulay's speech in the Charter Act Debate, House of Commons, 10 July 1833, cited in Stokes, *The English Utilitarians and India*, p. 45.

24 Rosselli, *Lord William Bentinck*, p. 266.

25 Bentinck also created at the apex another Sadar Diwani Adalat for the NWP at Allahabad in 1831, over and above the existing ones — the future Provincial High Courts — in Calcutta, Madras and Bombay.

26 Macaulay on the proposal to appoint a Law Commission, 10 July 1833, Parliamentary Debates, third series, Vol. 19, pp. 530–33, quoted in S. V. Desika Char (ed.), *Readings in the Constitutional History of India, 1757–1947*, Oxford University Press, New Delhi, 1983, p. 266.

27 Letter of the Government of India to the Judges of the Calcutta Supreme Court, 9 October 1830, House of Commons, Parliamentary Papers (hereafter PP), 1831, Vol. 6, Appendix 5, p. 147, cited in Stokes, *The English Utilitarians and India*, p. 189, fn 2.

28 Desika Char, *Readings in the Constitutional History of India*, p. 266.

29 Macaulay's Minute, 25 June 1835 and 6 June 1836, cited in Stokes, *The English Utilitarians and India*, pp. 209 and 213.
30 Stokes, *The English Utilitarians and India*, p. 228.
31 Ironically, later in 1860 when Macaulay's Penal Code became law, following some revision by Sir Barnes Peacock, these 'Notes' resurfaced as the standardized 'Statement of Objects and Reasons'.
32 Stokes, *The English Utilitarians and India*, p. 231.
33 Evidence of David Hill, 10 March 1853, PP, Vol. 27, p. 100, cited in *ibid.*, p. 261.
34 Macaulay was responsible for changing the nomenclature of 'regulation' into 'act' at the end of 1834, as well as, incidentally, for framing rules for the Supreme Government's Legislative Council.
35 S. N. Mukherji, 'Educational Policy', in K. K. Datta and V. A. Narain (eds.), *A Comprehensive History of India*, Vol. 11, People's Publishing House, New Delhi, 1985, chapter 11(c), p. 585.
36 Macaulay's Minute, 2 February 1835, in K. K. Datta and V. A. Narain, *A Comprehensive History of India*, Vol. 11, People's Publishing House, New Delhi, 1985, p. 599.
37 H. T. Prinsep's Note, 15 February 1835, in *ibid*.
38 Bentinck's Resolution, 7 March 1835, in *ibid.*, p. 600.
39 Auckland's Minute, 24 November 1839, in *ibid.*, p. 602.
40 Hardinge's Resolution, 10 October 1844, in *ibid.*, p. 601.
41 Macaulay was renowned for asserting hyperbolically at his flamboyant worst that 'a single shelf of a good European library was worth the whole native literature of India and Arabia'. See Macaulay's Minute, 2 February 1835, in *ibid.*, p. 599. Also available online at: http://www.columbia.edu/itc/mealac/pritchett/00generallinks/macaulay/txt_minute_education_1835.html (accessed on 7 May 2015).
42 According to Macaulay, any modernizing act, which especially belonged to a Government like that of India, owes wholly 'to an enlightened and paternal despotism'. Macaulay on the Law Commission, 10 July 1833, in Desika Char, *Readings in the Constitutional History of India*, p. 267.
43 Macaulay on the future of British rule in India, 10 July 1833, in *ibid.*, p. 211.
44 Ghosh, *Dalhousie in India*, p. 9, fn 5.
45 *Ibid.*, p. 11.
46 See R. J. Moore, 'Composition of Wood's Education Despatch', *English Historical Review*, Vol. 80, 1965, p. 85, and also his *Sir Charles Wood's Indian Policy, 1853–66*, Manchester University Press, Manchester, 1966, pp. 108–9.

47 Ghosh, *Dalhousie in India*, pp. 20–22.
48 R. C. Majumdar, H. C. Raychaudhuri and K. K. Datta, *An Advanced History of India*, Macmillan, London, 1950, p. 820.
49 Bentinck to Charles Grant, 10 March 1833, cited in Rosselli, *Lord William Bentinck*, p. 213.
50 Macaulay to Zachary Macaulay, 12 October 1836, cited in Stokes, *The English Utilitarians and India*, pp. 45–46.
51 Dalhousie Papers, 37/40, cited in Ghosh, *Dalhousie in India*, p. 14.
52 J. J. Lucas, *History of the North India Christian Tract and Book Society, 1848–1934*, North India Christian Tract and Book Society, Allahabad, 1935, p. 116.
53 Earl of Ellenborough, 9 June 1857, House of Lords, *Hansard Parliamentary Debates*, third series, 1857, Vol. 145, p. 1396.
54 Raj Bahadur Sharma, *Christian Missions in North India, 1813–1913: A Case Study of Meerut Division and Dehra Dun District*, Mittal Publishers, New Delhi, 1988, p. 31.
55 *Ibid.*, p. 32.
56 *Ibid.*, p. 164.
57 Survey of the Evangelical Work of the Punjab Mission of the Presbyterian Church in the U.S.A., 1929, p. 75, cited in *ibid.*, p. 212.
58 *Annual Report of IV Years*, Meerut Mission, 1852, p. 41, cited in *ibid.*, p. 89.
59 The Religious and Caste Disabilities Act, passed originally in 1832 and supplemented subsequently in 1850, removed all disabilities (namely, forfeitures of the rights of property and inheritance) due to change of religion. The act, known as the 'Hindu Black Act', invited the ire of a very numerous Hindu community, and resulted in 60,000 memorialists opposing it.
60 Ghosh, *Dalhousie in India*, p. 14.
61 *Ibid.*, p. 44; see also Dalhousie's Minute, 28 February 1856, on the administration of India, 1848–56, House of Commons, PP, 1856, Vol. 45, paper 245, p. 16, British Library, London.
62 Subodh Chandra Sengupta (ch. ed.), *Samsad Bangali Charitrabhidhan*, Vol. 2, Sahitya Samsad, Calcutta, 1988, p. 65.
63 Ghosh, *Dalhousie in India*, p. 43.
64 Secretary of State for India to the Government of India, 7 April 1859, in H. Sharp and J. A. Richey (eds.), *Selections from the Educational Records of the Government of India*, Vol. 2, Government of India, Calcutta, 1920–22, pp. 435–36.

65 Radhakumud Mukherji and R. C. Majumdar, 'Social Condition', in R. C. Majumdar (ed.), *The History and Culture of the Indian People*, Vol. 2: *The Age of Imperial Unity*, Bharatiya Vidya Bhavan, Bombay, 1968, p. 567. See also Romila Thapar, 'In History', in Andrea Major (ed.), *Sati: A Historical Anthology*, Oxford University Press, New Delhi, 2007, p. 453.

66 From young Gladstone's draft poem 'The Suttee' (1831), written during his last year at Oxford, cited in Sarvepalli Gopal, 'Gladstone and India', in Donovan Williams and E. Daniel Potts (eds.), *Essays in Indian History: In Honour of Cuthbert Collin Davis*, Asia Publishing House, Bombay, 1973, p. 2.

67 Dalhousie's Minute, 28 February 1856, on the administration of India, 1848–56, House of Commons, PP, 1856, Vol. 45, paper 245, p. 36.

68 *Ibid.*, p. 38.

69 Sir John Lawrence, Chief Commissioner of Punjab at the time, later served as Viceroy of India, 1864–69.

70 *Ibid.*

71 Ghosh, *Dalhousie in India*, pp. 52–53.

72 *Ibid.*, p. 55.

73 *Ibid.*

74 Dalhousie's Minute, 28 February 1856, on the administration of India, 1848–56, House of Commons, PP, 1856, Vol. 45, paper 245, p. 39.

75 Rosselli, *Lord William Bentinck*, p. 289.

76 *Ibid.*

77 Bentinck's submission to the Select Committee of the House of Commons, PP, 1837, Vol. 6, pp. 550–54, cited in *ibid.*, p. 292.

78 Dalhousie's Minute, 28 February 1856, on the administration of India, 1848–56, House of Commons, PP, 1856, Vol. 45, paper 245, pp. 28–29.

79 *Ibid.*, p. 16.

80 *Ibid.*, pp. 16–18.

81 Ghosh, *Dalhousie in India*, p. 108.

82 Dalhousie's Minute, 28 February 1856, on the administration of India, 1848–56, House of Commons, PP, 1856, Vol. 45, paper 245, p. 18.

83 *Ibid.*, p. 16.

# 2
# AGAINST FEUDALISM

The French Revolution of 1789 is acknowledged to be the outcome of an intensity of deprivation and injustice that the Third Estate (the commonalty) felt towards the First (the Church) and the Second (the nobility) Estates' domination over the *ancien régime* in France.[1] The Church's and the nobility's dominance, under absolute rule, was based on the feudal system of securing for them a monopoly on socio-political powers and privileges. With their declining fortunes in the second half of the 18th century, and conversely the growth in well-being and strength of a certain advanced section of the commonalty (the bourgeoisie and the *sans-culottes*), the former's monopoly on powers and privileges seemed incongruous against the latter's stark exclusion from any share in these advantages. To resolve the incongruities and the irrationalities of the existing socio-political arrangements, the bourgeoisie and the professionals, artisans and skilled labourers, merchants and shopkeepers had to confront the monarchy, the Church and the nobility, and challenge the country's feudal social structure in convulsive tumults between 1789 and 1799. Following the collapse of the old order, a bourgeois-controlled France stepped into the 19th century to herald capitalism and modernism in its history. Although the temper of anti-feudalism did not turn out to be as tempestuous and dramatic as in France, it nevertheless started rising in Britain in the 17th century, and stretched over a longer period of time till the mid-19th century.

The march of forces against feudalism in Britain commenced roughly with the onset of the civil war (1642), and reached an apparently conclusive stage in the 'Bloodless' or 'Glorious' Revolution (1688). These twenty-six years saw the squire-dominated national assembly or Parliament becoming all-powerful in Britain, with popular support veering around the bourgeoisie — the 'middling sorts', the lower orders and the urban elite — who felt their political and socio-economic aspirations were continuously being thwarted and undermined by the nobles, bishops and the greater gentry under a tyrannical monarchy. By the end of the 18th century in Britain, all instruments of tyranny (including the Prerogative Courts) were abolished and the royalty was prevented from suspending and dispensing with the laws passed by Parliament. It was not allowed to interfere with parliamentary elections and proceedings or impose itself on financial matters. Only Parliament could levy all the taxes and sanction standing armies as the legal and regular ones. The military character of the nobility was attenuated, forced loans abandoned, feudal dues discontinued, and feudal fiscal privileges withdrawn, forcing the nobles to pay taxes. Lands of substantial royalists were sequestrated (i.e., taken over by county committees), and the estates of more than 700 royalist nobles were confiscated.[2]

Coincidentally, throughout the 18th century, British manufacturers succeeded in expanding their markets at home and abroad, and urgently needed some production-boosting mechanism to continue with their success story.[3] Out of this dire need came about the Industrial Revolution in Britain, and it started replacing the feudal commercial base of economy by a capitalist industrial one. By 1800, with the onset of the Industrial Revolution in Parliamentarian Britain and the advancement of the social revolution in Republican France, feudalism was clearly on its way out.

The bourgeoisie had established their sway in both these powerful European nations, and in Britain additionally they stole the show over their counterparts in France by laying the foundation of a technology-based, forward-looking industrial society. Feudal elements in both countries tried in their own ways to adjust to the bourgeois political economy by entering more and more into entrepreneurial activities. The French nobles, who had already taken some interest in commercial profit-making, were becoming increasingly involved from the beginning of the 19th century in monopoly capitalist ventures or financial dealings. The British aristocracy, which had lost its hold over most institutions of privilege and a certain portion of its lands even in the 17th century, took on occasion thereafter to promoting manufacturing business. In the midst of the Industrial Revolution in the latter half of the 18th century, some of its members invested in industrial production, and many also profited from ground rents of industrial sites and royalties for mines on their estates. With the availability of capital, a good number of British landlords invested in improvements in farming, drainage and roadworks. Despite these attempted adjustments and improvements, the fresh memory of the nobility's dogged defence of their entrenched privileges in France, and the not-so-fresh recollection of the urbanite urgency for forfeiture of aristocratic concessions in Britain, contributed to the lingering public distrust of and intellectual disdain for the feudal social order. Feudalism being antithetical to industrial capitalism, the industrially advancing society in Britain was bound by nature to be hostile towards the continuance of the feudal order in any form — anywhere.

# I

Britain's colony in India could by no means be an exception, and the way the British bourgeoisie, their political strategists and ideologues (of Whiggish, Evangelical and Utilitarian varieties) were contemplating it at the junction of the 18th and 19th centuries more or less bears this out. Prompted by Whiggery, Charles Cornwallis, Governor General from 1786 to 1793, found the 'oriental form' of government (a euphemism for the Indian feudal order) to be fundamentally at fault, and its adoption by the Companyraj as the source of every ill.[4] He therefore decided to replace in the Bengal Presidency the hierarchy of the landed magnates and revenue collectors with the carefully devised great landholders (*zamindars*) on the model of the transforming British nobility of his time, expecting them — once they were bestowed with property rights and permanent tenure — to contribute to the country's stability and agricultural prosperity. More importantly, he wanted the *zamindars* to be deprived of all their powers and privileges so that they would not be able to trample India's civil and agrarian society. Consequently, he took away the *zamindars'* quasi-legal powers of the past, as well as their right to keep armed retainers and police in the *zamindari*s. That, despite the Government's oversight, the permanent *zamindari* system would deteriorate and revert eventually into an apparatus for massive economic exploitation and social oppression in the countryside was only vaguely suspected and not seriously considered at that point. Had it been possible to anticipate the deterioration, the British mercantile community would not have regarded the Permanent Settlement as enabling the landed estates in Bengal to pass steadily out of the hands of the aristocratic *zamindars* into those of the emerging Indian entrepreneur class, leading to a capitalist mode of agricultural production as well as an expansion of the Indian market.[5] A similar expectation for the coming into being of capitalist landlords (those investing surplus for improvement) out of the Permanent Settlement led Bentinck (1828-35), an illustrious successor of Cornwallis, 'to admit the place of great landholders — "the class of superborum" in the agrarian economy' of India.[6]

Although they did not share the hopes of Cornwallis (and also of Bentinck and some of the representative bourgeoisie in Britain) for the promising future of the Bengal *zamindars*, the Evangelicals and the Utilitarians agreed more or less with his adverse opinion of the Indian feudal order, and found it almost irredeemable. With vehemence, Charles Grant, the spokesman for Evangelical and Methodist opinion, denounced the unrestrained 'despotism' of the Indian political system and the 'tyranny' of the laws and religions associated with it.[7] Through evangelization and education, Grant thought of rescuing Indians from the clutches of medieval (and feudal) practices, thus ensuring the progress of their civilization and material prosperity (of course, with the help of British commerce). India would then be a suitable place for British capitalist displays — a condition the Evangelicals would have loved to see fulfilled as supporters of Lancashire capital. Like Grant and the Evangelicals, the Utilitarians also believed that the root cause of a retrograde society in India was 'despotism' — a vast political and religious 'tyranny'.[8] According to Mill, 'despotism' was the native form of government, and he believed that the only way India could be taken out of the morass was by emancipating its people from the 'despotic' rule, from the 'tyranny' of priests and nobles — the overgrown parasites — and by giving free scope to capital and labour.[9] Amidst industrial growth, Britain's responses to the prevalent form of feudalism in India were thus of two kinds: one, of trying expediently for its betterment on the Whig line, and the other, of audaciously rejecting it on the Evangelical and Utilitarian line. Both these lines had their followings among the men ('men' only, in an age of utter patriarchy) on the spot — the formulators and executors of British policies in India.

In India, the redoubtable Governor General Wellesley (1778–1805) belonged to the first category, and upheld to a large extent the position of his immediate predecessor Cornwallis (as Bentinck did about twenty-five years later), insofar as the promise of the newly created *zamindar*s were concerned. Well known for his 'haughtiness towards the Indian aristocracy',[10] Wellesley insisted in 1798 on the introduction of the Bengal system of permanent *zamindari* settlement in all the unsettled areas of the Madras Presidency,[11] and this he did on 'his own initiative', despite the Court of Directors' reluctance.[12] His stand, however, was never rigid, and in tune with his distaste for the nobility, he was willing in July 1805 to let the anti-landlord *rayatwari* experimentation to continue in Madras. Bentinck, who was still not enamoured with capitalist landlordism, also took the same position as a young Governor of the Madras Presidency. However, a good number of the East India Company's influential officials in India were, irrespective of their attitudes to the Indian aristocracy, particularly struck meanwhile by the entrepreneurial prospect of the Permanent Settlement. They felt that the security of landed property under the settlement, the property right, and the certainty of profit from such property's products should induce property-holders to invest capital into it — a major step towards 'improvement'.[13] Others in high office in India were opposed to having any intermediary (landed magnates and landlords) whatsoever in the country's land administration between the Government and the *rayat*, and committed themselves to the introduction of a *rayatwari* settlement in the rest of India as opposed to the permanent *zamindari* settlement. Despite the clear anti-feudal character of their commitment, at least two stalwarts among them — Mountstuart Elphinstone and John Malcolm in Bombay — suffered from a contradictory compassion for the Indian nobility. Both of them wished for the survival of the native aristocracy 'to preserve Indian society in all its rich variety'.[14] Additionally, Malcolm thought it expedient to conciliate the aggrieved, displaced aristocrats, and use them to counterbalance any adverse effect that direct alien rule might produce in the future.[15] But another opponent of all intermediaries between the Government and the *rayat*s, and a staunch critic of Permanent Settlement with the *zamindar*s in Bengal, Charles Metcalfe nevertheless remained a persistent denouncer of Indian feudalism in the north-western part of India.

A hard-core paternalist, and somewhat free from Utilitarian and Evangelical predilections, Metcalfe was at the fore of those who wanted to reject the role of the nobility altogether in the British-Indian political structure. Experience had shown him the worthlessness of its members, who were mostly indolent, extravagant and inefficient. Taking the aristocrats' titles to large landholdings to be thoroughly unreliable, and their social standing to be generally unworthy, Metcalfe planned to reduce the privileged class's power and influence,[16] and use every 'just occasion' to annex the Indian States and utilize their revenues to strengthen the British military machine.[17] Though not as vocal as Metcalfe, Governor General Auckland (1836–42) was also in favour of undermining the aristocracy's pre-eminence in India. Others in this category, although not at the top of the official hierarchy, were products of an industrializing British society and ideologically inclined to act as stern opponents of feudalism in India. Among many in the Company's service who were aware of bourgeois political economy, particularly noteworthy were Holt Mackenzie, Robert M. Bird, George Campbell, Alexander Ross, James Thomason, Edward Parry Thornton, George Wingate and Henry Edward Goldsmid. Together they represented the wholesale official British denunciation of the nobility's enjoyment of social dominance, political authority, administrative control and economic advantages. Many of these privileges, particularly those relating to the collection of land revenue and the hold over landed estates, sprang from questionable sources and had been wrested in dubious ways. Devoid of entrepreneurial drive, members of the Indian aristocracy were found to have contributed little to agricultural improvements anywhere, or to have justified the low, non-incremental Government demand on them under the Permanent Settlement. Clearly the aristocracy as a class, practically of unproductive, unremunerative and burdensome intermediaries between the peasants (individually or as a body) and the Government, deserved to be done away with so as to make room for a more direct, systematized and periodized settlement of land revenue. Agriculture should become rewarding business for both the agriculturist and the Government, and its profit should not be sucked away by 'the useless drones of the soil'.[18] If the profit was retained, shared and invested, it could push up the production of food and cash crops for a nascent income-generating market. Likewise, the Government could also use its augmented revenue in expanding the market (over and above bolstering up its administration and army) by providing for transport, communication and other infrastructural facilities. All these processes of commercialization, and eventual capitalization of agriculture, were dependent on the rejection and liquidation of feudalism in India. An offensive against the retrograde feudal order in the country, therefore, became the foremost task of the forward-looking opponents of aristocracy within the Government.

## II

The aristocrats usually held lands in pre-British India under an age-old system either of *jagir*s (royal grants) or of *taluk*s (a conglomerate of villages). The *jagir*s, or rewards for the noblemen's meritorious services to the state, were granted without liabilities, and, in accordance with popular perception, for life and in perpetuity. *Jagir*s proliferated in the 18th century when Moghul rule was declining and passing through a phase of confusion and anarchy. Adventurers and powerful men took advantage of the chaos by occupying estates through force and fraud, and proclaimed in course of time their de facto possessions as de jure *jagir*s. It is said that the number of *jagir*s that emperors from Babar to Aurangzeb granted in their rule for 274 years was only about a half of what Emperor Shah Alam granted in his rule of 48 years before the East India Company took over charge from him (through the grant of Diwani) in 1803.[19] On its part, the Companyraj also continued with the liberal distribution of largesse in order to buy over the loyalty of those personages who mattered locally. Innumerable villages and surrounding lands thus passed into the hands of the notables — the *jagirdar*s and *zamindar*s — who asserted their rent-free ownership over extensive estates on the plea of royal *sanad*s.

The *taluk*s had a slightly different kind of evolvement, and comprised vast stretches of lands from which the Government in the past used to collect revenue directly from village proprietors. Later, perhaps for the sake of convenience, the authorities made over by patents the right of collecting the entire revenue from the *taluk*s to the major landholders of the locality, called the *talukdar*s or *ijaradar*s. For undertaking this responsibility, the *talukdar*s were paid as remuneration a certain percentage of the total collection, and were offered other privileges. The wealth and influence thus acquired helped the *talukdar*s to become in course of time practically 'independent', enabling them to manage the estates as they pleased. The result was their infringing upon the rights of the village proprietors, ejecting them at will and appropriating villages for themselves.[20] Over the years, the patented rights or 'titles' of the *talukdar*s were often obtained, as it happened in the case of the *jagirdar*s and *zamindar*s, through fraud in connivance with village accountants. And also like them, the *talukdar*s and *ijaradar*s did enjoy rent-free lands simply by declining to contribute to the overall village revenue collection.

In the tradition of Mill, the anti-feudal officials of the Companyraj took the state to be the owner of all lands which the peasants cultivated and paid revenue for. Holt Mackenzie — a product of the East India College, Haileybury, Hertfordshire — considered Cornwallis's conversion of the revenue-collecting *zamindar*s into land proprietors (by giving them the right to alienate and sell their lands) as the original sin that downgraded and trivialized the right of all other agricultural classes. This mistake, he felt, should not be repeated in any other part of India, especially in its north-western and central parts where revenue farmers like *jagirdar*s, *zamindar*s and *talukdar*s hardly had any hereditary rights of collection and management. In most cases, they appeared to have assumed their position by dubious and questionable means during the troubled times of the 18th century. Therefore, the genuineness of their time-old hereditary rights and interests in the land should be confirmed, according to Mackenzie, through investigation — by undertaking detailed surveys and inspections. Following the outcome of these investigations, which, in Mackenzie's opinion, was likely to go overwhelmingly against the aristocrats, their lands ought in fairness to be resumed without exception. All losers of lands should also be deprived of their office of revenue collection for the Government, which could then be passed over advantageously to village community bodies — those in a position to represent the lower peasantry or the multitudes of peasants. Such peasants should include those who had lived in a locality for long periods, and cultivated lands occupied by them for thirty or fifty years, and yet possessed 'no rights beyond the year they commence the cultivation, having no *pattahs*, and the *Zamindars* being entitled to oust them at pleasure on the expiration of the year'.[21] Echoing Mill's view that the primary and substantive right to the soil belonged to the peasant, Mackenzie resolved to be protective of the *rayat* and aggressive towards those artificial creations of the state like the *talukdars*, *jagirdars* and *zamindars*. He was keen to devise such a custom-based scheme as would prevent landlords and *malguzars* (large-farming revenue collectors) from exercising their feudal control and 'usurping the property of the under-tenants, or force the village accountants (*patwaris*) to be instruments of exaction and fraud'.[22]

Theoretically, Robert Bird — another Haileybury product — seemed on the whole to have reinforced Mackenzie's position by trying to probe into the long past of the *jagirdari*, *zamindari* and *talukdari* land rights and expose their fragile nature. By citing past records and referring to translated documentations, he asserted that the land grants in India were, in principle, neither hereditary nor perpetual, and that the enjoyment of such grants depended 'solely' on the pleasure of a monarch during his reign; fresh *sanad*s had to be issued by every successive ruler for their continuation. In spite of this principle, however, Bird conceded that families did continue to enjoy grants for generations through several successions, sometimes out of their uncanny knack for currying fresh favours, and on occasion because of their popularity, so that forfeitures might result in the monarch's loss of reputation for liberality. Together, according to Bird, the land grants stood 'on a foundation — not of right, but of indulgences',[23] and the indulgences depended exclusively on the 'will' of the ruling authorities or the Government, who could annul these if they thought it fit to do so. That the Companyraj in the past did not interfere with the *jagirdari* as well as the *talukdari* estates, and even contributed to their spread, was because of 'ignorance' rather than for the sanctification of 'legality'. They were perfectly within their rights to resume all the nobility's lands if they wanted to, provided — for the sake of good government — they decided how to legitimately go about the business and set the rules of the game. Bird was confident that the resumption proceedings, the ascertainment of rights and the survey operations in the NWP could remove 'the evils which had eaten, like a canker, into the very vitals of landed property and agricultural prosperity'.[24] Resumptions, following in-depth examination of *sanad*s and other actualities, would not only help in bringing down iniquitous feudal structures in the country, but also lead 'to the regeneration that is to spring from their decay'.[25] A new India could be built up by using the returns from resumptions in good government — in education, in legal and administrative reforms, in public works and in setting up infrastructures for future development.[26]

James Thomason, a more successful Haileyburian (who rose to become the Lieutenant Governor of the NWP and a Governor-designate for Madras), was a committed anti-feudalist who found the *talukdar* to be an excrescence on the righteous original system of peasant proprietors. The *talukdar*'s overbearing presence in the *taluk*, Thomason noted with regret, relegated the separate village proprietors (*biswahdars*) almost to oblivion. Despite their primacy, no provision was made to protect their rights, though no one questioned the existence and the inviolability of these. Inaction and silence offered the *talukdars* golden opportunities to obtain whatever they wished to, and invariably 'succeed in their object'.[27] The onslaught on the rights of the *biswahdars*, and their being 'heavily encumbered with debt', adversely affected not only the agricultural prosperity of the country, but also the resources of the State.[28] In such circumstances, and on the lines recommended by Mackenzie and Bird, Thomason was anxious to prevail upon the high priest in the Government to look afresh into the *talukdari* proprietorship and take the chance of 'setting aside those Talukdars who were found to have no good title, and of restoring the village proprietors'.[29] Any considerable extent of resumption of the *talukdari* holdings was bound to result, according to Thomason, in the emergence of two kinds of proprietors on the NWP's agrarian scenario to augur agricultural stability: one, the chastened large proprietors or the *talukdars* with apparently valid titles, and the other, the relieved village proprietors or *biswahdars* with reinstated titles.

Thomason's position on the *talukdari* issue was appreciated by his superior, Governor General Ellenborough, who upheld it as 'the only one the Government can recognize under the existing state of things'.[30] Ellenborough and Thomason, however, were willing to compensate the *talukdars* for the loss of their superior position as revenue collectors and managers by conceding to them a certain percentage of the total annual revenue collection from the estates 'as a favour and not a claim'.[31] Similarly, all the detractors of feudalism in the NWP — whether Mackenzie or Bird or Thomason — had more or less been favourable to the payment of pensions to those whose estates were to be resumed, following invalidation. The pensions were meant to lessen the hardship resulting from their long dependence on such estates, and these would normally be paid for lifetime only. In the eyes of many in official circles, Thomason's and his predecessors' agreeing to compensation and pensions for the aristocrats added to their stature a rare statesmanlike quality. By the early 1850s, Thomason seemed to have become a cult figure among a sizeable number of civilians, collectors and settlement and revenue officers as an ideologue of social justice for the poor in confrontation with the powerful.

Despite the dominance of their standing, Thomason, Bird, Mackenzie and company did occasionally come across dissenting voices from within the Companyraj's officialdom. The battle between officers who supported the claim of the aristocracy and those who took the more popular view of opposing it 'raged with intensity in the course of the settlements'.[32] The ones who took the aristocrats' side believed that the landed magnates, in spite of their failings, still carried some popular sentiment with them — a kind of 'moral effect'. It would not be expedient, in their Malcolm-like opinion, to deprive the aristocracy materially to the extent that they would feel aggrieved towards the Companyraj, especially when the class preferred (the *rayat*s) lacked the countervailing political strength or any appreciation of their own gains.[33] Bird's anti-aristocratic stance also had its objectors at the apex official level. The Lieutenant Governor of NWP of the time (T.C. Robertson), in the face of the disappearance of 'every trace of superior existing rank', was rather panicky at the fearful prospect of 'trying to govern without the aid of intermediate agency of indigenous growth [the *talukdar*s]'.[34] Mackenzie was similarly accused of trying to impose an arrangement on 'the once wealthy, and comparatively speaking civilized landholders of our north-western provinces' which might result eventually 'in all the evil and none of the good'.[35] Even an ally of Mackenzie like Governor General Bentinck — whom he admiringly dubbed his 'Chancellor of the Exchequer' — did not fully share his trusted lieutenant's dislike for large and superior landholders. Bentinck accepted that the *zamindar*s or *talukdar*s were 'adventitious and artificial' creations of the Moghuls and were mere 'contractors with the Government for its revenue'.[36] Yet he was willing to let them continue, in spite of their lacking in documentary proofs, with the tenures under 'actual possession' (*uti possedetis*, i.e., 'if in possession, stay on') primarily to avoid raking up the past,[37] and getting into confusion — a 'jungle', 'most discreditable and injurious'.[38]

None of these criticisms and reservations, however, could stem the rising tide of the official offensive against the *jagirdar*s', *talukdar*s' and *zamindar*s' possession of vast stretches of rent-free lands, and a very stringent operation for their resumption to the Government continued to rock the country till 1857. The operation, spearheaded by the district officials (collectors, magistrates and revenue officers), was a vital part of the massive survey and settlement proceedings undertaken both in the Bombay Deccan and in the NWP In the NWP, these were guided in a disciplined manner by Mackenzie, a hard taskmaster; and it was at his instance that the great landlords' titles for and claims to rent-free lands came under severe official scrutiny. If found untenable on account of forgery and falsity, or if their veracity could not be authenticated, the *sanad*s and claims were summarily rejected, and lands under their cover subjected to resumption, forfeiture, fixation of *jama* anew, and also resale. All these were being carried out hurriedly by the district revenue officials, and the scope for examining and assessing their deliberations was somewhat limited.

Most of the settlements at this point were put into effect at a speed that 'ill-accorded' with their judicial character, and often without any 'pause to weigh the various merits of any claim that presented an obstacle to the high-pressure pace of its progress'.[39] Consequently, the settlement officers hardly pondered before sweeping up every patch of unregistered land, even of such formidables as the Raja of Mainpuri,[40] who lost *talukdari* rights over 116 out of

158 villages by the 1840s, and the Raja of Moorsaun (Murasan), Aligarh, who lost over 138 out of 216 villages of their respective estates.[41] The Etah Raja, Dambar Singh, was left in 1852–53 with but 19 of his 147 villages.[42] In eastern Muzaffarnagar, the Sayyids of the Ganges Canal Tract lost about 56 per cent of their lands between 1840 and 1860.[43] Bhopal Singh, the head of the Chauhan Rajputs in Mathura district, Khair Pargana estate, 'was reduced to a single village in 1857'.[44] Similarly, the Oudh *talukdar*s like Man Singh, Beni Madho or Hanwant Singh of Kalakankar suffered 'the excisions of many villages' from their estates.[45] Appeals against the revenue officials' findings were generally heard by the collectors who sympathized with the views of the Europeans working under them, and the legal processes in courts of law had been far too slow for any aggrieved party to expect prompt relief. Consequently, some arbitrariness or riding roughshod over matters was bound to be involved in certain cases of resumption of the nobility's lands, despite the Government's repeated resolve in the early 1830s to ensure impartiality and to stick to the actual *sanad*s in framing rules for the settlement of rent-free tenures in 1837,[46] and its further elaboration of the rules in 1840 for resorting to resumptions.[47] Even at the highest plane of the Governor, Governor General and the Court of Directors, who theoretically disliked 'harsh' and 'injurious' actions,[48] little consideration was shown in practice to petitioners who thought they had some case against resumptions ordered at the local level.

## III

A few examples should highlight the point, and one at hand is that of Shah Jaffir, who lost his *jagir* in Meerut on account of its *sanad* being found faulty by the collector. He petitioned the Governor General in December 1831 for the restoration of at least a part of the estate, i.e., *mauja* Bachkhari. He pointed out that when his *jagir* was taken away in 1823 (during the early years of Mackenzie), the provincial authorities agreed to return to him this *mauja* rent-free in due course, primarily to enable him to take care of his maintenance.

This had nevertheless not been done, and instead he was paid the annual revenue accrual of the village (fixed in 1823 at Rs. 700 per annum) — a sum inadequate for his maintenance. The Government of India, without being merciful, turned down his petition in May 1832 on the ground that Shah Jaffir had been reported to have given up his *istimrari* right (*zamindari* right) over the *mauja* rather discreetly for a small financial consideration.[49] The smallness of an amount obviously could never have mattered to the Companyraj, and what seemed to have spurred it on to action was the inability of any member of the aristocracy to keep to an understanding or a contract. Dayal Singh's and Bejoy Singh's pleadings with the Government against the forfeiture of their estate, Sarai Baghi, Jaunpur, for failure to pay revenue in 1830 practically fell on deaf ears. The amount involved was a paltry Rs. 3,043 and 12 *anna*s, which a person of Bentinck's liberality could have played down easily, but instead he refused to condone, and allowed the estate to be auctioned off.[50]

There were numerous such instances of harsh and strict application of the Sale Law for the recovery of moderate arrears of revenue from the landlords, big or small. Small or petty *jagirdar*s like Shah Jaffir, or Dayal Singh and Bejoy Singh and their dependants, desperately needed some financial support when they were suddenly caught in the web of forfeitures. Occasionally the Government did come to their rescue, as Mackenzie, Bird and Thomason had recommended, by offering them pensions. This was done in certain cases in Murshidabad, Bengal, a few *lakhirajdar*s[51] in Bihar, a number of *talukdar*s in the NWP, and *poligar*s in Madras. But it was mindful of restricting the duration of pension to the pensioners' lifetimes, dividing the amount in instances of more claimants and certainly not extending it to their heirs.[52] The officials always suspected that a dispossessed *talukdar* would try to dupe the Government into paying more pension than he actually deserved — 'sometime larger than he would have drawn in ordinary courses from the estate from which he was excluded'.[53] Such malpractices perhaps even led the Court of Directors in 1850 to call for the 'discontinuance' of the arrangement for pensions.[54]

Auckland, like his famous predecessor Bentinck, was also unyielding to the *badshahi lakhirajdars'* chorus of claims in 1836, and stuck to the Government policy on resumption. Led by Kabiruddin Ahmad, thirteen *lakhirajdars* of Bihar opposed the Government resumption of their rent-free lands, which, they asserted, had been received as royal grants, and hereditarily so for hundreds of years. On examination, the Government found the *lakhirajdari* claims to be untrue in the majority of cases (where they had occupied lands during troubled times, immediately preceding or succeeding the grant of Diwani), and even where it happened to be true in a minority of cases, the grant was never hereditary. As a result, the dispossession of *lakhirajdars* — to the utter dissatisfaction of the nobility — continued unabated under the Governments of Bengal and the NWP.[55] The issue of *lakhiraj* grant resumption came up once again rather forcefully in 1839, following the formation in 1837 for the first time in India of a powerful Landholders' Society in Calcutta, representing the *zamindari* and *talukdari* interests. The Society approached the Governor General soliciting the suspension of all resumption operations against the *lakhirajdars* till the whole issue — as had already been referred to the Court of Directors — was decided by it.[56] The Government of India was not in a mood to oblige, and since the resumptions in its opinion were fair and satisfactory, it felt the landholders had 'no just ground whatsoever for dissatisfaction'. Rather, according to the Government, the landed magnates should 'find abundant reasons to be satisfied with the indulgences extended to them'.[57] The Government, incidentally, was aware about this time of the need for relieving the *rayats* from the clutches of the landlords, and for getting ready 'in the most particular manner' not only to ascertain and protect the existing rights of the *rayats*, but to ameliorate their overall situation.[58]

All solo efforts of the landed aristocrats for restraining the resumption processes, like those of Dayal Singh and Bejoy Singh, came to naught almost without exception. In 1841, Raja Putnee Mall of Benares pleaded with Governor General Auckland for the annulment of the resumption of his *jagir*, Parganah Shahi. He argued that he had received the grant of this rent-free estate as a reward for his loyal services to the then authorities. The veracity of his claim, however, could not be proved beyond doubt and his plea was rejected in May 1841.[59] Similar was the case of the well-known Raja of Benares's contention for 'exclusion' of parts of his *zamindari* from revenue assessment (under some dubious arrangement of the past), and it was rebutted on the ground that he did not deserve any special privilege, and that he could only be treated identically with other *zamindars*.[60] Even in the case of a powerful feudal chief like Raja Narendra Singh Bahadur of Tributary Mahal, Singrowli, Mirzapur, whose title to his *zamindari* had already been established, any aberration of tenurial arrangement on his part was not countenanced. Some contiguous lands in Tappas Doolki, Poolwa and Burha were being used by the Raja for long as parts of his *zamindari*, though these had not been included in the document of Permanent Settlement. When the irregularity was discovered, the collector of Mirzapur declared the sites as *toofeer* (surplus), and liable for assessment and resettlement. The Raja's vigorous opposition to the collector's decision, first before the NWP Government and then before the Government of India, on the basis of some *pattah* granted to his ancestors in 1799, did not cut much ice with the authorities. Neither of the two Governments was convinced of his long-standing right, and even of its genuineness, and they refused to withdraw the resumption proceedings.[61]

The occurrence in Mirzapur was close to the great outbreak of 1857, and demonstrated that the Companyraj was not only not hesitant, but actually insistent on attacking feudal privileges. Almost an identical development took place during the outbreak of 1857, but since it happened in the turmoil-free southern part of the country, the happening could not have left any mark. Pusunuri Lakshminarasu of Nellore claimed to have inherited from his father the village of Murripad, granted by the Nawab of Arcot in perpetuity through a *sanad*. He alleged that when the neighbouring estate of Woodiagerry was being resumed by the Government, Murripad was also taken away by the collector 'erroneously'. When he found that his request to the Madras Government was proving ineffective, Pusunuri appealed to the Government of India for the restoration of the village to him. Not quite certain of the validity of the Nawabi grant or the collector's alleged proclivity for error, the Supreme Government turned down the appeal without any hesitation.[62] It may perhaps be added here further that even when a landlord's claim was found to be true and the resumption proceedings stopped, he/she was not allowed to alienate any part of the *jagir* lands through transfer, mortgage or sale.[63]

Apart from the large-scale resumption of misleadingly claimed rent-free lands, and the exercise of some control over their heavy revenue-yielding capacity,[64] the officials lost hardly any opportunity for grabbing the estates of those landlords whose inheritance was neither direct nor clear. Their succession was promptly declared to have 'lapsed', and their estates taken over by the Government and auctioned off for fresh settlement. In most cases, the pleadings against such forfeitures did not work out to the owning family's advantage, and the authorities stood by their decisions. The petitions of a good number of *sanad*-holders in western India (who had received their titles from the Peshwa or the Gaekwar) were rejected because of their being unable to prove themselves to be direct heirs.[65] Another example was the manner in which the petitions of the relations of Pandit Bishwambhar (a *jagirdar* of Ghazeepur, Benares) had been rejected by the Companyraj in 1837, following his and his wife's deaths. Succession to the *jagir* was declared to have 'lapsed', since the Pandit had no direct heir, nor had he any sanction for adoption, and the NWP Government faced no technical difficulty in resuming the estate without any loss of time.[66] Prior Government sanction was often made out to be the prime requisite for any adoption by childless *sanad*-holders, and because of its lack, certain adoptions had been squashed in Farrukhabad in 1840–41, resulting in the resumption of the 'lapsed' estates. Adoptions were also refused on the plea that the *sanad*s had not specifically mentioned the *jagirdar*s' right to adopt. In Fatehpur in September 1841, the estate of a deceased *maufidar* was declared 'lapsed' on this ground, and resumed in September 1841.[67]

The 'lapsing' of succession soon attained the high level of a politico-legal doctrine under Dalhousie (1848–56), the formidable

Benthamite and Utilitarian Governor General of India. Considering the Princely States to be the hardest and most archaic impediments to centralized India's progress along modern (bourgeois) lines, Dalhousie embarked on an aggressive campaign of annexations that Mill had sometimes toyed with, namely, by making war on them or taking over their administration by 'judicious means'.[68] Of as many as eight Indian States that he annexed during his eight-year rule, Dalhousie secured Pegu and Punjab by war, Berar by way of debt recovery, and Oudh by supplanting misgovernance, but the majority of them, namely, Satara, Sambalpur, Jhansi and Nagpur, he secured by employing the doctrine of 'lapse' — questioning, pressuring and casting aside the adoptions.[69] Dalhousie's crusade against the Indian aristocracy was demonstrated further in his Government's confiscation of princely properties, resumption of *jagir*s and *inam*s in these states, summary settlement of lands therein, and warding off pensions generally.[70] He also confiscated the plains territories of the hill state Sikkim over some jurisdictional dispute, deprived the Amir of Khyrpore (Sind) of lands which he had occupied 'wrongfully' under an understanding, secured the pledged ouster of the Moghul Emperor ('the king of Delhie') from his seat at the Red Fort (to 'a palace at the Kutub') in return for his grandson's recognition by the British as the heir-apparent, and declared the large stipend of the Raja of Tanjore as 'lapsed' on his death without a successor, and stopped thereby all pensions to his relatives.[71]

The notable victims of the Dalhousiean high-pressure tactics were some of the elaborately discussed iconic figures in the Revolt (1857) historiography, whose legends of anti-British armed opposition have remained alive for posterity. They included, among others, such stalwarts as Nana Saheb (Dhondu Pant), who lost his adopting father Balaji II's pension in 1851 and *jagir* (Bithur) in 1852; Rani Avanti Bai, who lost her regency for a minor son (Amar Singh) to a Court of Wards after the death of her husband, Raja Vikramjit of Ramgarh in Mandla in 1851;[72] and Rani Lakshmi Bai, who, along with her adopted son (Damodar Rao), were condescendingly granted a family pension and a few other facilities following the death of the Raja of Jhansi (Gangadhar Rao) and the annexation of

Jhansi in 1854. Though not of the same category of heroes, Nawab Wajid Ali Shah was similarly treated on the ground of his failure to rid his administration of alleged 'incompetency, corruption and tyranny',[73] and subjected to the annexation of Oudh at the beginning of 1856. By the end of Dalhousie's enlightened despotic tenure, feudalism in India was gasping for breath, living precariously through nightmares, despondencies and dumb rages.

## IV

The feudal system, its protagonists and beneficiaries were reduced in India to a moribund state within a span of roughly a quarter of a century. Between 1829 (1822 for the sake of strict historicity, when land administration started taking a new direction in the NWP) and 1856 (when Dalhousie, the most aggressive of the Governors General, left India for good), 'all superior tenures were extinguished', and in a 'systematic way', in the opinion of a perceptive observer, 'the aristocratic classes were set aside'.[74] Some of the Companyraj's standard-bearers uncomfortably noticed the manner in which 'every trace of superior [landlord] rank was fast disappearing',[75] and even those grave-diggers of feudalism in India were themselves aware of the contemporary 'outcry of spoliation, rapacity and cruelty' being raised against them, both in official and non-official circles.[76] Officials within the Government who were rather reluctant to support the anti-feudal Thomasonian method, did not quite appreciate the scale in which it diminished 'the power and authority of the Talukdars, individually and collectively'.[77] Evidently, anti-feudal officials under the Company's employment had not enjoyed the wholesale backing of their compatriots, or the service generally in India. But they did enjoy some superiority in the officialdom — not so much of number as of self-conscious belief in themselves,[78] of advanced politico-economic ideas and of distinct ideologuic support at home. The rest, or a considerable number of the 'others' in the Companyraj's bureaucracy, did not really know what to do with such a dogged anti-feudal thrust emanating from among themselves — whether to sustain or restrain it. Being the products of a steadily bourgeoized Britain like their counterparts — Mackenzie, Bird, Thomason and company — they could by no means be accommodative towards feudalism. However, since they had learnt to live with Indian feudalism in a hard way, and found it of some use in a semi-medieval set-up, and since they were uncertain as to the shape colonial India should eventually take or be led to take, many of them preferred perhaps to wait a while rather than hurry headlong. Their procrastination, or even inertia, hardly helped the harassed, troubled members of the Indian nobility. With the stepping up of the process of centralizing authority in British India, unlike the 18th-century state of decentralization that had offered scope for manoeuvrings and intrigues, they felt asphyxiated and helplessly depleted.

After all, the princes, *jagirdars*, *zamindars* and *talukdars* in India had throughout been habituated either to comply with the Government if it happened to be strong or to defy it if it was weak. The scenario was the same with the onset of British rule in India, and since British rule had uniformly been based on force of arms, the landed magnates remained more or less compliant towards it. During the early period of British rule, they were seldom interfered with by a demanding Government on financial, ideological and civilizational grounds, and resultantly their complaints against governmental authority, or acts of defiance against its commands, had been numerically rather limited if one takes the largeness and the diversity of territories into account. Acts of feudal resistance of any kind to the Companyraj also had very little chance of success, and practically no possibility of making any headway unless organized collectively for a burning cause and on a meticulously drawn up strategy. Even then, the best of resistance moves would not have the desired impact if it had not received the support, sympathy and active participation of the people at large. The *poligar* grand alliance in the feudal Southern Peninsula against the British in 1800–01,[79] for example, which earned impressive initial victories, could not involve the people in its struggle, and therefore failed to sustain itself. In an age prior to the rise of nationalism as an overarching emotive force, the mass of the people and the commonalty could hardly tide over the contradiction with their immediate social exploiters, and side with their elitist upper-category tormentors, if they did not feel convinced of the greater and sharper contradiction with their common opponents — the alien rulers. They had no means of guessing how widespread, penetrating and enslaving the alien imperialist exploitation could become in due course. But till that happened, or that misfortune struck, ordinary men and women had no grounds to believe the Companyraj to be their main enemy, more than their direct expropriators, especially when it was seen to be attacking feudalism in India, and that, too, professedly for the betterment of the lives of people in general. With little prospect for garnering popular support of any sort, the aristocracy and the great superior landlords in India were isolated, cornered and condemned. Having the circumstances so much in their favour, the bourgeois forerunners of the Company's regime could not but go for an all-out anti-feudal demolition work, by winning over the people through the attainment of some discernible public good — by a demonstration of evident popular well-being. What better way was there in an overwhelmingly agrarian country than to push forward and stimulate its stagnating agriculture by undertaking a theoretically sound and widely acclaimed scientific policy of land administration? The survey, settlement and assessment of land had, therefore, to become crucial for the Companyraj's success in India in the middle of the 19th century.

## Notes

1 Georges Lefebvre, *The French Revolution*, Columbia University Press, New York, 1962, chapter 8 ('The Bourgeois Revolution') and chapter 9 ('The Popular Revolution'), pp. 98–111 and 113–30. See also George Rude, *The French Revolution*, Weidenfield and Nicolson, London, 1988, pp. 4–5.
2 Christopher Hill, *The Century of Revolution, 1603–1714*, Routledge, London and New York, 1980, p. 144.
3 This point has already been clarified in Chapter 1, pp. 7–8.
4 Stokes, *The English Utilitarians and India*, p. 4.
5 *Ibid.*, pp. 61 and 86.

6 Rosselli, *Lord William Bentinck*, p. 250.
7 Grant, *Observations on the State of Society among the Asiatic Subjects of Great Britain*, p. 83, India Office/British Library (henceforth IO/BL).
8 Stokes, *The English Utilitarians and India*, p. 54.
9 *Ibid.*, p. 69.
10 *Ibid.*, p. 18.
11 Gupta, *Lord William Bentinck in Madras*, p. 63.
12 T. H. Beaglehole, *Sir Thomas Munro and the Development of Administrative Policy in Madras, 1772–1818*, Cambridge University Press, London, 1966, p. 5.
13 Peter Penner and Dale Maclean (eds.), *The Rebel Bureaucrat: Frederick John Shore (1799–1837) as Critic of William Bentinck's India*, Chanakya Publications, New Delhi, 1983, p. 108.
14 Stokes, *The English Utilitarians and India*, p. 17.
15 *Ibid.*, pp. 16–17.
16 D. N. Panigrahi, *Charles Metcalfe in India: Ideas and Administration, 1806–1835*, Munshiram Manoharlal, New Delhi, 1968, pp. 74 and 76.
17 Stokes, *The English Utilitarians and India*, pp. 16–17.
18 J. S. Mill, *Principles of Political Economy*, ed. W. J. Ashley, Longmans, Green and Co., London, 1909, pp. 325–28.
19 Fortescue's Report on Jagir Lands, 4 December 1819, paras. 19–20, Bengal Political Cons., 28 October 1820, 28, cited in Panigrahi, *Charles Metcalfe in India*, p. 72.
20 J. Thomason, Lt. Gov., N.W.P., to Ellenborough, Gov. Gen., Agra, 31 January 1844, Selections from the Records of the Government of N.W.P., Mr. Thomason's Despatches, Calcutta, 1856, Vol. 1, No. 9, p. 23, IO/BL.
21 Mackenzie's Memorandum, 19 October 1826, Selections from Revenue Records, N.W.P., Allahabad, 1873, p. 87, IO/BL.
22 *Ibid.*, p. 201.
23 R. M. Bird's Minute on Resumption of Rent-Free Tenures in N.W.P., 31 January 1840, Home Dept./Rev. Br. Cons., Proc. for 22 June 1840, Nos. 33/36, National Archives of India (henceforth NAI).
24 Extracts from the Proceedings of the Government of the N.W.P. during the Second Quarter of 1842, Agra, 18 July 1842 (No. 3), House of Commons, PP, 1857–58, Vol. 43, paper 181.
25 The N.W.P. Lt. Gov. T. C. Robertson's observations of 15 April 1842 on the Report on the Settlement of the North-Western Provinces by

R. M. Bird Esq. vide his Minute of 21 January 1842, House of Commons, PP, 1857–58, Vol. 43.
26 R. M. Bird's Minute on Resumption of Rent-Free Tenures in N.W.P., 31 January 1840, Home Dept./Rev. Br. Cons., Proc. for 22 June 1840, Nos. 33/36, N.A.I.
27 J. Thomason, Lt. Gov., N.W.P., to Ellenborough, Gov. Gen., Agra, 31 January 1844, Selections from the Records of the Government of N.W.P., Mr. Thomason's Despatches, Vol. I, Calcutta, 1856, No. 9, p. 18, IO/BL.
28 J. Thomason, Lt. Gov., N.W.P., to Ellenborough, Gov. Gen., 9 February 1844, Home Dept./ Rev. Br. Cons., 15 April 1848, Nos. 49–55, N.A.I.
29 J. Thomason, Lt. Gov., N.W.P., to Ellenborough, Gov. Gen., Agra, 31 January 1844, Selections from the Records of the Government of N.W.P., Mr. Thomason's Despatches, Vol. I, Calcutta, 1856, No. 9, p. 18, IO/BL.
30 Gov. Gen. Ellenborough's Minute, 13 January 1848, Home Dept./Rev. Br. Cons., 15 April 1848, Nos. 49–55, N.A.I.
31 J. Thomason, Lt. Gov., N.W.P., to Ellenborough, Gov. Gen., Agra, 31 January 1844, Selections from the Records of the Government of N.W.P., Mr. Thomason's Despatches, Vol. I, Calcutta, 1856, No. 9, p. 18, IO/BL; Gov. Gen. Ellenborough's Minute, 13 January 1848, Home Dept./Rev. Br. Cons., 15 April 1848, Nos. 49–55, N.A.I.
32 George Campbell, 'Essay on the Tenure of Land in India', in John Webb Probyn (ed.), *Systems of Land Tenure in Various Countries*, Cassal, Peter, Galpin and Co., London, 1876, p. 159.
33 Arthur D. Innes, *A Short History of the British in India*, Inter-India Publications, New Delhi, 1985, p. 204.
34 T. C. Robertson's Note appending the Report of R. M. Bird, 18 July 1842, House of Commons, PP, 1857–58, Vol. 43, paper 181.
35 Observation of Shore, cited in Penner and Maclean, *The Rebel Bureaucrat*, p. 111.
36 Bentinck's Minute, 26 September 1832, cited in Sulekh Chandra Gupta, *Agrarian Relations and Early British Rule in India: A Case Study of Ceded and Conquered Provinces (Uttar Pradesh, 1801–1833)*, Asia Publishing House, New Delhi, 1963, p. 301.
37 Rosselli, *Lord William Bentinck*, p. 258.
38 *Ibid.*, p. 255.

39 Extract Narrative of Proceedings of the Government of N.W.P. during the Second Quarter of 1842, Agra, 18 July 1842 (No. 3), House of Commons, PP, 1857–58, Vol. 43, paper 181.
40 Tej Singh, the Raja, was 'one of the most sorely stricken victims of the anti-magnate policy of the Thomasonian era of the 1840s'. Eric Stokes, *The Peasant and the Raj: Studies in Agrarian Society and Peasant Rebellion in Colonial India*, Cambridge University Press, Cambridge, 1978, p. 200.
41 *Ibid.*
42 Comm. Agra, Judicial 1(ii) 1857, File 13, Statement of Debts Filed on Estates of Raja Dambar Singh, cited in Stokes, *The Peasant and the Raj*, p. 204.
43 *Ibid.*, p. 188.
44 *Ibid.*, p. 194.
45 *Ibid.*, p. 133.
46 Rules for the Assessment and Settlement of Rent-Free Tenure, Saddar Board of Revenue, Bengal, Home Dept./Rev. Br., 5 June 1837, Nos. 1/7, N.A.I.
47 Resolution passed by the Gov. Gen. in Council, Calcutta, Home Dept./Rev. Br., 5 August 1840, Nos. 1–9(b)(H), N.A.I.
48 J. Thomason, Secy., Government of N.W.P., to Secy., Saddar Board of Revenue, 18 October 1841, Home Dept./Rev. Br. Cons., 27 December 1841, Nos. 1/2, N.A.I.
49 Home Dept./Rev. Br., December 1831, Nos. 73/74, and May 1832, Nos. 36/37, N.A.I.
50 Gov. Gen.'s Minute, Home Dept./Rev. Br. Cons., October 1832, No. 43A, N.A.I.
51 *Lakhirajdars* who were assigned by the Badshah (Emperor) in the Moghul period.
52 Letter of Court of Directors, 21 January 1849, Home Dept./Rev. Br. Cons., 4 April 1850, Nos. 25/28, N.A.I.
53 Home Dept./Rev. Br. Cons., 8 February 1836, Nos. 10/12, N.A.I.
54 Home Dept./Rev. Br. Cons., 4 April 1850, Nos. 25/28, N.A.I.
55 Home Dept./Rev. Br. Cons., 29 August 1836, Nos. 11–9, N.A.I.
56 Petition of the Secretaries, Landholders' Society, Calcutta, 20 August 1839, Home Dept./Rev. Br., 30 December 1839, Nos. 1/2, N.A.I.
57 Decision of the Gov. Gen. in Council, 30 December 1839, Home Dept./Rev. Br., 30 December 1839, Nos. 1/12, N.A.I.
58 Home Dept./Rev. Br., Proc. June–September 1841, Nos. 1–2, N.A.I.

59 *Ibid.*
60 Home Dept./Rev. Br., Proc., 25 May 1835, Nos. 5/6, N.A.I.
61 Home Dept./Rev. Br. Cons., 15 May 1857, No. 10, N.A.I.
62 Home Dept./Rev. Br. Cons., 23 October 1857, No. 4, N.A.I.
63 Home Dept./Rev. Br. Cons., 28 May 1852, Nos. 3/7, N.A.I.
64 The total revenue estimated to have been realized from the lands resumed in the N.W.P. between 1835 and 1848 amounted to Rs. 12,256,221. See Sulekh Chandra Gupta, 'Agrarian Background and the 1857 Rebellion', *Enquiry*, No. 1, February 1959, p. 77.
65 Home Dept./Rev. Br. Cons., April–May 1837, Nos. 2/5(d), N.A.I.
66 Government of India's decision, Home Dept./Rev. Br. Cons., 14 April 1837, Nos. 7/10, N.A.I.
67 Home Dept./Rev. Br., Proc., June–September 1841, Nos. 1/2, N.A.I.
68 Stokes, *The English Utilitarians and India*, p. 250.
69 M. A. Rahim, *Lord Dalhousie's Administration of the Conquered and Annexed States*, S. Chand, New Delhi, 1963, p. ii.
70 *Ibid.*, pp. 368–81.
71 Minute by Marquis of Dalhousie, 28 February 1856, reviewing his administration from January 1848 to March 1856, House of Commons, PP, 1856, Vol. 45, paper 245.
72 Pankaj Raj and Geeta Sabherwal, *The First War of Independence: Documents of Jabalpur and Mandla*, Directorate of Archaeology, Archives and Museum, Madhya Pradesh, Bhopal, 2007, pp. 324–25.
73 Draft Proclamation (B), Enclosure to the Despatch of the Gov. Gen. (Dalhousie) in Council to the Court of Directors, 22 February 1856, House of Commons, PP, 1857–58, Vol. 43, paper 282, p. 256, B.L.
74 Stokes, *The English Utilitarians and India*, pp. 114 and 115.
75 Minute of T. C. Robertson, Lt. Gov., N.W.P., Agra, 25 November 1842, House of Commons, PP, 1857–58, Vol. 43, paper 181.
76 R. M. Bird's Minute, 31 January 1840, Home Dept./Rev. Br. Cons., 22 June 1840, Nos. 33/36, N.A.I.
77 Innes, *A Short History of the British in India*, p. 204.
78 Bird was convinced that 'truth and reason are' with him. R. M. Bird's Minute, 31 January 1840, Home Dept./Rev. Br. Cons., 22 June 1840, Nos. 33/39, N.A.I.
79 Rising above the political standards of their times, feudal *poligar* notables like Marudu Pandyan, Gopala Nayak, Kerala Varma, Krishnappa Nayak, Dhoondaji Waugh and a few others threw up in the Southern Peninsula (covering parts of Tamil Nadu, Kerala, Karnataka, Andhra

and Maharashtra) a coalition to challenge in 1800–01 the British might that had spelt doom for their individual and collective existence. Despite significant initial success, the coalition eventually failed in its object, partly because of a lack of co-ordination among themselves, and partly on account of British vigilance and pre-emptive strikes.

# 3
# FOR RENT THEORY

In a profoundly agricultural country like India, the Companyraj, at the convergence of the 18th and 19th centuries, had to depend for its material well-being primarily on the administration of land. It was the revenue from land that provided the British with most of the finances to run the country as they wished, and to defend, consolidate and expand their vast possessions. Consequently, the settlement of land with its cultivators, the assessment of tax on their holdings, and the collection of the amount so assessed were the major concerns of the early British-Indian policy-makers. Taking care of these concerns involved the sorting out of a number of serious issues in respect of all the three aspects, namely, settlement, assessment and collection. As regards settlement, would it be practicable to settle with individual cultivators or their collectives, directly or through intermediaries, perpetually or periodically? Simultaneously, as regards assessment, would it be possible to strike a balance between over-taxing and under-taxing, or increasing the coffers of the Government without jeopardizing the fortunes of the cultivators? As regards collection again, would it be feasible to insure the Government against any pecuniary loss without being unduly harsh on the cultivators at difficult times, or mixing the realization of revenue with the liberality of its remission? On the resolution of all these issues together, and the one relating to assessment in particular, the well-being of agrarian society in India depended, and its resultant overall progress. It was incumbent on the Government of the time to try very hard to ensure that the conditions remained tolerable for those with whom land was to be settled, the tax levied, and the collection made. The goose that laid golden eggs must at least be allowed to survive if not actually cared for.

# I

During the evolvement of its rule in India, especially in the eastern part, the Companyraj was following more or less the pattern of land administration that had been set up traditionally by preceding Indian rulers. Usually, land had been settled by them either with the superior landlords (*zamindars*, *jagirdars* and *talukdars*) who enjoyed their holdings under charters (*sanads*) on condition of remitting to the Government a stipulated amount of revenue, or with such other intermediaries as the substantial farmers (*ijaradars*) and officials (*faujdars*, *amils* and *tehsildars*). The settlements were made with all these intermediaries for a period of one year on payment of a land tax roughly of one-third of the gross produce — an amount considered high enough in those days. No one was removed from the estate till proved a defaulter, thereby giving the intermediaries a kind of hereditary entitlement. Such general *bandobast* was then followed up by separate agreements between the tax collectors and the actual holders of lands — the tenants and cultivators — and the tax to be paid by them every year was nominally one-third of the gross produce, but actually considerably higher. Not being a party to these agreements, the Government took no interest in stopping the intermediaries from squeezing tenants and cultivators, extracting irregular cesses and levies such as *nazranas* and *salamis*, as well as free labour or *begar*. Taken together, the incidence of taxation on the *rayats* turned out to be so high that the Companyraj found any attempt on its part at raising the land revenue obviously to be 'destructive to the country'.[1] This was despite the fact that it could not have been wholly oblivious of the difference between what the landlords wrung out of the cultivating peasants, and what they paid as tax to the Government — the cause of their rolling in prosperity. Apparently some of those at the helm of British-Indian affairs then, including Governor General Cornwallis, himself a progressive landlord in England, were less bothered about the *zamindari* expropriation and more about the *zamindar*s' transformation into capitalist landed magnates to lead the country's agricultural prosperity.[2]

It was, however, Cornwallis who made the first significant move for a change in the administration of land in 1793, by introducing the system of Permanent Settlement. The system conferred, for the first time, proprietary rights on the *zamindar*s over the lands they looked after on payment of a fixed amount of land tax (calculated on previous years' assessment, ostensibly within the one-third gross produce framework) to the Government — the rightful owner of all lands. They were free, however, to raise the amount by apportioning it on their lease-holding cultivator-tenants, retaining one-tenth of the collection as collectors' fee. The most spectacular part of the arrangement nevertheless was the fixation of tenure of the settlement — not for one year or ten years (as originally thought of in 1789), but for all times to come, in perpetuity. The permanency of the settlement was devised not merely to free the Government from the yearly hazards of administering the nitty-gritty of land (or to conform to the Whiggish fad for minimum official interference), but also to boost the confidence of the superior landlords in themselves, to insure them against any spiralling of Government demand, to encourage them to take entrepreneurial risks so as to bring back deserted (in consequence of the famine of 1769–70) lands into cultivation and invest in artisanal village industries. For Cornwallis's landlordist utopia, the Companyraj seemed to be willing to forego the benefits of rising land prices and increasing agricultural outputs in the coming years. They were not even wholly reluctant to leave the peasantry in the lurch — exposing them to *zamindari* rack-renting and insecurity of tenure, and reducing them to the position of tenants-at-will.[3]

While the Permanent Settlement in Bengal thus turned out to be utterly elitist in character, its succeeding Rayatwari Settlement in Madras, and thereafter in Bombay, was in contrast remarkably egalitarian. The Rayatwari Settlement, which had initially been experimented with in Baramahal and the Ceded Districts (following the introduction of the *zamindari* system in certain locations in Madras Presidency), grew steadily in stages. The growth, corresponding to its founder Thomas Munro's rise from Captain in the army to Principal Collector, Special Commissioner of Justice and Governor, respectively, resulted in 1812 in a settlement that the Government entered into directly with the cultivators by leaving out the intermediaries. Preceded by some survey of the land and an observance on its fertility and yield, the assessment was arrived at by taking the previous rates into account, but not exceeding one-third of the gross produce.[4] The contracted settlement, conferring proprietary rights on individual cultivators, was to run for a fixed period (twenty or thirty years) instead of in perpetuity, and could be revised and renewed thereafter for further terms. The British authorities in Bombay Presidency were so impressed with these *rayatwari* principles of Madras that they decided to introduce a Bombay system around these, and by adopting it with the arrangements prevailing in the territories under them, such as the village and *talukdari* systems in Gujarat and the Peshwa or Maratha system in the Maratha countries. They abolished the farming out of revenue of an area to *malguzar*s and *talukdar*s, as well as to *mamlatdar*s and Patels, got rid of all the traditional cesses, and tried to settle directly with the *rayat*s. This they attempted to do by fixing the annual demand (about one-third of the gross produce) on the basis of village-wise revenue realized (as shown in the Marathi and Gujarati records) by their predecessors. However, the whole endeavour ran into serious difficulties over the heritage of inaccurate information and misleading accounts, and the persistence of widespread corruption and official arbitrariness. By the 1820s, the Government under Elphinstone felt a dire need for reliable data on the holdings, cultivation and resources of each cultivator to enable successful direct revenue settlement in the Bombay Presidency. The confusion and uncertainty over the Bombay authorities' opting for the Rayatwari Settlement continued for some time, till they decided in 1827 to appoint J.D. Pringle as Special Officer in the Deccan to devise a form of survey and settlement for Poona and the surrounding districts.

If the revenue administration in the Bombay Presidency thus remained in suspended animation awaiting finality, its condition about the same time in the Ceded and Conquered Provinces was worse — a hazardous mess in reality. Apart from the problem of the multiplicity of tenurial arrangements, such as with individual cultivators, joint proprietors or co-sharers (including *bhaicharas*), the *lambardari* village communities and the *jagirdari-zamindari-talukdari* intermediaries, the Provinces lacked the mechanism to scrutinize the landholding rights of each of these categories, decide upon the extent and the quality of lands they held, and determine the principles for arriving at the assessments. The revenue was still being calculated on the basis of unsound records of earlier settlements, and through hard bargaining between the collectors and revenue engagers. In the absence of rules and regulations, any proper assessment of revenue under such circumstances was bound to be a near impossibility. Consequently, what had been imposed as land tax during the early years of British administration in the Provinces was arbitrarily high for the actual cultivators — many of whom also lost, on account of the machination of the intermediaries, the land rights they and their ancestors had enjoyed for centuries.

At the beginning, it was felt by the Companyraj — though somewhat haltingly — that the land administration in the Provinces would be better run on the lines of the Bengal system, without of course being able to make up its mind conclusively on the permanency aspect. (Old Benares Province, however, including northern Mirzapur, Jaunpur, Ghazipur and Ballia, had been subjected to Permanent Settlement.) This fluid situation continued apparently for decades, during which the home authorities — in the post–Industrial Revolution phase — were retreating from mercantilism to the free trade economy, and hoping to turn their Indian possessions into both a market and a source of raw material for British capitalists. The unmistakeable 'make' of the Bengal system's feudal character, despite the pro-bourgeois, neo-aristocratic look, the 'losses' it caused to the treasury by putting an embargo on assessment for good, the 'mistake' it committed by perpetuating the tenure, and the *zamindari* 'injustice' it inflicted upon the cultivators, caused the

Permanent Settlement to be looked down upon a bit in the ruling circles. The authorities seemed to be moving steadily away from the Bengal system and tilting towards the Madras system of Rayatwari Settlement. Any system, whether a refined *rayatwari* one or a revised *zamindari*, had to be based upon the actual conditions prevailing at ground level, and these conditions — the determinants of the revenue assessment and the Government income — could only be ascertained through detailed survey and settlement operations in the Provinces (the North-West Provinces from the 1820s) as well as in the Bombay Deccan. These were undertaken in the 1820s, first in the former and then in the latter region, by those products of a technologically advancing society who had been imbued with the ideas of classical bourgeois political economy.

II

The classical theorists of an emergent capitalist economy in Britain, coinciding with bourgeois empowerment in Revolutionary France, had provided an ideological groundwork for generating British public hostility against the aristocracy. The anti-feudal trend in political economy was set, among others, by David Ricardo, who concluded, following his formulation of Rent Theory, that the landlords performed no economic service. They lived, according to Ricardo, as parasites on the community (a position which a charitable Thomas Robert Malthus took to be providential 'special bounty' for a 'leisured class'[5]), and their interest was 'always opposed to every other class or community'.[6] It was, however, Malthus who apparently 'discovered' the law of rent in 1815,[7] showing that rent was a special portion of the society's wealth, distinct from profits and wages. It originated in the rising rate of population, outgrowing food supply and consequently bringing the poorer or marginal lands into cultivation as society grew in numbers and wealth. Rent was the differential advantage enjoyed by all lands of higher quality over marginal lands being then put under tillage. On the lately broken lands the capital employed merely replaced itself, and yielded the ordinary prevailing rate of profit after paying for the wages of labour, also at its prevailing rate. In contrast, the yields of all other lands of higher quality continued to grow beyond this limit and produce a surplus which could be quantified by subtracting from the total or the gross produce the usual cost of cultivation, the charge for wages, and the ordinary rate of profit on the capital employed. Such a surplus or the 'net produce' happened to be the rent, which in classical economic language was

> that portion of the value of the whole produce which remains to the owner of the land after all the outgoings belonging to its cultivation, of whatever kind have been paid, including (apart from the fair and equitable wages for labour) the profits of capital employed, estimated according to the usual and ordinary rate of agricultural capital at the time being.[8]

Ricardo, on the whole, seemed to have approved of what Malthus thought about rent, but he found it to be a good description of rent and not a suitable definition — a calculation, and not a theory. He defined rent as 'that portion of the produce of the earth which is paid to the landlord for the use of the original and indestructible powers of the soil'.[9] According to Ricardo, the supply of land — not being endless — is inelastic, and land varies in fertility and favourable locations. If all land had the same properties, if it were unlimited in quantity and uniform in quality, at least superficially like air or water, no charge could be made for its use. Everywhere the most fertile and favourably situated land was cultivated first, and then — agreeing with Malthus — Ricardo observed that the land of inferior quality, and less advantageously situated, was called into cultivation under the growing pressure of population growth. With the cultivation of land of the second degree of fertility, rent immediately commenced to accrue on land of the first quality, and the amount of that rent depended on the difference in the quantity of these two profits of land.

Apart from the increase in population, land was subjected over time to a process of diminishing return, or marginalizing of its productivity. The same quantity of labour and capital would later return a lesser amount of produce and reduced rate of profit, leaving the surplus enjoyed by capital on superior land to be appropriated by the landlords as rent. Simultaneously, if it turned out to be increasingly difficult to enable production to keep pace with the natural rate of population growth and diminishing return, wages would tend to fall to their subsistence level and lead ultimately to a 'stationary level'. In this state or situation the rate of profit would fall so low that capital accumulation was likely to come practically to a standstill, and with the elimination of profits, the entire produce of the country might pass over as rent to the landlords (merely by virtue of their right to private property in land), except for the barest subsistence wage labour.[10] The landlord, according to Ricardo, is a unique beneficiary in the organization of economic society where the masses toil and are paid wages, capitalists work entrepreneurially and receive profit, but the landlord does practically nothing and yet benefits from the power of the land — gained without earning, and also without paying any price. Unlike interest as the price of capital, or wages as the price of labour, rent is a return of a special kind that is not held in check by competition.

Since rent thus maintained an idle 'leisured class' that had been reaping the harvest of economic advancement at the expense of all other classes, it became clearly iniquitous in the eyes of the bourgeoisie and the Government under their wing, and therefore, most suitable for taxation. Additionally, taxes on rent were not apprehended to hinder production, for it neither affected the rate of profit nor the prices of the produce (corn/grains) — both being governed by the costs of production (including wages and ordinary profit) on the marginal lands yielding little or no rent. The entire rent, therefore, of a country could justifiably be taken by way of taxation without in any manner infringing upon production and wealth. Demonstrating not only the efficacy of breaking away from the landlords, the Ricardian theory also provided the guidelines for a new, scientific taxation policy for land.

The search for a scientific land taxation system and turning away from the aristocracy seemed to be complementary moves. They were so synchronized in the context of consolidating British-Indian possessions as to anticipate developments in one singular direction, towards a common goal. Financially, the Government of India was dependent on the revenue from land, and it seemed a straightforward loss for the exchequer to share it with the great landlords and other intermediaries, especially when land in India belonged by indigenous precept to the sovereign or the state.[11] The only prospective aspect of intermediacy and landlordism was believed (under the Whig influence) to be their potential to contribute to society's prosperity in the countryside, by investing very considerably into its agricultural infrastructure and productivity. Since agriculture did not seem to be improving, if not wholly deteriorating, in spite of liberally endowing the Bengal *zamindar*s with full property right and permanency of settlement, and since the latter showed few signs of growing into capitalist landlords, the Companyraj's ideologues had to seriously consider the adoption of an alternative *rayatwari* experiment for all its territories, settling directly with the cultivators minus the intermediaries. As an impermanent arrangement like this did not appear to pose much of a problem in Madras, and was thought to be well worth trying in Bombay, it raised high hopes for agricultural development and resultant treasury gains by transforming *rayat*s into some sort of yeomen-cum-capitalist farmers, and by setting up a process of capitalization or industrialization of the agrarian system. Expanded agricultural productivity, bolstering up the state exchequer, and a transformed agrarian situation, all depended upon one fundamental tenet, i.e., that the Government should judiciously claim its due from the cultivators and proprietors of land without impairing their vital pecuniary interests. It was primarily on the authorities' ability to devise a modern, fair method of assessment, and their careful calculation of the amount, that much of the success of the British design of bourgeoizing India depended.

The modern scientific scheme for assessing individual farms was derived by the Companyraj's brain trust from Rent Theory, apart from obtaining from it a rationale for direct settlement with *rayat*s. Their derivation, expounded insightfully by Mill in his recommendations and evidence (before the Parliament Select Committee,

House of Commons, 2 August 1831), exposed the ills that plagued India for depending traditionally upon the 'gross produce' principle in arriving at Government demand. Since the poorer or marginal land hardly yielded any profit, the Government's extraction of a fixed share of the gross produce tended to result in the cultivation only of the superior land to the neglect and exclusion of the inferior land. Besides, such a tax collected indiscriminately, without taking the fertility of land into account, could only be met out of the ordinary profit of cultivation. It was bound in consequence to discourage the employment of capital in the marginal land, cause a fall in the ordinary rate of profit, and arrest the accumulation of capital. Cumulatively, this would lead to a general rise in the price of agricultural products in money (not real) wages of labour and in the level of rent.[12] All these ills, forcing India to continue to be caught in the mire of backwardness and poverty, could be remedied by casting aside the archaic and rather naïve 'gross produce' principle, by accurately surveying the individual plots of land, and classifying them according to their fertility and arability. These measures should then be followed up by fixing the land tax on the sophisticated Ricardian criterion of 'net produce', or on surplus after meeting from the gross produce the expenses of cultivation, the wages of labour and the normal profits of capital. Taxing the 'net produce', and not the gross produce, was the panacea that the classical political economists prescribed for India, and the home authorities had already been readying themselves for lapping it up by adjusting Government demand on the *rayat*s' lands in such a manner 'as fully to leave them the cultivators' profit'.[13] 'Net produce' soon became a watchword — almost an incantation — that would reverberate in the corridors of British power in the Presidency towns, provincial capitals and district headquarters.

### III

In the 1820s, Rent Theory and the 'net produce' criterion started influencing the processes of land revenue assessment in the Ceded and Conquered Provinces, as well as in the Deccan — those of the

Companyraj's territories yet to be decisively settled. It was discernible first in the case of the Provinces, where Mackenzie as Secretary, Territorial Department of the Government of Bengal, wrote his famous Memorandum of 11 July 1819 in response to some of the home authorities' queries. Opposed to the intermediate landed magnates, and protective of the cultivators, he favoured direct revenue engagements with the *rayat*s, not only as individuals and joint-holders, but also as members of the village community — a characteristic rural conglomerate in the Provinces. The engagements, according to Mackenzie, should be entered into in such a way as to leave the cultivating proprietors with some surplus after paying land tax to the state. They could use the surplus for agricultural improvements in much better a manner than the rent-absorbing landlord-intermediaries ever did, or were likely to do. Such a saving could be obtained from the rent of their land if the Government levied tax on the 'net profit' derived from it, i.e., the profit remaining after the payment of labour and all other charges with the profits of stock calculated according to the local rate of interest.[14] Although personally he would have preferred the Government to appropriate the entire rent or the 'net profit' (as an ardent follower of the Rent Theory), Mackenzie was rather keen to safeguard the saving to an extent by subjecting the land tax to a thorough investigation into the circumstances of the land — its quantity, quality and productivity. He wanted to collect data for the average gross produce and the average net produce of a *mahal* (revenue unit, also of *mauja* and fields), as well as the average prices of the produce prevalent in the locality for determining a judicious tax rate.[15] However, since the rent-yielding capacity of lands depended upon their differential fertility (in consonance with the Ricardian concept), no uniform rates of tax could in propriety be imposed on the produce in kind. The Government, therefore, had little alternative but to convert all its demands computed by division of the produce into money assessment to be paid in cash.

Endorsed by the authorities at home and in India, Mackenzie's scheme for the land revenue settlements in the Provinces was put into effect under Regulation VII of 1822. But for as long as eight years of their operation, the settlement proceedings were found to have made little progress beyond a small number of villages in various districts. Apart from some five districts in Bareilly and Meerut Divisions, the settlements were also not confirmed by the Government, primarily because they did not come up to the expectations and demands of their initiator. Mackenzie himself found them at a later date in 1826 to be incomplete and inadequate by his standards.[16] Simultaneously, the local revenue officials felt that the detailed Mackenziean settlement of all the villages under their districts would take an inordinately long time, perhaps sixty-five years,[17] or even 150 years as the then Governor General Bentinck recalled.[18]

Like Mackenzie, another young Haileyburian upholder of Rent Theory, Robert Keith Pringle, assiduously experimented with the assessment of land revenue in the Bombay Deccan and came up with a comparable outcome, but much worse in actuality. Ever since the introduction of the *rayatwari* system in their Presidency, the Bombay authorities felt a dire need for having in their possession authentic survey and assessment records to run the land administration without prejudice to the *rayat*s. Given the inadequacy of these essential data, the fixing of land tax turned out to be unsure and problematic — liable to be raised and lowered arbitrarily at the instance of local officers. To obviate the problem, the Bombay Government appointed Pringle in 1827 as Superintendent of Revenue, Survey and Assessment in the Bombay Deccan to devise a method of survey and settlement in Poona and the surrounding districts. A staunch believer in the 'net produce' criterion, Pringle made stupendous efforts to work out a method by calculating the average gross produce per acre for lands of different qualities, converting it into rupees on the basis of generally prevailing rates of prices of the past years, and finally deducting from it the cultivation costs, wages of labour and profits on stock to get the 'net produce'. Then he tried to ascertain the mean aggregate demand on a village or a district in past years and distribute it among fields on the basis of their 'net produce' value. Pringle, who thought, as Mackenzie did, of taking away the whole of the estimated 'net produce' as tax without impairing the resources of the country, decided to have one-half of it (about 55 per cent) in order to leave a rent property in private hands. Nobody apparently questioned the soundness of Pringle's principles at that point, and admirers of the 'net produce' principle like Mill and others were initially impressed by it.[19] Gaping cracks, however, appeared as soon as it was put into practice, exposing the deficiency of Pringle's data, which was collected by persons who were not very conversant with the country's agricultural operations. The classification of lands, the past years' demands on them, and the crop returns went awry at a time when agricultural prices showed a downward trend. All these cumulatively resulted in the assessments being proved to have been pitched too high. Severe over-assessment[20] soon led to accumulated arrears, necessity for remissions and modifications, and desertion of their homes and fields by peasants in large numbers.[21] The Pringle misadventure had to be called off, which the Bombay Government did in 1835 and started looking for fresh endeavours to tide over the crisis.

Seeing Pringle's failure and Mackenzie's lack of success as proofs against the 'net produce' principle, Governor General Bentinck decided to stay away from 'the introduction of our own fancies and schemes' that adversely affected 'some of the finest provinces of our empire'.[22] Guided by the opinion of a status-quoist Board of Revenue in the Provinces, he opted for an empiricist view of land administration, and effecting settlements expeditiously to suit administrative requirements. Although he accepted the merit of Rent Theory, Bentinck was not convinced of the suitability of its application in India, and found it 'decidedly impracticable' to ascertain profit or to convert gross produce into 'net produce' by any general rule.[23] He felt that if the Government assessment was not made incumbent on the 'net produce' or the 'net rent' of the land, the officials could be spared from the arduous task of computing 'net rent' for each field, as required by Regulation VII of 1822. Bentinck concluded, therefore, that 'a minute inquisition into the capacity of each field or each village of the country is unnecessary'.[24] In this situation assessment could be fixed, according to Bentinck, on such pragmatic grounds as past revenue collections, diminution or extension in the cultivated area, resourcefulness of the proprietors, facilities for irrigation and marketing, and of course the 'judgment and sound discretion' of the settlement officers.[25] All these called for a recasting of Regulation VII of 1822 and the enacting of Regulation IX of 1833, as well as the repealing of those earlier provisions that were related to the mode of determining *jama* on a *mahal*. The assessment could then be levied on rent collected by the intermediate proprietor or acknowledged landowner, and where there was no intermediary between the Government and the actual cultivator, it could be levied directly on the produce of the land after deducting the wages of labour and profits of stock.[26] Rather wishful of capitalist advancement in Indian agriculture with the help of both the forward-looking big landlords and the enterprising yeomanry and tenant-cultivators, Bentinck was willing to make agriculture a profitable business, and not unwilling to bend the Government demand a bit to leave useful agricultural profits. His Regulation IX of 1833 consequently became a curious amalgam of attempts at holding on to the glamour of the Theory of Rent, and replacing at the same time its complicated processes by certain assumed rates of rent on comparable lands, or by guessing their rental assets and potentialities.

It was Bird, a leading member of the Board of Revenue in the Provinces, who managed to dispel to an extent the element of arbitrariness involved in the 'assumed' or 'guessed' rate of rent. Although he himself was a rent theorist in complete agreement with the Mackenziean Regulation VII of 1822, Bird did not mind falling in line with the Governor General for practicality's sake, or abandoning the unrewarding search for an ideal 'net produce' measurement (e.g., deducting all charges of tilling, wages of labour and profits of stock from the gross produce of different lands). Rather, he thought of finding out the 'specimen' rent rates (actually being paid out of the gross produce for years together) by converting the existing rates in kind into money rates per acre.[27] Once an estimated rental value for the *mahal* was thus obtained by using 'specimen' rent rates for diverse kinds of lands, the settlement officer could arrive at an amount for the Government demand by leaving a portion of rent in private hands (two-thirds of the rental value, according to Bentinck). Such aggregate demand or a lump sum was then to be brought down to details, parcelled out to individual holdings and recorded in the register.

However compromisingly innovative Bird was in relation to Bentinck's dictats, he apparently remained firm in his Ricardian loyalty to the cause of tenant-cultivators in general, and especially of those cultivating under the landlords. In spite of curbing anti-feudal proclivities, and reluctantly conceding the British inability at that juncture to 'get rid' of the intermediaries,[28] Bird opposed the Governor General's advisors' move to keep the *rayat*s out of the settlement processes so that their taxes could not be fixed by the Government. Left aside, and compelled to adjust money-rent with their proprietors, they would then be subjected to landlordist fleecing on the plea of augmenting the Government revenue.[29] Since Bird believed that the augmentation of the Government revenue depended not on the landlords' squeezing ability but on the cultivators' enterprise in expanding and improving production, he was wholly opposed to leaving cultivators at the mercy of their landlords. In his opinion, the Government was duty-bound to fix the portion of the produce to be taken from the cultivators, or the money-rent to be received in commutation thereof. Bird claimed on behalf of the *rayat*s 'the right to have their payments fixed by the direct authority of the Government . . . founded as it is on the constitutional practice of the land and monitored by every authority'.[30] Bentinck apparently could not accept Bird's radical recommendation,[31] which did receive in due course the approbation of the home authorities.[32]

## IV

Despite the interlude of Bentinck's exuberant pragmatism, and more importantly, the setback of the promulgation of Regulation IX of 1833, the Haileyburian obsession with Rent Theory had not really waned in the Provinces (termed the North-Western Provinces from 1834). Although Bird could not hold on to his ideological position in the face of his official superiors, Thomason had little difficulty either in upholding it or in trying to live up to it as far as practicable. He elaborated his theoretical standpoint, as Mackenzie and Pringle had attempted to do before him, by emphasizing the urgency of creating private property in land as an essential precondition for the improvement of agriculture, or — if stretched a bit further — for the modernization or capitalization of agriculture. Being the sole owner of land, the State could, in the opinion of Thomason, and in accordance with the Ricardian precept, absorb the entire 'net produce', or exclude all other persons from enjoying any portion of it. Viewing the situation conversely from this premise, he felt that 'the first step, therefore, to the creation of a private property right in the land was to place such a limit on the demand of the Government as would leave to the proprietors a profit, which would constitute a valuable property'. The process, he believed, could be effected 'by providing that the assessment shall be a moderate portion, say two-thirds of the net produce at the time of the settlement, and that the proprietor shall be allowed all the benefit from improved or extended cultivation'.[33]

Who could, however, be the proprietors to benefit from the limitations of Government demand and the enlargement of cultivation? Proprietorship being varied in the NWP, there were several categories to qualify for this, namely, those original settlers in a locality from the long past, those who occupied land by cultivating it themselves or by employing tenants and labourers and paying tax through the village headmen, those who owned lands jointly and severally as members of the village communities, those who owned lands under joint proprietorship or as co-perceners, and those *jagirdar*s, *zamindar*s and *talukdar*s who owned lands by special grants of the ruling power to collect tax from the cultivators for the state coffers, after deducting a service charge.[34] While proprietorship of lands in a *mahal* was being screened by the settlement officers, the surveyors laboured hard to find out the size and position of each field, and the quality of its land and the crop it yielded. It was incumbent on the settlement officers and surveyors, according to Thomason, to work in close co-operation with each other.[35] The survey would be undertaken mainly for revenue purposes, and the settlement for both revenue and legal requirements. Once the proprietary or the landholding right was decided, the settlement officers must take up the fiscal part. The aim of this part was assessing or fixing the demand upon the land for a certain period 'within such limits as may leave a fair profit to the proprietors and create a valuable and marketable property in the land'.[36]

For fixing the demand, it was necessary, according to Thomason, to ascertain the 'net produce' of the estate, meaning — as already known — the surplus it might yield after deducting the usual expenses of cultivation, including profits of stock and wages of labour. Such estimates of net produce had to be worked out for estates held entirely by cultivating proprietors, but not for estates held by non-cultivating proprietors and leased out to cultivators (where an estimate of gross production should suffice). Once the estate-based net produce (and gross produce in case of landlords) was known 'pretty nearly', and aggregated to get the figures for a village or a number of villages, these could be compared with the previous assessment figures of the same tract for the past years. Armed with this data, and the knowledge from survey returns of the cultivated and cultivable areas of the village, of the irrigated and unirrigated lands and their qualities, the settlement officers ought to be in a position to fix a fair tax demand which should not be 'more than two-thirds of what may be expected to be the net produce . . . leaving to the proprietor one-third as his profits and cover expenses of collection'.[37] Any slight tilt in deciding upon the produce could jeopardize the peasant cultivators' precarious financial well-being. The precariousness had been brought out by the contemporary analysis of a rural district (Kanpur) whose statistical returns showed that 'the greater number of cultivators realized about Rs. 5 per year'. Paying the land tax, rent, and defraying the cost of seed, tools, animals, etc., a family of four was left with above 12 shillings per annum for supporting each individual[38] — the princely figure of a little more than a penny a day! Thomason was mindful (more anxiously perhaps than his fellow rent theorists in India) of the difficulty of correctly ascertaining the net produce in the face of the proprietors' presentation (sometimes deliberate) of misleading information, and the lower officers' furnishing inaccurate accounts. Besides, the net produce of one year was no certain guide to the produce of the years to come. The future produce might be more for some reason (e.g., addition of wastelands to cultivation, favourable weather and fresh irrigational facilities, use of better seeds and more effective manures, greater demand in the local market, etc.), and also might be less (if the reasons for more production got somehow reversed). The net produce, according to Thomason, should be used as a useful indicator of facts and figures and not accepted as the biblical truth. The settlement officer 'should not harass himself to attain accuracy in this respect, nor, when he fancies that he has ascertained the actual net produce, should he treat this as any certain basis on which he found his settlement'. The assessment in its ultimate analysis, as concluded by Thomason, was 'not one of arithmetical calculation but of judgment and sound discretion, and to proceed openly on that assumption'.[39]

It was expected in Bombay that Pringle's successors in 1836 would pursue like him the doctrinal craze that Rent Theory was at that point, and try to make up in its light all the lapses that had crept into the settlement proceedings. Both H.E. Goldsmid and G. Wingate — the in-charge of survey and settlement who was to undertake the task of settling land revenue in the Deccan — also kept up the show of being ardent followers of the 'net produce' criterion. In 1840 and again in 1862,[40] they (more specifically, Wingate) continued harping on their acceptance of the theoretical soundness of Rent Theory, and also on giving effect to it in the method they introduced. But the fact of the matter was that Goldsmid-Wingate had in actuality found the search for the net produce to be rather hazardous and inconvenient, and had therefore decided to call it off altogether in their operations. Instead of trying to be true to the theory, howsoever scientific, they attempted to build up a system on a rigorously empirical foundation through meticulous survey of lands, even of the individual fields, by classifying their soil (into nine grades) authoritatively on the basis of natural productive qualities. Thereafter they decided to separately assess each field, not only for the land's profitability or rentability (to express it in Ricardian concept) but also for its capability for improvement — for its contributing to general agricultural progress. By aggregating the findings, they expected to get the picture of homogeneous groups of villages and fix 'the approximate amount' of tax by taking into account the present condition of the agricultural classes, the state of particular villages, the amount of the Government realizations, the prices of produce and similar considerations, compared with those of preceding years, 'affording us the chief groundwork for determining satisfactorily what abetment or addition should be made to the existing *jamma*'.[41] In their own pragmatic way, they thought they were carrying the teaching of Rent Theory forward by fully coinciding 'in the justice of limiting the Government demand to a portion of the true rent', and believing '50 to 80 per cent thereof would form a liberal assessment [leaving a good portion of rent with the cultivator], and . . . would prove an invaluable blessing to the agricultural classes in India'.[42]

Irrespective of whether it lived up to Rent Theory as a whole or in part, the laborious experimentation of Wingate-Goldsmid hinged crucially on the knowledge, judgement and sagacity of the survey and settlement officers — the men on the spot. According to Goldsmid in 1840: 'It must be considered that in any revision of assessment, Government had only the judgment, and what may be termed the practical tact of the superintending officers to rely on'.[43] This finding in the Deccan was a typical reiteration of the NWP policymakers' hopeless dependence — be it Thomason, Bird, Bentinck or Mackenzie — on the men of destiny, the revenue officials in the Provinces. But, were those in the ranks reliable enough to bear the heavy burden of their authorities' total — almost unqualified — reliance? Did they also try incidentally to ease the Companyraj's tightened grip over revenue collection at times of distress?

## Notes

1 Bengal Select Committee Proceedings, 8 July and 12 October 1769, cited in Harry Verelst, *A View of the Rise, Progress and the Present State of the English Government in Bengal*, Nourse, London, 1772, p. 76.
2 This point has been made in Chapter 2.
3 It became necessary later to pass the Rent Act of 1859 and the Tenancy Act of 1885 to offer some protection to the *rayat*s against rack-renting and ejectment.
4 Stokes, *The English Utilitarians and India*, p. 34.
5 T. R. Malthus, *Principles of Political Economy Considered with a View to Their Practical Application*, Basil Blackwell, Oxford, 1951 [1836], pp. 194–217.
6 David Ricardo, *Principles of Political Economy and Taxation*, Everyman's Library Edition, London, 1949, p. 33.
7 Stokes, *The English Utilitarians and India*, pp. 87–88.
8 Malthus, *Principles of Political Economy*, as quoted by Sir Barnes Peacock, Chief Justice, Calcutta High Court, in a historic judgement, 30 August and 4 September 1862, cited in S. Ambirajan, *Classical Political Economy and British Policy in India*, Cambridge University Press, Cambridge, 1978, p. 120.
9 David Ricardo, *An Essay on Profits*, John Murray, London, 1815, Vol. IV, p. 10.
10 Ricardo, *Principles of Political Economy and Taxation*, Chapters V and VI, cited in Stokes, *The English Utilitarians and India*, p. 89.
11 The British in India had no qualms at this point in accepting this theory by which they could legitimately fill the state coffers to their maximum extent with the help of land revenue.
12 Stokes, *The English Utilitarians and India*, p. 93.
13 Revenue Despatch, Court of Directors to Bengal Government, 10 November 1824, Appendix p. 105, Report of the Select Committee 1832, Vol. III, cited in Gupta, *Agrarian Relations and Early British Rule in India*, p. 165.
14 *Ibid.*, p. 178.
15 *Ibid.*, p. 183.
16 Mackenzie's Memorandum, 19 October 1826, Selections from Revenue Records, N.W.P., Allahabad, 1873, Microfiche MFI/2862, pp. 84–100, IO/BL.

17 Minute by Gov. Gen. Bentinck, 20 January 1832, cited in Gupta, *Agrarian Relations and Early British Rule in India*, p. 239.
18 Rosselli, *Lord William Bentinck*, p. 253.
19 Stokes, *The English Utilitarians and India*, p. 101.
20 Pringle himself conceded over-assessment by 33 per cent; *ibid.*, p. 100, fn. 1.
21 Bombay Administration Report, 1872–73, pp. 41–42, cited in *ibid.*, p. 134.
22 Rosselli, *Lord William Bentinck*, p. 262.
23 Gupta, *Agrarian Relations and Early British Rule in India*, pp. 298–99.
24 *Ibid.*, p. 298.
25 *Ibid.*, p. 299.
26 *Ibid.*, p. 298.
27 Stokes, *The English Utilitarians and India*, p. 105.
28 Minute by Mr. Bird, undated (1833?), Selections from the Revenue Records of the N.W.P., Allahabad, 1873, Microfiche MFI/2866, pp. 466–69, IO/BL.
29 Gupta, *Agrarian Relations and Early British Rule in India*, p. 293.
30 Minute by Bird, 25 September 1832, cited in *ibid.*, p. 288.
31 *Ibid.*, p. 292.
32 Stokes, *The English Utilitarians and India*, p. 121.
33 Remarks on the System of Land Revenue Administration prevalent in the North-Western Provinces of Hindoostan, J. Thomason, Simlah, 25 August 1849, House of Commons, P.P., 22 July 1853, Vol. 75, paper 999.
34 *Ibid.*
35 'Directions for Revenue Officers in the North-Western Provinces of the Bengal Presidency', Promulgated by the authority of the Hon'ble Lt. Gov., Agra, 1 November 1849, House of Commons, P.P., 1852–53, Vol. 75, paper 999.
36 *Ibid.*, Section IV, Assessment.
37 *Ibid.*
38 John Capper, *The Three Presidencies of India: A History of the Rise and Progress of the British Indian Possessions*, Ingram, Cooke and Co., London, 1853 (reprinted in 1997 by Asian Educational Services, New Delhi).
39 *Ibid.*
40 Goldsmid-Wingate Report, Section II, 17 October 1840, Ahmednuggur, Appendix No. 1, House of Commons, P.P., 1852–53, Vol. 75, paper

999; and also Wingate's Memorandum of 2 May 1862, cited in Stokes, *The English Utilitarians and India*, p. 128.
41 Goldsmid-Wingate Report, Section II, 17 October 1840, Ahmednuggur, Appendix No. 1, House of Commons, P.P., 1852–53, Vol. 75, paper 999.
42 *Ibid.*
43 Bombay Survey and Settlement Manual, cited in K. L. Punjabi, *Bombay Land Revenue System*, Praja Bandhu Press, Ahmedabad, Broach, 1938, p. 25.

# 4

# AGAINST PEASANTRY

The superintending and supervisory officials of the Companyraj in India — whether deciding upon the assessment of land or collecting the amount of land tax — laboured hard to live up to the expectations of their superior authorities. The collection of revenue between the 1820s and the 1850s, as carried out in the NWP by the collectors and their subordinates, was not only highly efficient but also coldly severe. It had to be so from the British point of view in an age of imperialist expansion, culminating in expensive military campaigns in Afghanistan, Sind, Gwalior, Punjab and Burma, and resulting in financial deficits from 1838 to 1848. 'The Government must draw from the country as large an income as its resources can be made to bear upon, not only for meeting the war expenditure but also for spending on internal security and good government all around.'[1]

## I

That a sizeable amount of land revenue was being collected annually and punctually in the Provinces till 1858 (more than £4,000,000), with a 'small amount of outstanding balances',[2] spoke volumes of the revenue officials' skill in revenue collection and settling tax arrears, and their promptitude in auctioning off deficient plots and estates. Repeatedly the higher authorities impressed on them 'the expediency of a stricter application of the sale law for the recovery of the arrears of revenue'.[3] Some official heartlessness was apparent in matters of revenue collection, and it was compounded further by competition among the tax collectors for the 'rewards' for extracting the highest amount in an area within the shortest period. That the system of 'rewards' (which came into practice in the Provinces from December 1820) raised apprehensions of oppression seems to have been known to those at the top echelon of power as early as 1835, and they, therefore, called for the local authorities' extreme caution in recommending their subordinates for such 'rewards'.[4]

Even without the irresistible lure of 'rewards', the survey and settlement officers worked as enterprisingly perhaps as their tax-collecting counterparts did, and succeeded in covering wide ground. Within about ten years between 1834 and 1844, they had surveyed 72,000 square miles of the Provinces, having a population of more than 23 million.[5] The proprietary right, as ascertained and recorded in the surveys, had thereafter been confirmed in perpetuity, but the Government assessment was fixed generally for thirty years.[6] Since the survey and settlement operation was meant ideologically to indicate the 'net produce' of the land, and to help calculate the tax on its basis, its data had to be reasonably reliable, if not wholly accurate. Despite the official exertions, the survey and settlement findings apparently did not prove to be good enough for setting up even an approximation of the net produce criterion. Reviewing as many as 1,012 completed settlements in the Delhi territories, the Commissioner, William Fraser, did not come across even one 'on a thorough based estimate of cost produce, and profit as the ground work, and advertence to local free-will rent as the rule'.[7] The redoubtable rent theorist Holt Mackenzie eventually had a clearer idea of what led to the net produce misadventure in the Provinces. 'The causes of failure have been many', he ruefully discovered,

> the vastness of the country, our ignorance of its circumstances, the inaccuracy of language, and erroneous notions and principles originated in that ignorance, unwilling to admit new notions, reluctance to confess our blunders, the defective education and discipline of European officers . . .

inefficiency of government and of subordinate authorities of control, misuse of patronage.[8]

Thomason also had his own reservations about the settlement officers' ability to deal competently with the assessment operation, known to be 'undoubtedly a very difficult one . . . in which error may be committed, and injustice may be done'.[9] To guard against such errors of judgement, he thought that the settlement officers' 'determination of assessment' should invariably be closely supervised by senior officers at the district and provincial levels — officers of 'matured experience'.[10]

Apparently, the survey and settlement officers in the NWP, from the 1820s to the 1860s, did not live up to the expectations of their ideologist hard taskmasters. Despite the serious effort they had put into their work, they were often not able to maintain a fine balance between understanding and information, dexterity and deliberation, preference and decisiveness. (Was it realistic to expect all this from men in a comparatively lower rank, lesser education, and having limited knowledge of the social diversities and ways of life in the Indian countryside?) Consequently, they were uncertain of themselves, became authoritarian in the absence of 'any fixed rules' for their conduct,[11] and even turned arbitrary, or at times intolerant. But providentially, by some miracle, had they managed somehow to keep their cool, track down the land prices, scan through the local markets, juggle with the agricultural data (of the past and the present), would they have succeeded in giving some effect to the Classical Rent Theory, pinpointing the net produce and arriving at an assessment for the good of Indian agriculture and agriculturists? Perhaps they still would not have been able to deal with such corollaries of the Rent Theory as, for instance, the problem of over-assessment.

In Indian conditions, the application of the net produce method was likely to result in over-assessment. A simple example bears this out: a hypothetical comparison of the land tax calculated on the net produce with that of the one fixed on the gross produce. If the gross produce of a small plot was assumed to be worth £1,000 a year, its assessment by conventional practice was expected to be fixed at one-third of it or about £333. To arrive at the net produce value from £1,000, however, it would be necessary to deduct from the amount a sum of about £400 as the expenses of cultivation, the wages of labour and the profits on stock. The deduction would leave £600 as the net produce value, and the two-thirds (alternately 70 to 80 per cent) of it as per the usual demand recommended, or £450 or so, was liable to be fixed as the demand. It would signify in this case a considerable rise by £117, or about 35 per cent in land tax under net produce over that under gross produce. Such tendencies of over-assessment were damaging to the interests of cultivators and proprietors alike, and consequently contributed to the slackening of agricultural progress. Altogether, therefore, and in a broader context, it was indicative of a certain restrainment of the process of capitalization of agriculture — the very politico-economic objective that the Companyraj's doctrinaire policy-makers had been hell-bent on achieving. In their desperation to make expeditious use of an innovative, sound method that worked well in Europe, they either refused seriously to ponder or decided to ride roughshod over the difficulties of implanting the ingenious net produce device on untested territories like the NWP of India. Did the circumstances of the Provinces call by any chance for an adoption of the Rent Theory there, and was it eminently suitable for this region?

## II

It is apparent in hindsight that the NWP was far from being in readiness for the introduction of Rent Theory, or for experimentation with the net produce criterion. This is because the conditions prevailing in India at the time were not favourable for such an endeavour. The land market, for example, had not so far enjoyed much freedom, and landlords ordinarily exercised considerable influence in the sale of land services to tenants. The conditions were effectively contrary to the Ricardian assumption of pure competition among landlords, and 'the freedom of entry and egress from agriculture' did not hold.[12] Market conditions were generally imperfect without any competition for capital, and offered no facility for the transfer of capital from one economic activity to another, resulting in an immobility of capital. There appeared also to be an immobility of labour, for the peasant proprietors had no alternative sources of revenue, and were bound to stick to their respective agricultural callings. Besides, hardly any system seemed to exist of the Government knowing and keeping farm accounts of the estates, and it was difficult to decide what had been 'a normal harvest and a normal level of prices'.[13] Since good and bad seasons came in circles, many years' findings would be required to discover a satisfactory 'average' — a fundamental for revenue assessment. All these factors clearly did not allow for a neat separation of an estate's total income into wages, rents and profits. Unlike rent theorists in India, James Mill in England did appear to have had an inkling of these handicaps, but still, like them, he decided to put his faith entirely in 'a good civil servant' (even if 'ignorant' by the Mackenziean standard) to estimate the net rent 'with a high degree of accuracy'.[14] Deeply impressed with the use that England and a few European countries had been making of Ricardian Rent Theory, Mill started regarding it as universally applicable. He was in favour, therefore, of exporting it to India as a useful tool to carve out the Companyraj's taxation policy. By doing this, he anticipated that the Government would tax the net produce in such 'moderation'[15] as to take enough so as to cater to public needs, as well as to leave enough for cultivators to reinvest.

There were, however, contemporaries of both Mill and Ricardo in Europe, more specifically in England, who seriously questioned the Rent Theory itself, its supposed universal application and the urgent need for applying it to India. Most prominent among them happened to be Reverend Richard Jones, a successor of Malthus as Professor of Political Economy at the East India College, Haileybury, and as one renowned for his attempts at 'sociologizing' economic categories and institutions. Jones considered it his function to test and correct prevailing notions of political economy against historical developments, and frame new view-points. Of a number of such frameworks, the most outstanding one was his discovery of 'transfer' that took place in England from an economy of independent peasants and handicraftsmen to capitalism, in which they became propertyless and immiserized. Such a 'transfer' — the loss of economic independence through the loss of ownership of the means of production — was what prompted Karl Marx to look for 'primary accumulation' or the antecedent of capital formation.[16] Similar to his questioning of the concept of capital formation through thrifty 'savings', and the attempt to replace it by the mechanism of 'transfer', Jones wanted to take on the Rent Theory and examine its validity in the light of institutional practices in various societies.

Although lower in celebrity status than Ricardo, Malthus and Mill, Jones, with his inductive method, did not do too badly in disputing the deductive method-based Ricardian formulation. The objections that Jones raised against the Rent Theory were of three varieties: methodological, analytical and epistemic. To begin with, Jones had serious methodological differences with Ricardo, with Jones following induction and Ricardo following deduction as their respective methods. Jones was against calling any formulation a 'theory' if it was not backed up by a rigorous assemblage of data. He asserted that any 'snatch at general principles' without the widest possible support of evidence turns out to be 'frequently false'.[17] He was unwilling to accept Ricardo's formulation on rent as a well-founded theory,[18] and consequently questioned its supposed universality. Jones contended that the Rent Theory had but limited validity, and it would be workable only in 'the small portion of the earth's surface', or England, where Ricardo's presupposition might perhaps agree with the actual conditions.[19]

Analytically, Jones thought he found a sizeable chink in the rent theorists' armour — in the Ricardian emphasis on diminishing returns resulting in poorer lands being brought into cultivation as the population grew. He argued that the increase in rent as a result of extension of the cultivated area could be more on account of agricultural improvements than on account of the cultivation of poorer grades of land.[20] So he argued that the farmer's rent might rise, against the basic premise of the Ricardian view, without requisitioning marginal lands and without further diminishing returns upon lands already in use.[21] In fact, by citing historical facts, he showed that rents were actually the highest in those countries where agriculture was most productive.[22]

Jones was nevertheless at his epistemic best when he tried to draw lessons from the development and content of rents in diverse social conditions and at different times. His survey of the economic patterns of the countries he was familiar with revealed two basic kinds of land rents, namely, the farmers' rents and the peasants' rents. Since farmers were generally capitalist tenants in the mould of English farmers, the nature of their rents came closer to the subject of Ricardo's scrutiny. Beyond the gaze of Ricardo, however, remained the pre-capitalist peasants whose peasant rents needed further to be classified into various types, such as serf rents (paid in labour, in Russia), 'metayer' rents (paid in produce, in Italy), 'cottier' rents (paid in cash, in Ireland) and, of course, 'ryot' (*rayat*) rents (paid in cash/produce in India). Jones pointed out that, by trying to formulate a theory in relation to farmers' rents in capitalist England, or barely 'about one per cent of the globe', the Ricardians could not by any stretch of imagination claim its general applicability.[23] More relevantly, therefore, like the cases of all other pre-capitalist rents, the Rent Theory should not be applicable — in Jones's opinion — to the 'ryot' rent in India.

## III

According to Jones, rent under the 'ryot' tenure was 'in no degree dependent upon the existence of different qualities of soil, or different returns of the stock and labour employed in each'.[24] The *rayat* was not a capitalist farmer, and his rent had been determined not by competition of capital on land but solely by competition among tenants for land (as was the case with the cottiers in Ireland). Mill had put it more cogently than Jones: with growing pressure of population on limited availability of land, he observed, 'the competition for land soon forces up rent to a point consistent with keeping the population alive'.[25] Tenantry had to bear any increase in the State's (or landlord's) share of the produce, and consequently a certain decrease of its own share if it wanted to subsist. Handicapped in the market facility, as well as in alternative employment opportunities, the peasant in India produced primarily for subsistence. He was for all practical purposes a subsistence cultivator in the position of a farm labourer, forced to raise his wages from the land or starve. The mechanical imposition of a capitalist economic dictum on a pre-capitalist subsistence economy was not only impracticable,[26] but also damaging for the peasants, and self-defeating for the rent theorists in India.

The pet theme of the rent theorists, namely, the turning of peasants into capitalist farmers, would not work if the tenantry were overburdened with taxes, and thereby held back from accumulating surpluses or generating capital. That was precisely what seemed to have happened in the Provinces during the four decades of Ricardian experimentation. Ordinarily, the usual proportion of tax fixed on the net produce principle was known to be much higher than the standard amount traditionally demanded on the gross produce. The rent theorists — the typical offspring of a capitalistic England — therefore sought to be cautious in using such difference, or the enhanced amount, to meet the costs of modernizing governmental infrastructures. The enhancement nevertheless had been a vital part of their overall taxation strategy — one that was expected to give some impetus to peasants' surpluses and investments. In their intense pre-occupation with the theory, they did not bother to notice the steep rise in land revenue demand that their policy had caused, and lulled themselves into believing that it was well within the limits prescribed by political economy.[27] In 1848 their patrons, the home authorities, even stoutly denied before the House of Commons Committee the charge that the high pitch of assessment was damaging to India.[28] The excessiveness of assessment in India in general, and in the Provinces in particular, did not escape the notice of alert knowledgeables like J.R. McCulloch[29] and Richard Jones. As early as 1827, McCulloch found the land tax of India (in the Provinces and in Bombay Deccan) to be 'so heavy that it was bound to interfere with the country's development'.[30] Jones also felt that extraction by the State, as well as by the landlords, 'reduced the peasant tenantry to penury',[31] and that the only way to raise production under peasant tenures was to lower rent. The 'constant tendency to take an excessive share' impoverished the 'ryot', and undermined the sources of all agricultural improvement and growth.[32] Both Jones and McCulloch, as well as Marshall much later in the 1890s, suggested that the imposition of excessive over-assessment led to 'too severe a drain of resources into the Government', and that the 'drain' inhibited the development of capitalist farmers in India.[33]

All the above impressionistic views were corroborated by instances at the ground level. The trend of pitching the Government demand too high started practically from the beginning of the Companyraj in the Provinces. The young officers who were usually entrusted with settlement operations were known to have a careerist interest in keeping both the demands and the returns on the up.[34] Since its formation, the NWP's statistics suggested 'an overall increase of about 88 per cent in the land revenue demand during the forty years following 1806–7'.[35] In the Conquered Provinces, including Bundelkhand and the entire Doab upwards of Agra, the assessment was raised from Rs. 36 lakh in 1805 to Rs. 118 lakh in 1818, and in Delhi, separately assessed, from Rs. 6 to Rs. 17 lakh.[36] In Rohtak, it was found later, the assessments were 'injudiciously heavy', and in Hissar the demand of the first settlement from 1815 to 1825 exceeded by about 20 per cent the revenue fixed even in 1890.[37] The arbitrarily imposed assessments till the mid-1820s did not seem to have abated much from the theory-based assessments of 1822 and thereafter. In Bundelkhand, the *jama* was raised in the eastern parts by as high as 46 per cent between 1806–07 and 1815–16.[38] Resultantly, the persistent increase in the Government demand over the years forced cultivating proprietors to live so much on the razor's edge that any fluctuation in production and grain prices would jeopardize their fortunes. In 1833–34, a certain decline in the cotton trade and some depression in agriculture in Banda district led to mounting arrears of revenue and consequently a massive resignation of *malguzar*s (who paid the revenue assessed on an estate to the Government, either on their own behalf or as representatives of others) from their rights on estates (588 out of 1,098) by placing them under the direct management of the Government.[39] In 1844, following a decline in the prices of grains, the cultivators in Lalitpur could scarcely manage to pay both the land tax and cultivation expenses. A similar situation in 1851 resulted in the accumulation of a large outstanding balance of land revenue in the district of Jalaun.[40]

The situation was no better in the western districts above Agra, including Rohilkhand, where Rs. 45 lakh of tax was outstanding in 1818 out of a total of Rs. 65 lakh for the Provinces. The revenue officers in Rohilkhand and upper Doab were convinced in 1832 that the severity of the demand left negligible proprietary surplus — almost none at all.[41] Oppressive assessment, levied with cruel precision, was reported to have caused popular disaffection in Mainpuri and south-west Saharanpur.[42] Throughout the 1850s, the Jat peasants in the ecologically disadvantaged areas west of the Gangetic valley suffered impoverishment from severe British revenue assessments.[43] The weight of the revenue rates fell heavily on the peasantry in Aligarh and Mathura districts, especially in the *pargana*s of Tuppul and Noh Jil. In Aligarh the assessment was 'avowedly based on extracting 80 per cent of the rental assets',[44] and it did not allow proprietors in Mathura to pay their tax without distress. 'In good seasons they made little, in bad seasons they were ruined', observed Mark Thornhill, the Collector of Mathura. The story was not very different in Budaun where even the landed magnates found it difficult to meet the Government demand in spite of incurring huge loans.[45] However, the experience was astounding for a revenue officer at the time of revising the settlement of Meerut district in 1867. He discovered, to his utter dismay, that the assessment of Chhapruli *pargana*, 'prior to the revolt of 1857', was 'fearfully heavy'.[46]

Almost an identical finding, though not as dismal, emerges from the comparison of revenues of the pre-Revolt with the post-Revolt days of the Hissar district (see Table 4.1[47]).

It is pertinent to point out here that the general area of the *tehsil*s in both periods under study was the same. But, of course, the

*Table 4.1* Comparision of Hissar district revenues pre-Revolt and post-Revolt

| Tehsils | Pre-Revolt revenue (in Rs.) | Post-Revolt revenue (in Rs.) |
|---|---|---|
| Bhiwani | 81,181 | 73,206 |
| Hansi | 160,209 | 141,739 |
| Hissar | 101,204 | 89,885 |
| Barwala | 63,743 | 56,438 |
| Fatehabad | 79,006 | 69,438 |
| Total | 485,403 | 430,739 |

cultivated area in the post-Revolt period increased by roughly over 30 per cent. There is all the more reason now to feel that the earlier settlements were 'really ruinous'.[48]

Likewise, a comparison of land revenue settlements before the annexation (February 1856 or 1262 Fasli under the Nawabi Government) with those soon after it (1856–57 or 1264 Fasli under the Companyraj) also reveals a hint of the British penchant for high assessment in Oudh. Under the Summary Settlement, some *parganas* of Sitapur district marked a 28 to 63 per cent increase in the Companyraj's demand over the Nawabiraj's. Similar increases had taken place in a large number of *parganas* in such districts as Faizabad, Sultanpur and Unnao. But in other districts like Lucknow, Rae Bareli, Pratabgarh, Bahriach, Hardoi, etc., barring of course the pockets of over-assessment within them, the English restrained themselves to put up a show of good governance by scaling down the demand. Thus, the Summary Settlement of 1856–57 in Oudh seemed to witness 'gross over-assessment in certain areas, despite some reduction in the over-all assessment in others'.[49] Apart from such reluctant liberality as shown occasionally in Oudh, the Companyraj's assessment in the Provinces till 1857 appeared in their own eyes in the post-1857 days to be so high a proportion of the real average assets that it could hardly be paid by the peasant proprietors. The administration reports of the later years did concede the oppressive character of the pre-Revolt assessment in NWP and Oudh: 'It is now generally admitted that the proportion of the rental to the proprietors in the N.W. Provinces was much less than was absolutely necessary to provide for the support of themselves, and their families, bad debts, expenses of management and vicissitudes of season.'[50]

## IV

The exorbitant revenue demand, and the severity of its collection, evidently had a disastrous effect on the Province's agrarian society. Whether high or low in the social ladder, everyone groaned under the heavy weight of assessment. It was well known in Azamgarh 'that the British assess lands very highly' and that had been the cause of the landed classes' 'ruin'.[51] William Edwards, the Collector of Budaun, and C.J. Christian, Commissioner of Sitapur, recalled later how the evils of over-assessment had reduced the landed gentry to such straits as to force them to sell family jewellery to save their ancestral properties.[52] In the Gangetic canal tract of Muzaffarnagar, the traditional elite seem to have lost about 56 per cent of their land to urban money-lenders between 1840 and 1860.[53] Obviously the cultivating proprietors were bound to be the worst off, and they had to incur very heavily burdensome loans at high interest to meet their tax liabilities and family commitments (mostly on social ceremonies and religious rites). Their debts increased in leaps and bounds following the famines or famine-like conditions of 1833–34 and 1837–38 throughout the Provinces, leading to a sharp rise in land alienation. Lands were alienated either by enforced sale (the auction sale of confiscated land under the Court's and Government's orders) or by consensual sale (the transference of rights on land under the pressure of circumstances or on the advice of the revenue officials). Both auction sales and land transfers were the cumulative effects of the high demand of Government revenue and the *mahajani* returns — the consequential outcome of peasant indebtedness. Auction sales and land transfers became rampant by the middle of the 1840s, and the Board of Revenue of the Provinces found the districts of Aligarh, Mainpuri, Mathura and Banda in

1846 to be particularly afflicted with the sales of proprietary rights for revenue default, and ascribed this to the pressure of revenue demand.[54] But for the high assessment and increase in land sales, 'the rural classes would never have joined in the rebelling with the Sepoys'.[55] The beneficiaries of these sales and transfers were the *mahajan*s, *bania*s and the urban nouveau riche who spotted at this time a steady rise in land and agricultural prices,[56] and decided to invest increasingly in land and its products — food grains in the main. More than 50 per cent of land titles changed hands between 1838 and 1858, and the money-lending and trading classes continued to register a gain of 9 per cent during this period and thereafter.[57] Land transfers in certain districts of the Provinces were in fact too many, covering as much as 30 per cent of the total area of the districts.[58] The bulk of new purchasers of these lands came from cities and towns, but operated their businesses and enterprises largely in the villages.

Among all other 'outsiders' on the village scenario, the money-lender particularly was in an advantageous position because of the absence at that time of any law regulating rates of interest. He was free not only to take recourse to dishonest practices like manipulating accounts books, but also to charge inflated interests at compound rates. When all restraints and postponements of the execution of money decrees were removed in 1846,[59] the money-lender received the bonanza of dragging his debtors to the law courts for non-payment, and swiftly getting their properties or lands auctioned in discharge of the borrowed amounts. The auction-purchasers (both money-lenders and businessmen, especially grain dealers) secured lands for straightforward pecuniary reasons — for getting quick profitable returns. What is baffling here, however, is the fact that they lost no opportunity in procuring all those encumbered estates whose owners turned indebted primarily on account of excessive tax demands. Apart from a dubious form of esteem which the exploitative landlords enjoyed locally and in rural society, for which the non-elites could have an attraction or even a craving, the realists in business and money-lending would never go for vain social status without making hefty profits from their investments in land. Since landlordist profit was not guaranteed in an era of notorious over-assessment, why should these hardboiled men have taken on all the litigational and managerial obligations of owning the once-encumbered estates? It was apparently because the *bania*-cum-trader anticipated that more and more land would be brought under cultivation to mitigate the high State demand, and that the market for agricultural produce would resultantly also become enlarged. With this perspective in mind, he wanted through the auction purchase an enhanced control over the grain producer, enabling himself 'all the more surely to buy cheap and sell dear'.[60] But the auction-purchaser's major interest lay in squeezing — in typical landlordist tradition — as much profit out of the estates and plots of land as possible. He would ensure that the proprietor from whom he had purchased the estate departed from the scene, bag and baggage. However, he would not mind allowing a cultivating proprietor to stay on, but only as a tenant like all others. In either way, the auction-purchaser was in a position to extract from his tenants and under-tenants the maximum possible rent, as well as other inherited *zamindari* exactions, to the extent practicable under subsistence requirement. Such rack-renting and exaction of *zamindari* dues[61] should leave him, according to his calculations, enough profit after paying the over-assessed taxes.

The peasantry's frustration and impoverishment in NWP and Oudh were mounting rapidly around the central issue of oppressive over-assessment. All other ills, such as the rigours of revenue collection, the mounting rural indebtedness, the spurt in alienation of land, the rise in auction purchases and even the incitement to *zamindari* rack-renting were its by-products or fallouts. No one in rural society was spared from suffering proportionately, not even the *jagirdars*/*zamindar*s and *talukdar*s, but the worst sufferers quite obviously were the cultivating proprietors — the peasants and their dependants, like the sub-tenantry and agricultural labour of various kinds. According to H.D. Robertson, the Magistrate of Saharanpur, 'no class seem to have acted with so vindictive a hate against us [the Companyraj] as the smaller class of landholders'.[62]

Soon the peasants' initial dismay at the sharp deterioration of their conditions was transformed into deep resentment and spontaneous resistance and protest. Protests took diverse forms, from desertion of one's hearth and home to refusal to cultivate land, and from jacquerie to killing themselves — from murder to suicide. A few cursorily found instances offer a glimpse of what the countryside in the Provinces was agonizingly passing through.

The commonest form of peasant protest against the oppressions inflicted on them in India was their collective desertion of the place of sufferance. It was reported by a settlement officer in Karnal district that 'the inhabitants of some villages, nearly in mass, had abandoned their lands and homes to distant parts'.[63] Similar reports came from Sonepat *pargana* in Delhi district where nine villages were discovered to have been completely deserted in 1842.[64] The situation appeared to be no better in Rewari *pargana* and Rohtak district, and the settlement reports of the district were replete with such observations as 'this village is entirely abandoned', or 'half the villagers of this village have run away', or 'only five families are left in this village', etc.[65] Of the fifty to sixty houses in the village Kurkurnah in Lalitpur, Banda district, in 1848–49, only ten had been found to be occupied by the settlement officer in 1851.[66] Some of the best tenants of Lalitpur Sub-division were known to have migrated to the neighbouring Banpur state 'which offered more reasonable terms'.[67] In the not-too-distant Betul, a number of cultivators from Atner *pargana* left in 1831 for better conditions of life in Berar.[68] Peasants' refusal to cultivate (approximating an industrial 'strike') was, however, a more advanced form of protest than desertion, and it did mark the protesters' raising their protest to a new high. This happened in Jalaun in 1851 when the cultivators refused to plough over the issue of payment of taxes, and thereby paralysed the entire agricultural operation for some time.[69]

However, the highest or the most advanced form of protests were the ones in which the peasantry demonstrated its anguish vociferously and violently. One such delirious outburst took place in 1842 at the urban centre of Rath in Hamirpur, resulting in the looting of *bazaar*s and raiding of *bania* shops and *mahajani* establishments. It apparently coincided with some landed magnates' (*thakurs*') disaffection in south Bundelkhand, and possibly led to disgruntled *thakurs* and harassed and tormented villagers of Panwari and Rath to join forces.[70] Almost in an identical fashion, according to the Board of Revenue in the Provinces,[71] the peasants in Aligarh, Mainpuri, Mathura and south-western Saharanpur were found to be restless and aggrieved since 1840, and any further rise in their temper could prompt them to join an open rebellion. Unrest had in fact also been brewing in the Rohilkhand districts over the years, and William Edwards, an officer of considerable experience, reminisced how during 'the fifteen years preceding the Mutiny' discontent grew so fast as to render the country 'ripe' for revolt.[72] Jacquerie and rebelliousness became quite pronounced in NWP and Oudh by the early part of 1857. In a number of places, notably in Banda district, peasants of Buberoo and Mow on the Jamuna were actively engaged in such activities.[73] Simultaneously with such militant manifestations of collective discontent came a tragic and morbid form of individual protest, namely, the peasant and his family taking recourse to suicides.[74] The galloping rate of suicide rocked Bundelkhand in the 1840s and 1850s; nearly as many cases were reported in Hamirpur in one year as were reported in Kanpur in five years. Incidents of suicide in Hamirpur were the highest in its poorer areas like Rath and Panwari. 'It was most common among women and the cultivating castes, certainly the hardest hit.'[75]

Even in their wildest dreams, the rent theorists in India had not had any inkling as to their hard labour causing such havoc on the peasant proprietors in NWP and Oudh. Both in theory and in practice, they were devoted to the cause of the peasants and desired their all-round advancement, whether it was Malthus, Ricardo and Mill in England, or Mackenzie, Bird and Thomason in India. Malthus and Ricardo together were interested in a gradual bourgeoization of Indian agriculture for its own good, and encouraged Mill to expect from so significant a development the eventual emergence of the self-confident capitalist farmers. Mill in fact pinned his hopes for bringing in such a transformation on a Ricardian revenue policy in India, and also, for playing a pivotal role in it, on the original holders of land in the country — the *rayat*s and peasants. Mackenzie, like Mill, felt that the future of agricultural enterprise depended not on the aristocracy but on the peasantry, and that 'the cultivator was the sole hope of Indian agriculture'.[76] His follower Bird was anxious to help the *rayat*s by correcting the raw deal they had received under the prevalent revenue arrangements, under which nothing had been done 'for those to whom so much owed', and who 'alone had the right [over land] before our times — the cultivating classes'.[77] Thomason for his part also championed the *rayat*s' cause by upholding the village proprietors' rights — whose 'existence and inviolability' could not be questioned — and by opposing all the *talukdari* attempts at nullifying the *biswahdar*s' rights and appropriating their properties.[78]

Never before the 1820s or ever after the 1850s had the peasantry had more committed sympathizers within British ruling circles in India than perhaps the rent theorists — the visionaries from a developing industrial society, and the anti-feudal policy-makers of an increasingly stabilized Companyraj. And yet ironically, whether they were wholly unaware of it or not, Messrs. Mill-Mackenzie-Bird-Thomason could be held morally and administratively responsible for the economic devastation that had been forced upon the peasants. Both were the realities of the situation: the fully conscious sympathy for the cultivators of land, and the largely unconscious tormenting of them, and both had curiously been true almost in equal proportion, and emanated from actions of the same brand of people. It is difficult, indeed, to try to explain the tragic character of this contradiction, except by taking our cue from what Jones and McCulloch contemporaneously contended about the Rent Theory and India.

Jones forcefully argued, and McCulloch tended to agree, that the Ricardian formulation on rent was meant essentially for dealing with the farmers in capitalist England, and that it could not automatically be applied to the peasants in pre-capitalist India. At the height of their modernist exuberance, and their great desire to replace an unscientific with a scientific system, the rent theorists failed to diagnose the subsistence nature of agrarian India. What was worse, they did not leave any margin for unforeseen error and had not tried to anticipate any damage that might result from forcing an English method on an under-prepared India. The disastrous consequence that followed turned out dramatically to be a prelude to an upheaval, and the English ideologist romanticists of the second quarter of 19th-century India faded out of the pages of its history as unsung, failed prophets.

## Notes

1 Minute by R. M. Bird, 31 January 1840, cited in Stokes, *The Peasant and the Raj*, p. 72.
2 'Memorandum of the Improvements in the Administration of India during the Last Thirty Years' (Petition of the East India Company to Parliament, London, 1858, Anon.) [written actually by J. S. Mill], B.L.
3 Government of India Cons., 4 April 1850, Nos. 25/28, Home Dept./Rev. Br., N.A.I.
4 Government of India, Cons. 6 April 1835, No. 2, Home/Rev. Br., N.A.I.
5 'Memorandum of the Improvements in the Administration of India during the Last Thirty Years' (Petition of the East India Company to Parliament, London, 1858, Anon.) [written actually by J. S. Mill], B.L.
6 *Ibid.*
7 Bentinck citing Fraser in his minute of 20 January 1832, para. 54, Selections from the Revenue Records of the Government of the N.W.P., Vol. 2, 1822–33, Allahabad, 1872, p. 369, B.L.
8 Mackenzie's letter to the Select Committee of the House of Commons on East India Affairs, 1832, cited in Gupta, *Agrarian Relations and Early British Rule in India*, p. 241.
9 Remarks on the System of Land Revenue Administration in the North-Western Provinces of Hindostan by J. Thomason, Directions for Revenue Officers in the North-Western Provinces of the Bengal Presidency, Agra, 1 November 1849, House of Commons, P.P., 1852–53, Vol. 75, paper 999.
10 *Ibid.*, section IV, 'The Assessment', para. 68.
11 *Ibid.*, para. 60.
12 W. L. Miller, 'Richard Jones: A Case Study in Methodology', in Mark Blaugh (ed.), *Pioneers in Economics (18): Thomas Tooke (1774–1858),*

*Montford Langfield (1802–1884) and Richard Jones (1790–1855)*, Edward Elgar, Aldershot, 1991, p. 142.

13 Alfred Marshall, *Principles of Economics*, Macmillan and Co., London, 1890, p. 656.

14 W. L. Miller, 'Richard Jones's Contribution to the Theory of Rent', in Mark Blaugh (ed.), *Pioneers in Economics (18): Thomas Tooke (1774–1858), Montford Langfield (1802–1884) and Richard Jones (1790–1855)*, Edward Elgar, Aldershot, 1991, p. 356.

15 As a tough Utilitarian, Mill originally wanted the State to exact 'full' economic rent of the land as revenue.

16 'What Jones calls "transfer" is what I call "primary accumulation"', said Marx, finding it to be a historically correct view. Karl Marx, *Mehrwerttheorien*, III, p. 477, cited in Henryk Grossman, 'The Evolutionist Revolt against Classical Economics in England — James Steuart, Richard Jones, Karl Marx', part II, *Journal of Political Economy*, Vol. 51, No. 6, December 1943, p. 510.

17 Grossman, 'The Evolutionist Revolt against Classical Economics', p. 508.

18 It is noteworthy that for his own part, Jones had not formulated a theory of rent, nor even a hypothesis of it. He talked only of 'comprehensive views of facts' for arriving at 'principles truly comprehensive'. Richard Jones, *Literary Remains, Consisting of Lectures and Tracts on Political Economy of the Late Rev. Richard Jones*, ed. William Whewell, 1859 (reprinted by J. Murray, New York, 1964, pp. 569–70).

19 Miller, 'Richard Jones: A Case Study in Methodology', p. 199.

20 Miller, 'Richard Jones's Contribution to the Theory of Rent', p. 80.

21 *Ibid*.

22 Grossman, 'The Evolutionist Revolt against Classical Economics', p. 513.

23 Richard Jones, *An Essay on Distribution of Wealth*, 1831, cited in N. C. March and R. P. Sturges, 'Malthus and Ricardo's Inductivist Critics', *Economica*, new series, Vol. 40, No. 160, November 1973, p. 383.

24 B. N. Ganguli, 'Foreword', in Gupta, *Agrarian Relations and Early British Rule in India*, p. x.

25 Mill, *Principles of Political Economy*, p. 319.

26 Looking back at the end of the 19th century, Alfred Marshall, the renowned economist, felt that the British policy-makers were mistaken 'in trying to force the English system of land revenue on India and Ireland'. See Marshall, *Principles of Economics*, p. 656.

27 Stokes, *The Peasant and the Raj*, p. 92.
28 *Ibid.*, p. 93. Discreetly, in the heart of their hearts, they suspected the charge of high assessment to be true to an extent, and so decided to bring down the proportion of assessment from two-thirds of the net produce in 1833 to one-half in 1855. The damage by that time, however, had conclusively been done.
29 J. R. McCulloch was a well-known journalist economist in the first half of the 19th century, and had much to say on British policies in India.
30 J. R. McCulloch, 'Revenue and Commerce in India', *Edinburgh Review*, March 1827, p. 354.
31 Stokes, *The Peasant and the Raj*, p. 117 and fn. 54.
32 Jones, *An Essay on the Distribution of Wealth*, cited in *ibid.*, p. 109.
33 Ralph B. Price, 'The "New Political Economy" and British Economic Policy for India', *American Journal of Economics and Sociology*, Vol. 35, No. 4, October 1976, p. 413.
34 They, according to Thornhill, Collector of Mathura, kept the assessment so high that the peasants 'were not long able to pay'. Surendranath Sen, *Eighteen Fifty Seven,* Publications Division, Government of India, New Delhi, 1957, p. 32.
35 Habib, *Essays in Indian History*, p. 310.
36 Stokes, *The Peasant and the Raj*, p. 89.
37 K. C. Yadav, *The Revolt of 1857 in Haryana*, Manohar, New Delhi, 1977, p. 27.
38 Tapti Roy, *The Politics of a Popular Uprising: Bundelkhand in 1857*, Oxford University Press, New Delhi, 1994, p. 206.
39 *Ibid.*, p. 211.
40 *Ibid.*, p. 217.
41 Stokes, *The Peasant and the Raj*, p. 89.
42 *Ibid.*, p. 135.
43 Eric Stokes, *The Peasant Armed: The Indian Revolt of 1857*, Clarendon Press, Oxford, 1986, p. 117.
44 Rudrangshu Mukherjee, 'The Revolt of 1857 in the North-Western Provinces', in Barun De (ed.), *Essays in Honour of Professor S. C. Sarkar*, People's Publishing House, New Delhi, 1976, p. 485.
45 Sen, *Eighteen Fifty Seven*, p. 33.
46 Stokes, *The Peasant Armed*, p. 220.
47 Table 4.1 is sourced from Yadav, *The Revolt of 1857 in Haryana*, p. 36, fn. 33.

48 *Ibid.*
49 Rudrangshu Mukherjee, *Awadh in Revolt, 1857–58*, Oxford University Press, New Delhi, 1984, p. 62.
50 The North-Western Provinces and Oudh Administration Report, 1882–83, p. 46, cited in Stokes, *The English Utilitarians and India*, p. 133.
51 Proclamation of the Azamgarh rebels, Foreign Dept. Cons. No. 197, 8 October 1858, cited in Sen, *Eighteen Fifty Seven*, p. 34.
52 *Ibid.*, p. 133.
53 Mukherjee, 'The Revolt of 1857 in the North-Western Provinces', p. 483.
54 Stokes, *The Peasant Armed*, p. 219.
55 Edwards, Collector of Budaun, on his personal experiences during the Mutiny, cited in Judith Brown, *Modern India: Origins of an Asian Democracy*, Oxford University Press, Oxford, 1984, p. 86.
56 Gupta, 'Agrarian Background and the 1857 Rebellion', p. 78.
57 W. H. Smith, Aligarh Settlement Report, Allahabad, 1862, p. 65, cited in Eric Stokes, 'Traditional Elites in the Great Rebellion of 1857: Some Aspects of Rural Revolt in the Upper and Central Doab', in Edmund Leach and S. N. Mukherjee (eds.), *Elites in South Asia*, Cambridge University Press, Cambridge, 1970, pp. 16–32.
58 Settlement Reports of the Second Settlement of Allahabad, Cawnpore, Gorruckpore etc. in the 1870s, cited in Gupta, 'Agrarian Background and the 1857 Rebellion', p. 79.
59 *Ibid.*
60 Stokes, *The Peasant and the Raj*, p. 137.
61 Bird apprehended this torturous situation for the *rayat* as early as 1832, and opposed keeping the *rayat*s out of the Government settlement with the landlords, thereby leaving them unreservedly in the landlords' hands. See Chapter 3, this volume.
62 H. D. Robertson, *District Duties during the Revolt in the North-Western Provinces of India in 1857*, London, 1859, pp. 135–37.
63 Yadav, *The Revolt of 1857 in Haryana*, p. 27.
64 *Ibid.*
65 *Ibid.*
66 Roy, *The Politics of a Popular Uprising*, p. 215.
67 *Ibid.*
68 P. S. Mishra, *The Revolt of 1857: Saugor and Nerbudda Territories*, Sharada Publishing House, New Delhi, 2001, p. 22.
69 Roy, *The Politics of a Popular Uprising*, p. 216.
70 *Ibid.*, p. 213.

71 Stokes, *The Peasant Armed*, p. 219.
72 S. B. Chaudhuri, *Civil Rebellion in the Indian Mutinies, 1857–59*, The World Press, Calcutta, 1957, p. 11.
73 Roy, *The Politics of a Popular Uprising*, p. 218.
74 Even in the first decades of the 21st century, in a period touted as one of radiant economic well-being, farmers — those unable to cope with the socio-economic maladies — still commit suicides in many parts of the country.
75 Mayne, Collector and Magistrate of Banda, to Chester, Commissioner, 4 Division, 20 June 1856, Selections from the Records of the Government of N.W.P., Vol. V, 1856, cited in Roy, *The Politics of a Popular Uprising*, p. 218.
76 Stokes, *The English Utilitarians and India*, p. 113.
77 Minute of Bird (1833?), Selections from the Records of the Government of the North-Western Provinces, Allahabad, 1873, p. 467, Microfiche, MF 1/2866, IO/BL.
78 Thomason's letter to Gov. Gen. Ellenborough, 31 January 1844, Selections from the Records of the Government of N.W.P., Mr. Thomason's Despatches, Vol. I, Calcutta, 1856, pp. 17–18, IO/BL.

# 5
# FOR CONFRONTATION

By the 1850s, grating discontent in northern and central Indian rural society over high assessment and harsh collection affected its migrant members wherever they went to earn their livelihood. Whether at a marketplace or a waterfront, a manufacturing centre or a construction site, they tended to identify themselves with their near and dear ones living in their ancestral homes and encountering steep rise in Government demand, incurrence of growing debts to meet it, and loss of land from the inability to pay. The sepoys of the Bengal Army, or the army of the Bengal Presidency, like some of those of the armies of the Madras and Bombay Presidencies, were recruited largely from the NWP countryside. The majority of them — the *purbia*s — came from the villages of the Provinces' easterly parts: Benares, Gorakhpur, Basti and southern Oudh, as well as from the region stretching to Shahabad in Bihar. Consequently, being tied by an umbilical cord with village fortunes, they shared a similar agony as most migrants were experiencing. They thoroughly disapproved of the manner in which the Companyraj extracted revenues of 'Rupees 300/- where only Rupees 200/- were due, and Rupees 500/- where but Rupees 400/- were demandable', and the manner in which it had 'doubled or quadrupled and raised ten fold the Chowkeedaree [village policing] tax', over and above charging 6 pies 'every soul' and 4 to 8 *anna*s every cart as toll to be permitted to travel on the 'public roads'.[1] Apart from deeply resenting the too-conspicuous Government apathy towards the sufferings of their own village people, the sepoys — the professional, well-drilled armsmen — had their own quota of grievances.

# I

The sepoys' main grievances grew out of the dire financial straits they were subjected to — the consequence of the Companyraj's overall allocation of funds for its army. To cater to the needs of an entire Indian army personnel of 315,520, it spent £9,802,235, and out of this sum, no less than £5,668,110 was expended on 51,316 European officers and soldiers.[2] That left £4,134,125 to be spent on 264,204 Indian sepoys by keeping their pay and pension at the lowest possible limit. While a *sowar* (cavalryman) received a salary of Rs. 27 per month, a sepoy got monthly Rs. 7, and both amounts included payment for their respective uniforms. The sepoy's pay would not exceed Rs. 9 per month for years of service unless he was promoted, and the chances of promotion to higher posts were severely limited. At most, one out of twenty or thirty sepoys would become a *jamadar*. Of another 35 *jamadar*s, one perhaps would turn out to be a *subedar*, and only a fortunate few of the *subedar*s might make it to a *subedar* major — the highest among the Indian ranks.[3] By the time the sepoys received promotions, they were usually too old: one Sitaram was promoted to *subedar*ship at the age of 65 after 48 years of service.[4] To begin with, an ordinary sepoy's first few months' paltry salary had to be spent on illegal gratification by paying about Rs. 16 to the Indian drill *havildar* and the European sergeant of the Company where he was posted. He had also to pay for his daily ration on credit from the *bania* in the regimental *bazaar*, and after settling his accounts on pay day, he was left with a bare rupee or a rupee and a half.[5] Without sharing the Indian sepoys' burden of rough and rugged service duties, the European soldiers were lodged, fed and paid in a manner unknown to the non-Europeans.[6] The racial divide in the army was clearly very wide, and the treatment the Europeans meted out to their Indian counterparts was characterized by harshness on issues of military discipline, and haughtiness and abusiveness in matters of personal intercourse. Put together, all these condemned the Indian section of the Companyraj's military machine to a permanent position of emphatic inferiority. The army not being attractive by any standard for career prospects, the urbane, educated and well-to-do Indians did not attempt to join the British Indian Army. Despite the presence of a good number of Brahmins, Rajputs and Pathans in their midst, those who enrolled themselves in its lower ranks came by and large from the hard-pressed rural categories with scant education and little literacy. Consequently, they were steeped as much in religiosity as in superstition. Since superstitious religiosity dictated against their going out of Hindustan or crossing the seas (*kalapani*), the Companyraj had to coax the sepoys to take part in its campaigns in Afghanistan (apparently by going over Hindustan's last frontier — the Indus) and in Burma (by crossing the seas), and compensate them monetarily for their fall into disgrace in the public eye at home and for facing hardship in unfamiliar lands. The monetary compensation or the grant of special *batta* did financially help a lot of the sepoys who were called upon in 1842 to serve under General Pollock in the first Afghan war beyond the Indus through Sind and Punjab. However, when the British annexed Sind the next year in 1843 and moved into Punjab, the Companyraj decided against paying any *batta* on the ground that these places had turned into an integral part of its territories in Hindustan, and could not, therefore, be formally considered as foreign lands. The sepoys were baffled by this legal sophistry, because to them the Indus had not ceased to exist, and life beyond it in 1843 remained as hard as a year before. They thus took the authorities' refusal to pay the *batta* as a breach of an assurance justifiably given to them by the Government. They felt convinced of it when in 1844 the Companyraj frowned upon the Commanding Officer Mosley of the 34th Bengal Regiment for conceding *batta* to his sepoys marching into Sind, or when in 1849 Governor General Dalhousie severely censured Commander-in-Chief Napier for granting *batta* to the regiments stationed in Rawalpindi (in the newly annexed Punjab).[7]

Any promise which appeared to have been broken thus by the authorities was likely to raise a disquieting suspicion in the sepoys' religiously touchy minds: what if the Government withdrew for some intricate reasoning its pledge of religious non-interference, and encouraged the Churches to Christianize those linked closely with it, such as the Hindu and the Muslim armymen? Their misgivings could not have been altogether imaginary, since they had to countenance racial and religious contempt day in and day out from missionaries in regimental chapels, and even from the evangelist British officers on the parade ground — a ceaseless haranguing as to how bad their religious beliefs were in comparison to the Christian faith. The climax was reached when the sepoys learnt that the cartridge they were to load into the new Enfield rifle by biting off the seal (rather than removing it by hand) was smeared with repugnant animal fat.

The rifles made in Enfield were found by the British in the Crimean War to be more effective than the earlier Brow Bess ones, and were consequently introduced in 1856 for use in the Companyraj's Bengal Army. The new rifle was proved further to be useful because its greased cartridge slipped more quickly into the barrel than others. Besides, biting off the cartridge seal made reloading much faster than breaking it with one's fingers; 'for the sepoy, too, the time gained might make all the difference between life and death in the battlefield'.[8] That the composition used in greasing the cartridges was a mixture of tallow and bees' wax had been apparent to many, but it could not be said with certainty that the fat came from beef (unacceptable to Hindus) or pork (repugnant to Muslims) or mutton (largely inoffensive to both communities). No precaution seemed to have been taken to ensure that the animal fat used was above objections, though some fancied the use of 'hog's lard', and some others did not rule out offensive tallow, since the Brahmin contractor for supplying the fat (in Dum Dum) would go for the cheapest material in the market and save 'a few shillings' to give pig's and bullock's fat.[9] The authorities of military ordinance also confirmed that the tallow used was what the contractor supplied, and so rejected outright the suspicious sepoys' plea for 'a high-caste Hindu and a Mahomedan' overseeing the manufacture of cartridges.[10]

The suspicion deepened and the sepoys felt that the Companyraj had a secret to conceal — the secret of polluting and defiling them and rendering them helpless before the machination of the Christian missionaries. With the suspicion gaining ground, the sepoys felt alarmed, then grew agitated, turned defiant and eventually became mutinous. Their mutiny thereafter could hardly be stemmed by the half-hearted and belated attempts at allaying apprehensions and making concessions. The sepoy mutiny consequently broke out in fits in Barrackpore, Bengal, on 26 February and 29 March 1857, but exploded earth-shakingly in Meerut, NWP, on 10 May 1857 in violent protest against the authorities' diktat on the use of greased cartridges. Clearly, in hindsight the sepoys' distrust over the use of forbidden animal fat does not appear to have been entirely unfounded. However, their allegations that the Government had used cow's or bullock's tallow (vis-à-vis the Hindus among them) or that of the pig (vis-à-vis the Muslims in their midst) seem to be too contrived and neat to cause widespread apprehensions, and perhaps had been ingeniously twisted a bit by the leaders among the sepoys for mobilizational purposes. For identical purposes, perhaps another bogey was similarly raised through a whisper campaign that certain animal bones (selectively again of cows and pigs!) had been mixed with the sepoys' *atta* (wheat flour) or poured into their wells for polluting water.[11] That the sepoys' anti-greased cartridges posture had probably been built up for rallying them (both Hindus and Muslims) against the Companyraj was apparent from the mutineers' use, throughout the great Revolt of 1857, of the same Enfield rifle in their possession, and biting the same condemned bullets for firing upon the British, their families, allies and minions. This was noted very conspicuously by the Prosecutor of the Government at the trial of Bahadur Shah 'Jafar' in March 1858 in Delhi, observing that the fact that 'neither Mussalman nor Hindu had any honest objection to the use of any of the cartridges' was

> sufficiently proved by the eagerness with which they [the sepoys] sought possession of them, and the alacrity [with which] they used them when their aim and object was the

murder of Europeans or when . . . they for months constantly went forth to fight against the power [the Companyraj] to which they owed fidelity and allegiance.[12]

It is also useful to remember in this connection that the men in the three regiments, one cavalry (3rd Cavalry) and two infantry (11th NI and 20th NI), which first broke into mutiny on 10 May 1857, had not had 'in reality' been supplied with 'a single greased cartridge'.[13]

That the greased *tota* (cartridge) which was believed to be responsible for the outbreak of the sepoy mutiny in Meerut, and its spread over vast stretches of land, could not have been its main cause or a prop behind the sepoys' inter-religious joint front against the British, was apparent even to the then authorities, and they did smell 'some deeper and more powerful [cause] than the use of greased cartridges' to be at work.[14] They could not, however, discern then what this 'something deeper' was — not because it was not wholly discernible, but on account of their reluctance to raise any doubt whatsoever as to the Companyraj's self-righteous position in India. In the lingering flush of British military successes in Afghanistan (1842, though dubiously), Sind (1843), Punjab (1849) and Burma (1852), and in the smug contentment over setting up a process of bourgeoizing Hindustan between 1829 and 1856 (on the basis of doctrinal novelties in the administration of land, and of modernist initiatives in the spheres of governance), the masterminds of the British rule had not had enough curiosity to glimpse what tension India might have silently been undergoing beneath the surface. They felt hardly any need to know what social realities dominated the troubled world of the 'native' mercenary sepoy at this juncture — the confines of which he wanted to break open in search of a more congenial and dignified human existence. It was for a promising future, not merely the despondency of the present, that he wanted to storm out of the torturous monotony of low pay, lack of promotion, racial discrimination and alarming news from home of the family's inability in his village to meet Government demand, mounting debts, and failure to prevent the loss of land

and avoid the ignominy of going down the peasantry's hierarchical order. The rebellious disdain for the present and the promise of the future must also have driven one who was superstitiously devout to make common cause with similar others from different faiths. Objective conditions do crucially mould the subjectivities — the orthodoxies and traditionalities of the neglected categories of society — and encourage them to try together, to go all out for a lunge forward.

## II

The sepoys' mutiny in 1857 signified a serious setback for the British in India, most certainly in military terms, though it was not by itself in a position to shake the very foundation of their rule in India. For causing such a turbulent convulsion, it required the supportive rising simultaneously of the commonalty and various other sections of people, especially deep inside the country. When that actually happened — to the bewilderment of all concerned — the mutiny stepped out of its bounds, grew tumultuous and turned into the great Rising it is known to have been. The British in India had always coped with mutinies of one kind or the other, small or not so small; and despite considerable losses in men and money they succeeded in quelling them. Some of the mutinies were so perilous and life-threatening that they could have thoroughly jeopardized or even overturned the Companyraj, had they received some popular support and attracted a certain participation of the people in them. The Vellore mutiny of July 1806 in Madras Presidency was one such delirious occurrence that had the possibility of becoming an upheaval had it succeeded in drawing popular support on a substantial scale. Like the mutineers of 1857, the Vellore sepoys also suffered from poor pay and pension, lack of promotional avenues and racial ill-treatment. More importantly, their superstitious religiosity was affected almost in the same way as that of the Meerut sepoys in 1857. The effect of forcing the 'dress regulations' and the 'new turban' upon the prejudicially objecting Hindu and Muslim sepoys in 1806,[15] was similar to the imposition of the Enfield rifles and greased cartridges on them in 1857. But unlike the storm that broke out in 1857 in apparent spontaneity, the outbreak in 1806 had been the outcome of careful planning (with the help of chosen leaders among the sepoys) under an astute leadership (comprising Tipu Sultan's two imprisoned sons and a skilful agent),[16] and with a straightforward political objective (the overthrowing of the Company's rule over the southern peninsula and the restoration of Tipu's dynasty in Mysore).[17] Clearly the mutineers at Vellore in 1806 were far in advance organizationally and programmatically than the mutineers of 1857, whose only political mobilizational objective was to reach Delhi from Meerut and hoist up as a symbol of anti-British resistance the tottering Moghul Emperor Bahadur Shah 'Jafar' in India, whose writ in reality barely ran beyond the precincts of Delhi's Red Fort.

What, however, the mutineers in 1857 got readily beyond all calculations and expectations, and also without striving much for it, did not come so very conveniently to aid the Vellore sepoys in 1806. In Vellore, the Hindu and Muslim sepoys under the princely and the native army official leadership awaited breathlessly but in vain for the favourable reactions of the towns' people to their 'action' — the commotions in the local *bazaar*s and the stirrings in the tranquil countryside — or for any other visible signs of growing popular support for them. The common Velloreans were rather nonplussed about the event and did not feel much interest in taking sides, and the tradesmen and the well-to-do became alarmed by it and looked up to the Companyraj to ensure their security. The masses also lacked enthusiasm for the happenings in the Vellore fort, since they found the Companyraj's attempt from 1802[18] to settle land on *rayatwari* lines — directly between the *rayat* and the Government — ostensibly to their advantage. It seemed to offer the possibility for restraining the high demands of both an unrelenting state and a rent-receiving intermediary — the exploitative landlord, or aristocrat. It was only those feudal overlords — whose sociopolitical authority and land-based profiteering had been threatened by the Companyraj — who dared to be openly anti-British. But even their hostility was not of much consequence following the rout of the *poligar* opposition and the defeat of their confederacy at British hands in 1800–01. Besides, they had not proven themselves to be very reliable, and when the Mysore princes at Vellore contacted a few of them (notably the *poligar*s of Kalastree and Venkatagherry)[19] before the mutiny and solicited their help in the course of it, they failed to rise to the occasion and join the fight as promised. So the occurrence at Vellore in 1806, despite the requisite leadership, organization and subaltern heroism, could not attain the height of a full-fledged rising, failed to get the popular support, and remained an isolated, unconnected mutiny of the sepoys. Consequently, the Companyraj faced no insurmountable difficulty in suppressing it and recovering the Vellore fort, within eight hours of its falling into the hands of the mutineers, by sending reinforcements under Colonel Gillespie from Arcot. What the mutineers of 1806 sadly missed or lacked at Vellore, their counterparts in Meerut and Delhi, however, received in abundance — not only popular support but also the people's participation on a large scale — the sublime magic touch that transformed dramatically a military mutiny into an uproarious violent uprising.

Who crucially formed the multitudes whose support and participation had so qualitatively changed the status of the sepoy mutiny in 1857? They appear to have included both the elites and the commonalty, the social exploiters and the socially exploited, the masters and the masses — mainly those connected with land in the rural sector. The masters, the social exploiters and the elites — at the upper level in the countryside — were the holders of landed estates and upholders of the feudal system in India, like the princes, the intermediary aristocrats, landlords of all hues and their dependants, such as the courtiers-cum-*musahib*s, the *diwani* and *cutcherry* employees, the personal attendants and retinues. The commonalty, the socially exploited and the masses — at the lower level in the rural sector — were unbreakably tied with land as its cultivators under feudality: the peasants (with or without occupational rights), the sharecroppers, the agricultural labourers and the survivors on agro-entrepreneurship like the handicraftsmen, the boatmen and fishermen, the washermen and masons, and the village menials. In the urban sector, however, despite being under the shadow of feudal magnates, those at the upper level, like the *mahajan*s, the *bania*s and the *dalal*s (agents) at one end, and the traders and the professionals, the English-educated and the public servants at the other, had little to do with the uprising and seemed to prefer the overbearing continuance of the Companyraj — the safety, security, orderliness, technology and the blindingly dazzling modernity it offered. At the lower level, somewhat varyingly, the artisans (notably ironsmiths, cotton-carders and weavers[20]), the domestic workers, the labourers, the semi-employed and the unemployed riff-raff did constitute a volatile section which could jump into any fray and act as ready combustibles in inflaming a great Rising.

The fortunes of those at the upper rural level had been impaired severely by the anti-feudal precepts and practices of the Companyraj's bourgeoized high priests — the products of the milieu emanating from the Industrial Revolution in Britain. These deprecators of feudal India launched their offensive by questioning the estate-owners' jurisdiction over the land they lorded over by investigating its legality with excessive rigour. If the investigations proved the landlord's claims to be unsustainable, wholly or partially, the land was forcibly 'resumed' for sale or settlement afresh. The Companyraj also examined the landed magnates' titles of inheritance and grants of pension, and cancelled and circumscribed these if found wanting in any way. Similarly cancelled were their successions if the lines of these were not proved to be direct and the 'adoptions' not deemed to be acceptable, and such 'lapsed' estates and domains were passed over to Government agents or Courts of Wards for supervision. Over and above these measures, the rulers of powerful kingdoms were also liable to be charged with maladministration, be 'deposed' and have their territories 'annexed' and administered directly for the 'good of the subjects'. Resumptions, life pensions (in place of family pensions), lapses, assumptions and annexations together under the Companyraj's bourgeoizing dispensation signified the Indian feudal components' rapid dispossession during the several decades preceding the outbreak of 1857.

The rapidity of dispossession nevertheless could hardly cover up the fast-deteriorating circumstances of the rural poor underneath, and those who might be held responsible for it were paradoxically the same anti-feudal luminaries of the Companyraj — those who dreamt of agricultural advancement and peasant well-being by replacing the feudalistic decline in production with the capitalistic flourishing of productivity. Despite all pious intentions, their obsessive dependence on importing the Ricardian Rent Theory from a capitalist Britain into a pre-capitalist, under-prepared India was bound to be problematic, and even disastrous if ineptly handled. That was exactly what happened, resulting in the imposition of exorbitantly high revenue demand on all holders of land, big or small — from *zamindar*s to *rayat*s — but most excruciatingly on the middle, poor and marginal peasants, over and above the suffering they (and their sharecroppers) underwent due to various landlordist exactions. It was the over-assessment that triggered the all too familiar (and quite repetitive) torrents of high State demands, harsh collections, rack-renting by intermediaries, mounting indebtedness, defaulting on payments, sales and transfers, and land alienation or speedy dispossession. Apart from the recently dispossessed peasant innumerables and the princely and intermediary numerables, in addition to the perpetually dispossessed agricultural labourers, artisans, menials and outcastes, there were also some others in Indian society who — out of their overall dislike of and reservations about what the Companyraj stood for — could not wholly be disagreeable to any anti-British confrontation.

Most people were thoroughly alienated by the aggressive proselytizing of the Christian missionaries in India, by their abusive denunciation of all non-Christian religions. Since it was known to belong to a so-called Christian nation, and despite its attempts at following a policy of secularity and religious non-interference, the Companyraj invariably felt the ire of various other religionists of an overwhelming number, the staunch Hindus and Muslims in particular. It was the orthodox and the conservative *maulavi*s, as much as their *pandit* counterparts, who derided the alien *feringhee* rulers and denounced whatever they tried to do, especially in matters of the educational advancement of their subjects. The steady promotion of English education and educational institutions and the contrasting decline of education in Arabic, Persian and Sanskrit, as well as of the *madrasa*s, *pathsala*s or *tol*s, did not receive the approbation of the status-quoist Indian society at large. The Companyraj's replacement of Persian by English as the Court language, and its emphasis on the knowledge of English as essential for Government employment, so jeopardized the career prospects of a large section of the Indian intelligentsia that they could not but have turned into bitter critics of the authorities.

The endeavours on the part of the Government to put an end to some of the long-standing social abuses, especially those affecting women (such as *sati*, female infanticide, neglected Hindu widowhood and widow remarriage), were thoroughly disapproved of and resisted by the Indian (Hindu) orthodoxy who took these efforts to be calculated meddling by the arrogant, Christian, Western imperialists into Indian ways of life so as to demean an ancient civilized society's morally acclaimed practices. Besides, a highly stratified and self-absorbed Indian people — though marvelling at the British introduction of railways in their country — were not comfortable with the idea of persons of differing communities, of high, low and 'polluted' castes, of rich and poor backgrounds, travelling together on the same train and sometimes interacting with each other in the same compartment. The backward-looking medieval trends of thought continued to hold their ground despite the challenges, with a certain landlordist backing under a feudalistic environment in which even Lord Ellenborough's epoch-making anti-slavery legislation of 1843 went practically unnoticed. At the time of the sepoy mutiny, thus, there were many of traditional and conservative disposition who dominated Indian society, as they so frequently did in most other societies in the world, and who were resentful and disapproving of the Companyraj's doings, particularly between 1829 and 1856. Their resentment might or might not have led them to join the anti-British camp, but they by no means were likely to be wholly or unexceptionably on the side of the British. Their show of some forced neutrality was heavily tilted against the British and prone to encourage the rebels who could count on their implicit sympathy. The mute dissenters of British rule did contribute to the building up of the Revolt, but not so much in its actuality — they remained in the fringes, and not in the thick of it.

### III

In the thick of it were, apart from the forerunning mutinous sepoys, the commonfolk — people from the lower strata of urban and rural societies, the latter heavily outnumbering the former — the hydra-headed 'mob' and 'rabble' in official and elitist parlance. The very day (10 May 1857) the mutiny broke out in Meerut, the so-called lawless Gujars of the neighbouring villages scented instability, descended upon the city, broke open its jails to release the prisoners, attacked and plundered the European quarters and selectively looted and burnt down the shops and houses of the local *bania*s.[21] The pattern was more or less the same in most urban centres that the rebellion engulfed — country people marching in to join the mutineers, ransacking the European establishments and overpowering the *feringhee*s and their henchmen. Additionally, in Muzaffarnagar, Saharanpur, Bareilly and Bijnore, the raiding peasants of Banjara, Mewati, Gujar and Jat origin looted the Government treasuries, destroyed the official records[22] and *mahajans*' papers and burnt down the Government premises. The story was identical in Farrukhabad, Shahjahanpur, Fateabhad and Fatehpur, and anarchy and arson reigned supreme in Budaun, Aligarh and Mathura, where 'the cultivating classes constituted ninety per cent of the people in civil rising'.[23]

While the rebellious villagers around the urban centres and military cantonments had thus succeeded in breaking through the well-secured British barriers, they had little difficulty in overwhelming the loosely run and remotely controlled vast countryside of their own. The large-scale participation of the Oudh peasants in the revolt is illustrative — 'about three-fourths of its [Oudh's] adult male population'[24] armed themselves to the teeth with swords, spears and firearms,[25] and turned themselves into single-minded insurgents with the appearance of a rabble. They became so powerful that when Sir Havelock (and his battle-seasoned army) 'tried in the first instance to force his way into Oudh, he was obliged to retreat before the 'rabble' enemy'.[26] Similarly in Bundelkhand, as soon as the news of the departure of British officials from the headquarters in Banda 'spread . . . like wild fires, villages rose in arms in all directions',[27] and their inhabitants took to plunder and pillage — the typical assertion of people's power — arming themselves with 'Talwars and matchlocks . . . spears and scythes and iron-bounded lathis, and extemporary axes, formed of chopping knives fastened on sticks'.[28] The manner in which the English were hounded out of the countryside by belligerent peasants and forced to scamper for safety is described in Capt. P.G. Scot's *Narrative of the Escape from Nowgong to Banda and Nagode*,[29] among other narratives. The armed peasantry forced European officials to flee from their stations, thus confirming the collapse of British power as well as of the belief that 'once overthrown, the British rule would never return'.[30] The Bundelkhandis apparently offered a joint front to their common oppressors, irrespective of belonging to disparate caste categories like the Sangar Rajputs, Ahirs, Lodhis, Mochis and Gujars.[31]

Despite the regional variations and differences in caste, clan and class among the diverse sections of landholders, the British officials were literally 'flabbergasted' by their 'spontaneous, universal upsurge' in the various vital parts of NWP.[32] The Jats in Meerut and Muzaffarnagar and their Gujar and Pandir Rajput counterparts in Saharanpur were at the forefront in spreading the conflagration.[33] The rising was also 'tumultuous' among the peasantry as a whole, notably in the interiors of Mathura and Aligarh,[34] as well as of Mainpuri and Agra, though somewhat of fractured mobilization.[35] Generally speaking, the peasants were acknowledged to be the 'prime movers' in the uprising in most places in the NWP.[36] The picture of the rebellion that Central India and the Norbudda Territories presented in 1857 was hardly different from what had been happening in the rest of the Provinces. While 'anarchy was the order of the day' in all parts of Hamirpur,[37] the British Deputy Commissioner in Mandla sorrowfully conceded: 'two-thirds of my district have thus risen in rebellion against the Government'.[38] Even in November 1857 — when the Rising's momentum seemed to have diminished a bit, following the Companyraj's reoccupation of Delhi — the British officials in Jubbalpore had no doubt whatsoever that 'the number of the followers of the rebel chiefs has increased greatly'.[39] About the same time the Deputy Commissioner of Hoshungabad reported of the ease with which 'the Mewati rebels' were plundering 'the villages of his district,[40] or the negligible administrative and judicial work done there 'owing to the disturbed state of the country for the four or five months'.[41]

Peasants also took to arms outside the Provinces in Shahabad and Gaya in the permanently settled Bihar where the state demands (taxes) were not as burdensome as the landlords' exactions (rents). Their sporadic acts of rebellion continued on 'a wide scale', especially among 'the war-like population of the Rajput villages'.[42] Such merging of the disaffected Bihari villages with the widespread rural risings all over the NWP and Central India so seriously threatened the very existence of the Companyraj in India that the feudal sufferers at its hands not only took heart from the developments, but also saw themselves in a position to take advantage of them. The *raja*s and the chiefs, the *jagirdars/zamindar*s and *talukdar*s, the big estate-holders and landed magnates, or those rich and powerful whom the awe-struck rural societies had traditionally been habituated to look up to, felt like joining the peasant rebels and hoped for gaining control over the proceedings by dint of their high social position. It was not easy for them to contemplate confronting the mighty Companyraj and take the side of the rebels, and therefore, a good number of them did not actually dare. But the desperate ones, especially those who had been left in the lurch by the British authorities in particular, overcame their hesitation in joining the revolt of the commonfolk and took leading roles in it in the great expectation of carving out niches for themselves. Nana Saheb craved for Peshwaship; Rani Lakshmi Bai for the sole rulership of Jhansi; Begum Hazarat Mahal for securing the succession of her son (Burjis Qadr) in Lucknow; Hanumant Singh, Beni Madho and Muhammad Khan for the recovery of their lost land and local authority in Oudh;

Khan Bahadur Khan of Bareilly and Mahmud Khan of Bijnore for becoming the virtual independent rulers of their respective regions; Walidad Khan for the glory of dominating Bulandshahar; Maulavi Ahmadulla of Fyzabad for immortality in a *jihad* against the *kafir*s; Teja Singh for making his *gadi* undisputed in Mainpuri; Kunwar Singh for relieving his debt-ridden estate in Shahabad; and so on and so forth.

Spearheaded by the mutinous *kisan*s-turned-sepoys and strongly backed up by the peasant rebels in the rural sector, joined by the dispossessed feudal elements and a sprinkling of urban firebrands, the engine of the Revolt of 1857 rolled on from Meerut to Delhi, and from Delhi to various other places. It reached Kanpur on 4 June and had travelled to the major cities, like Allahabad, Lucknow, Agra and Benares, by July 1857. The Rising also covered within the month of July itself the relatively quieter and smaller urban centres — and their widely spread and remotely placed interiors near about towns like Hissar, Rohtak, Panipat, Saharanpur, etc. (around Delhi); Bulandshahar, Aligarh, Etah, Etawa, Mathura and others (Agra); Unnao, Farrukhabad, Fatehpur, Rae Bareilly, Faizabad, Jaunpur, etc. (Kanpur-Lucknow); Azamgarh, Ghazipur, Mirzapur, Gorakhpur, Basti and the like (Benares). The Revolt had already run over from July 1857 the whole of Rohilkhand (Bareilly, Moradabad, Shahjahanpur, Budaun and Bijnore), as well as Bundelkhand (Jalaun, Jhansi, Hamirpur, Lalitpur Sub-division and Banda), and passed through the Saugor and Norbudda Territories, including Jubbalpore, Mandla, Narsingpur, Hoshungabad, Damoh and Seoni, etc. Simultaneously, the Central India Agency Areas within the Provincial set-up, such as Gwalior, Panna, Rewa, Sohagpur, Tonk-Sirdi, Indore, Dhar, Mhow and others, fell in its way. Clearly the NWP — under British rule from 1801, and experiencing the fallout of the unforeseen Ricardian debacle since the 1830s — constituted the extensive actual arena within which the uprising of 1857 was primarily enacted. Secondarily, of course, in Rajasthan it threatened to come over to Ajmer, and seriously affected the Cantonment towns of Nasirabad and Neemach. Downward of Benares, similarly, in Arrah (Bihar), the Danapur sepoys joined Kunwar Singh and his followers at the end of July 1857 to start a general rising. Likewise in Punjab at the periphery, the sepoys also mutinied as early as 13 May 1857 in Ferozepur, but could not hold up against the British, and they marched either into Patiala to take refuge or towards Delhi to swell the rebel ranks there. Sir John Lawrence, the Chief Commissioner, not only ensured British safety in Punjab but also converted it into a base from which attempts at the recovery of Delhi could effectively be made. He sent all European armymen to Delhi, rallied the Sikh sepoys in their support and opened up a line of steady supplies for them. 'The men he sent [to Delhi] and the materials he supplied turned the table in his country's favour.'[43]

## IV

The recovery of Delhi — the emblematic and strategic centre of independent Moghul Hindustan — was obviously the most pressing task before Britain for reasserting its imperial hold over India. The Companyraj's ability to fulfil this task on 20 September saw an agreeable reversal of British fortunes, somewhat gradually but unfailingly, between September 1857 (reoccupation of Delhi) and March 1858 (restoration of Lucknow). The reversal demanded a stupendous effort: the commissioning of a massive reinforcement of 60,000 British soldiers (over and above the 36,000 already in India) from abroad, the rallying of troops within from the Presidential armies of Bombay and Madras, as well as from the Punjab Frontier Force and the Gurkha Regiment of an obliging Nepal. It also called for making the fullest use of the British generals' experience in conducting military matters, arranging supplies, ensuring finances and enjoying a technological superiority in arms, armaments and telegraphy.[44] Despite the rebels' obvious numerical superiority — not so many military professionals (sepoys) as hordes of armed peasants and civilian volunteers — they could not cover up their deficiencies in armour, inadequacies in supplies and funds (causing frequent desertions and withdrawals at the desperate call of livelihood) and, more decisively, their lack of expertise in running military machines in the way a Colin Campbell, a Hugh Rose, a Henry Havelock, or a James Outram could. A *subedar* major (the highest in the Indian ranks) was trained at the most to command 100 men, and not a thousand nor tens of thousands, and the others among the mutinous sepoys from *subedar* downwards hardly had any education and therefore capacity for issuing written instructions, comprehending strategies, working out tactics and devising field movements of large numbers of troops.[45] Compounding their gaping gaps in military understanding (which does not seem to have been filled by the princeling and *jagirdar-zamindar* rebel leaders and their agents, with the exception of Tantia Tope, possibly of Bakht Khan and probably Kunwar Singh), the rebel forces were handicapped by not having Enfield rifles, field-guns, howitzers, mortars, revolving pistols. Their 'pathetic attempt' at manufacturing guns and shells[46] did not help them get over their dependence on plundering the enemy's arsenals and military stores. Similar reliance on the looting of British treasuries, establishments and residences did not go far enough to keep up the flow of funds to pay for the expenses of wages, arms and provisions. It became further problematic on account of the pro-British wealthy *mahajan*s' and *bania*s' reluctance to contribute to the rebel coffer unless coerced to do so.

The military disparities between the Companyraj and the rebels seemed so distinctly wide that these were bound to play a conclusive role in the outcome of the civil war, following the six months of Delhi's recapture. Determined to recover their major centres of power, the British succeeded in overcoming the rebel resistance first at Allahabad in July, and then at Benares in August and Agra in October 1857. The more demanding task of reoccupying Kanpur was completed by the British armies towards the end of the year, subsequent to their running over Gurgaon, Hissar and Rewari, storming Fatehpur (November) and taking on the rebels in Rajasthan (beginning of 1858). Following protracted resistance, Lucknow fell into British hands in March 1858, signalling a clear swing in the war in favour of the Companyraj. The trend was discernible in the simultaneous recovery of Etawah and Azamgarh, as well as of Banda and other Rohilkhand strongholds like Kalpi, Hamirpur and Lalitpur Sub-division by May 1858. It was, however, the month of

June that proved militarily to be most crucial for both the warring parties: first Bareilly was lost to the British in this month, making way for the surrender of entire Rohilkhand, then came the reoccupation of Mainpuri and Aligarh, to be followed by the confederated rebel armies coming face to face with the British armies in Gwalior. The British victory over the rebels in the battle of Gwalior on 20 June 1858 marked the end of the more than a year old Great Rebellion for all practical purposes. What remained thereafter were the mopping-up operations by the British forces between July and October, or till the British Queen's Proclamation on 1 November 1858, such as the taming of the rebels in Malwa and Indore; Rewa, Mhow, Karwi and Nagoda; Saugor, Mandla and Jubbalpore; the obstinate Oudh *talukdari*s and similar other 'trouble-spots'.

Some non-combatants invariably got entangled in any confrontation between the contesting armies and suffered inconsolably and irreparably. Such sufferings — howsoever regrettable — are different from the inhuman atrocities and bestialities the rival parties wilfully perpetrated on the civilians *en masse* as retribution of one against the other. Both the contending armed forces had engaged in unprovoked assaults and retaliatory actions throughout 1857–58 — the rebels against the Europeans and their loyalists and the Companyraj against Indian people of all categories. Obviously the victims in most of the cases were the defenceless and the innocent, the dignified and the ordinary, the aged and the infirm, the women and the children. Properties of both Europeans and Indians were looted and gutted, putting often an entire village or a whole locality into flames, massacring their inhabitants and ravishing and killing their women. All these were let loose in the Rising's initial stage by the rebels on a considerable number of Europeans and Eurasians mainly in Meerut, Delhi, Kanpur (notably in Sati Chaura Ghat and Bibighar, where hundreds of women and children were slaughtered), Jhansi, Bareilly, and in a scattered manner in various other places. The vengeful reprisals of the Companyraj on a very wide scale were horrific and unparalleled in the annals of British-Indian history. The British commanding officers carried out acts of retaliation practically limitlessly in Benares, by the continuous plundering of its inhabitants' properties, burning of their *mohalla*s and hanging of persons without a semblance of discrimination. A similar fate awaited the residents of Fatehpur, and the mutineers in Peshawar, Hoti Mardan and Mian Mir (Punjab) were either butchered or blown away by cannons as soon as they had been overpowered. Retaliatory carnage in Kanpur was believed to have resulted in the killing of 10,000 of its residents,[47] 20,000 of such in Delhi,[48] about 5,000 in Jhansi,[49] countless others in Lucknow and Oudh and in innumerable places in Rohilkhand and Bundelkhand, Saugor and the Norbudda Territories, Malwa and Indore. The Companyraj's re-conquest of the NWP and Central India was replete with the traditional conqueror's typical terrorizing treatment meted out to the defiant and obdurate conquered — through rapes, plunders, arsons and killings (by bayoneting, shooting, hanging, burning alive and blowing up by cannon) without sparing the aged, women, juveniles and even infants.

The great Rising and its aftermath may thus appear to posterity to be incorrigibly medievalist (at the onset of modernity), unabashedly jingoist and utterly racialist. The occurrences may even seem to be indicative of a kind of civilizational clash between the last-ditch efforts of the decadent and a hard-hitting emergent, as well as a conflict of staunch religiosities — of a *jihad* or a crusade between the 'Kafrush Fujah Nisara' (fraudulent Christian infidels) and the 'Diabolically False and Fanatic Faiths', with General Neil systematically following in Kanpur the policy of 'burning' the bodies of Muslim victims and 'burying' those of the Hindus so that 'both might be visited with eternal perdition'.[50] How relevant are such impressionistic issues for evaluating the Revolt of 1857 — in which manner and to what extent — can perhaps be gauged from some tentative attempt at understanding the nature of the great upheaval.

## Notes

1 Foreign Secret Cons., No. 14, 30 April 1858, N.A.I, cited in Sen, *Eighteen Fifty Seven*, p. 1.
2 *Ibid.*, p. 20.

3 Irfan Habib, 'Rashtriya Vidroha ki Kahani', Special Issue on 1857, *Naya Path*, No. 21, May 2007, p. 7.
4 Sen, *Eighteen Fifty Seven*, p. 47.
5 *Ibid.*, p. 21.
6 R. C. Majumdar, *The Sepoy Mutiny and the Revolt of 1857*, Firma K. L. Mukhopadhyay, Calcutta, 1963, p. 31.
7 Sen, *Eighteen Fifty Seven*, pp. 17–20.
8 Irfan Habib, 'The Coming of 1857', in SAHMAT, *Red the Earth That Year, That Year* . . . , New Delhi, 2007, p. 7.
9 Sen, *Eighteen Fifty Seven*, p. 40.
10 *Ibid.*, p. 41.
11 *Ibid.*, p. 43.
12 The address of the Prosecutor of Government, Major F. J. Harriott, Deputy Judge-Advocate General, 9 March 1858, the 21st Day of the Proceedings, reproduced in K. C. Yadav, ed., *Delhi in 1857*, Vol. I: *The Trial of Bahadur Shah*, Academic Press, Gurgaon, 1980, p. 351.
13 *Ibid.*, p. 352.
14 *Ibid.*, p. 353.
15 Gupta, *Lord William Bentinck in Madras*, p. 174.
16 Princes Mohiuddin and Muizuddin were assisted by an agent-cum-relation, Alauddin.
17 Maya Gupta, 'Vellore Mutiny, July 1806', in Maya Gupta and Amit Kumar Gupta (eds.), *Defying Death: Struggles against Imperialism and Feudalism*, Tulika, New Delhi, 2001, p. 31.
18 Gupta, *Lord William Bentinck in Madras*, p. 62.
19 *Ibid.*, p. 181.
20 S. A. Khan, *Sar-Kashi-i Zila 'Bijnor*, Agra, 1858, ed. Sharafat Husain Mirza (Delhi, 1964), p. 178, cited in Irfan Habib, 'Understanding 1857', in Sabyasachi Bhattacharya (ed.), *Rethinking 1857*, Orient Longman, New Delhi, 2007, p. 62.
21 Sen, *Eighteen Fifty Seven*, p. 59.
22 The deliberate destruction of official records and reports was widespread in most of the places under Meerut, Agra, Rohilkhand, Allahabad, Benares and Jhansi Divisions of the N.W.P. and Oudh. See Home/Rev. Proc., 1859 (January–December), No. 81, Fort William, 4 March 1859, pp. 149, 357–58 and 504–8, N.A.I.
23 Majumdar, *The Sepoy Mutiny and the Revolt of 1857*, p. 119.
24 Forsyth to Secy., Government of India, 27 June 1857, Foreign Dept. Secret Cons., No. 223, cited by Rudrangshu Mukherjee, 'Awadh in

Revolt', in Biswamoy Pati (ed.), *The 1857 Rebellion*, Oxford University Press, New Delhi, 2008, p. 28.
25 The List of Arms Surrendered, 16 December 1858, in *ibid.*, p. 228, fn. 44.
26 Chief of Staff to Edmonton, 26 June 1858, Foreign Dept. Secret Cons., No. 77, in *ibid.*, p. 228, fn. 42.
27 Roy, *The Politics of a Popular Uprising*, p. 22.
28 *Ibid.*, p. 225, fn. 121.
29 *Ibid.*, pp. 229–30.
30 *Ibid.*, p. 226.
31 *Ibid.*, p. 246.
32 Stokes, 'Traditional Elites in the Great Rebellion of 1857', in Biswamoy Pati (ed.) *The Rebellion of 1857*, p.196.
33 Stokes, *The Peasant and the Raj*, p. 188, fn. 7.
34 *Ibid.*, p. 200.
35 *Ibid.*
36 *Ibid.*, p. 213.
37 Majumdar, *The Sepoy Mutiny and the Revolt of 1857*, p. 122.
38 Waddington, Deputy Commissioner, Mandla, to Erskine, Commissioner, Saugor Division, Jubbalpore, 28 September 1857, in Raj and Sabherwal, *The First War of Independence: Documents of Jabalpur and Mandla*, p. 180.
39 Deputy Commissioner's Report, 2 November 1857, in *ibid.*, p. 67
40 Deputy Commissioner's Report, 15 November 1857, in *ibid.*, p. 100.
41 Deputy Commissioner's Report, 8 November 1857, in *ibid.*, p. 80.
42 Majumdar, *The Sepoy Mutiny and the Revolt of 1857*, pp. 141–43.
43 Sen, *Eighteen Fifty Seven*, p. 345.
44 Deepkanta Lahiri Choudhury does not, however, believe that the telegraph network helped the Companyraj much in India in 1857–58, since it was infrastructurally oriented to the colonial port city, leaving out most of the hinterlands, and 'completely' isolating the NWP and its capital, Agra, from Calcutta and Bombay. See Deepkanta Lahiri Choudhury, '"1857" and the Communication Crisis', in Sabyasachi Bhattacharya (ed.), *Rethinking 1857*, Orient Longman, New Delhi, 2007, p. 273.
45 Kaushik Roy, 'Structural Anatomy of Rebel Forces during the Great Mutiny of 1857–58: Equipment, Logistics and Recruitment Reconsidered', in Sabyasachi Bhattacharya (ed.), *Rethinking 1857*, pp. 287–88.
46 *Ibid.*, p. 294.

47 Majumdar, *The Sepoy Mutiny and the Revolt of 1857*, p. 204.
48 *Ibid.*, p. 215.
49 *Ibid.*
50 Col. G. B. Malleson, *History of the Indian Mutiny*, London, 1880, Vol. III, p. 515, cited in *ibid.*, p. 205.

# 6

# AGAINST QUALITATIVE CHANGE

As the civil war of 1857–58 rapidly progressed, both the warring parties — the Companyraj and the Indian rebels — appeared to have become increasingly incensed with each other. If one had gone berserk while opposing the oppressor, the other ran amok in wreaking vengeance on the opponent. The jingoist extremities that both sides thus displayed — despite some disparity between them in extent — was actually their collective response to an inflammable situation, and had not caused that situation; the jingoism was more its product or by-product than its direct initiator. Some of the components of jingoism, i.e., antagonism over racial superiority, conflict of religious faith and practice, or divergence of cultural approach, could, nevertheless, play some contributory role in bringing the war about. And, indeed, jingoism did seem to have indirectly spurred the conflict in 1857–58.

## I

Racial discrimination and disparagement of the coloured skin had been discernible to some degree throughout the Companyraj's in India — underneath, of course, an officious liberalist veneer. The European treatment of most of the natives of the country, barring a few aristocratic notables, was generally one of superiority, indifference and negligence bordering on total rejection. The common man and woman were often subjected by them to harassment and ridicule, and the masses to abuses and even physical violence on the slightest pretext. Self-respecting Indians invariably found the day-to-day European behaviour towards them to be extremely difficult to put up with, and their brewing resentment was bound to ventilate itself sometime or the other. In the case of the British Indian Army, the sepoys' discontentment over racial discrimination by the authorities in the conditions of service and their racial ill-treatment at the hands of the European soldiery contributed substantially to their turning into mutineers, and receiving the sympathy and support of the racially looked-down-upon general public — some of whom had little hesitation in joining an anti-British showdown.

The racial arrogance of the ruling categories went in concert with a conviction in the superiority of the religious faith they followed over all others in a land of multiple religiosities. Christianity and its aggressive disseminators during the Companyraj so alienated and upset the religious sensibilities of the common man and woman that they started suspecting every single act of the Government or its officials — howsoever innocuous — as deliberate attempts at Christianizing them. Simultaneously, however, the Church missionaries' offensive against all the major religious faiths in India, the stress that they laid on Christianity's monopoly of truth and virtues, and their boisterous campaign in its favour for rescuing the fallen and the doomed through conversion to Christianity, also effected a sort of anti-Christian joint front of all the Indian religionists. The coming into existence of a combination of religiosities, more significantly of the unity of Hindus and Muslims *vis-à-vis* an alien Christian power — apart from its being an oppressive imperialist one — added strength to the great Rising against the British. It might have helped in building up, around a certain intense localism or regional patriotism, the quasi-ideological and proto-nationalistic justification for encouraging the innocent commonalty to take up arms against the British in defence of 'Deen and Dharma'. One can hardly set aside in this connection what Rajat Kanta Ray saw in the meaning of the defence of 'Deen and Dharma', i.e., of the entire community of righteous people's collective way of life, or that of the brotherhood of the two principal religious communities (Muslims and Hindus) of a single land.[1] The artless people who upheld

'Deen and Dharma', and relied on their status-quoist standing, were bound to be startled and to feel insecure if they had suddenly to face on a noticeable scale the importation of forward-looking Western socio-political concepts and technological novelties. The tendency for them naturally would be to cling to their traditional ways as tightly as possible, and to harden their hostility towards the importers of Westernism. This was broadly what happened between the reforming governors generalship of Bentinck and Dalhousie, and every modernizing effort that was tried in that phase — be it in the sphere of education, the legal system, social uplift, or communication and transport — invited conversely and proportionately ill-informed popular resentment.

The resentment was particularly bitter when the common man and woman witnessed the emergence in their midst of a generation of English-educated, unbelieving, non-conformist and iconoclastic young people. They were outraged by the radicalist excesses of the Young Bengal movement, or the Derozians' utter contempt for conventional Indian society,[2] and believed these flamboyant greenhorns — the shock minority — to have been bred and nurtured surreptitiously by the British to sabotage the edifice of the Indian value system. Bentinck's and Mrs Bentinck's patronization of the Derozians and their appreciation of the Young Bengal proceedings in Calcutta, as well as their action of rewarding some of its Hindu College student activists,[3] for instance, might have raised strong popular apprehensions as to the corrupting ways of the British. This attitude backfired in a way, by engendering a modernist temper and the process of Westernization in India along Utilitarian lines, and appeared to push the general public to the ways of anti-Britishism and contribute to the creation of an environment of discontent against the Companyraj. It is in this context that one may perhaps appreciate a liberal British attempt at viewing the Great Rebellion as 'a last convulsive movement of protest against the coming of the West on the part of traditional India'.[4] The breaking into the open of a socio-cultural clash, the raising sky-high of the standard of Christianity and the deliberate downgrading of a subject race — all contributed to the average Indian commoner's disenchantment with the Companyraj, his or her willingness to lend ears to anti-British exhortations and even passively or actively side with those who dared to challenge British authority. In other words, these were the components on which the popular base of an upsurge could be built up, but these by themselves would not be likely to create a popular rebellion. For that, a rebellious thrust was essential, one that was occasioned and simultaneously backed up by the most numerous and self-conscious section of a populace. From among the ranks of the numerically overwhelming and socio-economically aggrieved and agitated multitudes of peasants marched out the mutinous sepoys, who heralded the commencement of the fiercest and the most widespread of the anti-imperialist outbreaks of its time.

As has already been observed in this study, the misapplication of the Ricardian Rent Theory by those who were *kisan*-phile in the Companyraj, and the resulting demand on land, proved ironically to be catastrophic for all peasant-proprietors — substantial and marginal. In the two decades prior to 1857–58, it resulted in mounting indebtedness, land mortgage, distress sale, ejectment, immiserization and destitution. In utter desperation, and in the face of a bleak situation, the peasant had no alternative but to take arms up against his direct, visible oppressors — an alien Government and its officials — the authorities. Its back against the wall, it was the peasantry who unleashed the propulsive force into the great Rising of 1857–58, and who was willing to carry it on to its finality. Eric Stokes almost hit the bulls-eye when he termed the Revolt that engulfed the Indian countryside (the NWP and beyond) 'a peasant revolt'.[5] His inference was very close to the target, but not quite: as noted earlier, apart from the innumerable active and passive participants in the Rising from the rural elites and the common masses in the countryside, there were many others from the urban and semi-urban centres who joined the fight and upheld its cause. More than a peasant rising, it was a popular anti-imperialist Revolt, the only one of its kind to threaten the very existence of the Companyraj in the subcontinent. Clearly, the initiative and the impulsion came from the peasantry of all varieties, of course with the nod of the respective caste and clan *beradari*s;[6] and they, by themselves, were quite capable of producing their own leaders through the baptism of insurgency, though not intellectually groomed for setting up political goals. Being conscious of the limitations of their world view, therefore, they did not, or dared not try to, become the arbiters of the Rising's destiny.

Rather, the peasants preferred to leave the crucial role of piloting the upsurge to the care of the competent and the worldly wise in rural society. And who could be more knowledgeable and capable in their eyes than those belonging to the higher, wealthier and more resourceful categories (the owners of estates, *taluk*s, *jagir*s and *zamindari*s and operators of rural credit)? Habituated to treat these powerfuls with deference, and despite their subjection to the feudal exploitation of the landed magnates and the *mahajani karbari*s (the extractors of irregular levies and exorbitant loan interest), the rebellious peasantry in northern and central India of the 1850s were still not as prepared to confront their internal social exploiters as they were to confront their external strangulators. In their semi-conscious preference for anti-imperialism to anti-feudalism, the peasant-rebels had by themselves — at the first flush of seizing the initiative — approached the rural elites and the country high-ups to take care of the Revolt's political and military directions. Many of the aristocratic notables and the landed luminaries naturally fell for the distinctive role that was offered to them on a platter, rightfully, by their reckoning, without having much idea, however, as to the basic qualities of leadership that a stormy, rebellious situation called for. Apart from the anger and hatred they nursed against the Companyraj for dispossessing and incapacitating them for decades, they had not planned or prepared themselves for a counter-attack on their tormentors or to unleash retribution on them in the future — even if a distant one. None of the feudal stalwarts had shown, in the entire length and breadth of the great Rising arena, any particular talent in conducting military affairs and giving political directives. Militarily, in comparison with some of their subordinates and junior partners like

Tantia Tope, Mehndi Hasan of Sultanpur and Daulat Singh Sangor (with a few exceptions in an ageing Kunwar Singh and a fumbling Rao Saheb), and politically in contrast with some of those in the second rung, for example, the demagogic Maulana Ahmadullah Shah, the diplomatically seasoned Azimullah Khan and an unperturbed Bakht Khan (barring such equivocal personages as Firoz Shah, Khan Bahadur Khan and Begum Hazrat Mahal), the leadership qualities were generally missing, often palpably. Only Rani Lakshmi Bai was credited popularly for combining some military virtue with political acumen, though there were not many tangible proofs of it in the whole proceedings, except of course her heroic military exploits and death in the battle area. The Rani's resolve not to allow her (and also all the Jhansiwallahs') beloved Jhansi to be annexed by the Companyraj (*Mera Jhansi nahin dungi* [I shall not give up my Jhansi]) was laudatory, and even stirring in terms of local patriotism. However, one can not but ponder a little more and ask oneself: which Jhansi was the Rani so passionately talking about — the one ruled by a Regent under the surveillance of an overbearing Companyraj, or the one to be ruled by a dynastically adopted dependant of the British authorities? And would that Jhansi — ruled in either of these ways — be looking backward towards the 18th century, or forward towards the 20th?

In the answer to this question lay the crux of the situation: the prospect or otherwise of both the unfolding great Revolt and its emerging political leadership. The tumult that had been taking place, and was being led, stood in effect for breaking the mid–19th-century status-quo — for struggling out of the Companyraj's stranglehold. It could not stand still thereafter, and had to move on — either retreating into the confluence of the Moghul and British regimes in a feudal Hindustan, or advancing on to a self-governing India within the British-led world capitalist system. Since striving hard to reach for the 20th century was infinitely more difficult than sliding habitually down to the 18th, aspirants to political leadership of the Rising needed to be endowed with some vision of its lasting effect, an awareness of the popular mind, and perhaps a certain world view.

## II

A world view is generally that by which thinking persons ought to examine the world around themselves and decide upon a course of action for its betterment, or even transformation. The more precise way of expressing such an approach is to ascribe to it the term ideology: a system of ideas and ideals for bringing in suitable changes in society and its political economy. As leaders of the Rising of 1857 at the height of their anti-imperialist confrontation, the *rajahs*, chiefs, *jagirdars/zamindars*, *talukdars* or the social elites could not have politically been bereft of some ideology, or unconcerned about its application in the course of the tumult. They must have kept before them the promises of the kind of society and the form of state or government they were striving to set up on the ruins of the Companyraj in India. One may possibly get an inkling of these, not so much by listening to the exhortations in the Rising's heroic hymnodies and folklores, as by referring to the jargonistically recorded numerous proclamations and advisories that its leaders had issued to the general public.

The emphasis of most of the declarations was on the sacred duty of the people of Hindustan to take up arms against the alien rule of an oppressive Christian power — to declare a religious war and make sacrifices for it: 'since the real purpose of this war is to save religion, let every Hindu and Mussalman render assistance to the utmost'.[7] What seems remarkable was the attempt at building a united front of the Indian religious faiths, especially of the Hindus and Muslims, with the fervent desire that 'all Hindoos and Mahommedans should be of one mind in this struggle'.[8] In the name of the Ganges, Tulsi and Saligram, as well as in the name of God and the Koran, the Hindus and Muslims were reminded that 'these English are the common enemy of both, that you unite in considering their slaughter extremely expedient, for by this alone will the lives and faiths of both be saved'.[9] It was considered 'indispensable for both the Hindoos and the Mahommedans to direct their united efforts to the extermination of the Christians — enemies of lives and faith'.[10] To maintain the cherished Hindu–Muslim unity, the leaders were willing to go even to the extent of prohibiting irritants to the practitioners of the opposite faith. It was declared that

> if the Hindus will come forward to slay the English, the Mahommedans will from that very day put a stop to the slaughter of cows, and those of them will not do so will be considered to have abjured the Koran, and such of them as will eat beef will be regarded as though they have eaten pork.[11]

In the season of Baquar Eid, before or after, anyone who stealthily slaughtered or sacrificed cow, calf or buffalo 'will be treated as enemy of the King and will be condemned to death'.[12] As events showed eventually, the rebels' attempt at forging a kind of populist religious unity did seem substantially to have worked out, despite perpetuating irrational practices.

In the affirmative footsteps of bringing Hindus and Muslims closer to each other, the rebel leaders of 1857 also proceeded quite methodically and in a balanced manner with the administering of their newly liberated territories. In spite of giving primacy to the interests of the landed aristocracy,[13] the creation of a central Court of Administration (*jalsa-i-intizam-i-fauzi wa mulki*), or the devising of a system of military-cum-civilian governance to deal with an emergency situation, speaks rather highly of some leadership ingenuity — comparable to the well-established Western practices. The Court was an 'appointed (or elected) Court of Ten', six from the military (two each from the Infantry, Cavalry and Artillery) and four from the civil side. One among these ten was chosen unanimously as the President, and another as Vice President, and all the members were senior in service, competent and experienced. However, seniority itself did not bar younger and capable persons from serving at the Court where all the important military and civil matters were discussed and decided upon. The acceptance of the decision and the issuance of the final order remained nevertheless in the hands of His Majesty the King-Emperor. Giving effect to the final order was left to the charge of the secretaries appointed in the Military and Civil Departments.[14] The entire mechanism for the making and implementing of decisions was rendered so full of deliberations by persons of competence and experience — and not by men merely of wealthier birth, superior position and higher social status — that it brought the process almost out of the feudal and medievalist fold and gave it an expert-oriented, specialized, modernist look. What was more, those who had been called upon to lead the Rising showed at times some concern for the lesser humanity, of 'guarding and protecting the people and the subjects, who were a unique trust placed in us by the Creator'.[15] Even the thought of protecting the 'ryot' [rayat], of remitting the 'ryot's one-fourth of the Revenue',[16] and very magnanimously of providing 'for subsistence of the indigent and poor' did cross their minds occasionally.[17]

But none of these sparks of altruism could actually detract from the aristocracy's and the elite's abhorrence for the 'contempt and disrespect' they suffered at the Companyraj's hands 'at the instance of', or on the complaints against them by the lower grades, such as the *chamar*s.[18] They could never forget that 'on the institution of suits by a common Ryot, a maid-servant, or a slave, the respectable Zamindars are summoned into the courts [of law of the British], arrested, put on gaol and disgraced'.[19] They could hardly erase the memory of the degradation their fellow *zamindar*s and landed magnates had to undergo in the Companyraj's courts, imprisoned or fined 'on the assertion' or on the accusations of the 'mean and the low[ly] people'.[20] That the *rayat* and the *zamindar* would stand in the same court of law made the British rule as 'savoury to the masses' as it did to the 'heaviest of oppressions to the elites'.[21] Antipathy against the British could and did override religious disparities, but not class contradictions, nor the disdain and hostility against the under-privileged and the unprivileged. In fact it was the safeguarding of their own privileges, their socio-economic and political advantages — and more importantly, how to protect and extend these — that dominated the elitist rebel leaders' line of thinking. This they longed to do by guiding the rebel regime to restore them to their former position, to reduce or remit their tax liabilities, and to pat their own backs by rewarding themselves for leading the rebellion. They declared that all the rent-free lands which had been resumed during the British rule, and on which revenue demand had been imposed thereon, should be 'restored and treated as *muafi* to the original holders and their heirs'.[22] Also, all the forfeited rent-paying lands of the landed magnates would be restored to them discounting 'the arrears for the period of disorders'.[23] If any *zamindar*, unjustly deprived of his lands by the English, joined the fight against the Companyraj, 'he would be restored to his Zamindaree and excused from paying one-fourth [concessionally fixed by the Badshahi Government] of the revenue'.[24] Those *zamindars* who sided with the Peshwa Nana Saheb against the Companyraj would 'receive a remission of the whole of the revenue for two years, and afterwards of four *anna*s in the rupee per annum for eight years'.[25] All the remissions were declared to have been granted for opposing the English, and the grantees would be required 'to furnish men at arms' when needed by the *Sarkar*.[26] Additionally as a reward for their 'meritorious service', the *zamindar*s, *talukdar*s and *malguzar*s would obtain 'a remission of 4 *anna*s in a rupee [perpetually] on account of the revenue payable to the Sarkar'.[27] There was also talk of conferring on them 'adequate reward in the shape of honour [titles] and riches' (jewellery, precious stones, a good amount of gold coins, etc.),[28] as well as of occupying 'those provinces . . . exclusively in the British possessions', and arranging for their 'distribution to such Chiefs' as were devoted to the cause of the Revolt.[29]

It was the avowed object of the Badshahi Government to make 'the dignity and honour of the Zamindars safe' and ensure 'every *Zamindar* to have absolute rule in his Zamindaree'.[30] They believed the *zamindar*s, *rajah*s, chiefs and aristocrats in general to have been sent by Providence 'into the world in [their] elevated position and given [them] dominion and Government'.[31] The Badshahi regime's great liking for the socio-politically powerful did not, it is held, preclude them altogether from sympathizing with the commoners, notably the *rayat*s. But unfortunately, and despite its pompous guarantee to commit 'neither disturbances nor oppressions on the ryots',[32] and tall talk of the *rayat*s' welfare, there was no trace of any attempt on its part at understanding — not to speak of ameliorating — the basic ills from which the peasantry had been suffering under feudal exploitation all through the ages. There was no mention of the *jagirdars*', *zamindars*' and the *talukdars*' own lands (*khas* and *sir*) which they got cultivated either through wage labour (*khetmajdoors*), or through tenants-at-will and sharecroppers, pressing down the wages to the minimum and raising up the rents (cash/produce) to the maximum (rack-renting). There was hardly any hint of concern at the *rayats*' suffering at the hands of their overbearing social superiors on account of the extractions of forced labour (*begar*), irregular levies (*abwab*s), *nazrana* and *salami*.

Clearly the rebel leaders of 1857–58 and the Badshahi regime were given in the main to reverting Hindustan to the Moghul and Maratha ways of sustaining the 18th-century set-up. The centrality of this point should not be lost sight of in the variety of ways the great Revolt has been marked out, i.e., the contagious mutiny of the sepoys, a furious protestation against the vituperative Christian missionaries, a subterranean contest between traditionalism and modernism, a crucially widespread rising of the peasantry, and a massive anti-imperialist struggle of the people. All these attempts at its depiction could be quite true in their own ways, and also not at variance with each other: a *kisan*-cum-sepoy outbreak in the traditional social circumstances was consistent with popular resistance to British rule. It might similarly be realistic that this epic struggle of the people had taken place amidst an 'extremely feudal' scenario,[33] dominated by the chiefs, princes, title-holders and landlords, and that its participating peasantry and commonalty — in the absence of adequate ideologues or messianic leaders — had little alternative to falling back upon their social superiors. After all, despite their exploitative role vis-à-vis the peasant masses, the landed high-ups, with some education and worldly wisdom, were commonly believed to have a certain understanding as to how places and peoples were governed, and how powers and forces used for government.[34] That these elites themselves had been harassed, humiliated and dispossessed by the Companyraj, and grown disgruntled and hostile, had rendered them — in the eyes of their social inferiors — more or less suitable for heading an anti-imperialist movement against the common enemy. Instances are far from rare in history where the ordinary public have strengthened the nobility's hands against an absolutist authority — the persecutor of them both.

The landed notables' assumption of a leadership role in a popular movement need not necessarily have turned it into a feudal one, unless they themselves were numerous and enjoyed a countless following. Their own participation in the great Rising, and the support base they commanded (including relatives, courtiers, dependants, retinues and servants) — though 'quite undeniable'[35] — had not perhaps been as decisive as they sometimes are made out to be. However, in characterizing a movement or a great Revolt like that of 1857–58, one should not be guided only by the number of participants, the categories they belonged to, and the relative strength and weaknesses of their combinations. More importantly, it is worth one's while to make out what they (the rebels and their leaders) were found in the ultimate analysis to have stood for, what they wanted to achieve, and also how they expected to perpetuate the achievement. The declarations and proclamations the rebels and their leaders issued from time to time — from Delhi, Lucknow, Kanpur, Allahabad, Jhansi, Bareilly and similar other places — do reveal their intention to revive and reactivate the feudal rule all over Hindustan. Irrespective of their participation, large or not so large, and their strength, imagined or real, the aristocrats and the landed magnates had succeeded in committing the entire movement, somewhat anachronistically, to the exclusive upholding of the feudal system. Of course, they were able to do it with the support of the sepoys, the peasantry and a large part of the general public who had not had a glimpse of any other system, or visualized another kind of world. To them, and to the *rajah*s, chiefs, *zamindar*s, *jagirdar*s and *talukdar*s, the destruction of the Companyraj meant the re-establishing of Badshahi rule (under the Moghul Emperor), retrieving the Moghul or later-Moghul *hukumat*, and restoring their brand of the feudal system. Despite the accretions that might, in the meantime, have crept into it, the feudal system and the social relations based on it appeared crucially to have determined the rebel military and political proceedings in 1857–58. If that indeed was true, then one cannot be in a position to accept the grandiose assertion that characterizing the Revolt as 'feudal' would not only be wrong but 'be unhistorical'.[36]

## III

The popular anti-imperialist feudal upsurge in India had blown over by the end of 1858, and the Companyraj managed to survive by a whisker. It had to do much more than survive: it had to get over the shock of the most unexpected, recover from an overall European demoralization in the colony, and most importantly, restore in full the comprehensive governance in India. Since the Indian empire was the 'boast' of Britain, and 'one of the chief sources' of British wealth, Benjamin Disraeli unequivocally discovered that 'our power and authority'[37] had to be put firmly on its feet again, without much loss of precious time. It could not be allowed to drift uncertainly in the fervent hope that someone like William Ewart Gladstone would prepare India 'for independence and self government', and to govern India 'for India', and practicably 'by India'.[38] Both the emerging heavyweights in the British Parliament (Gladstone in the Liberal opposition and Disraeli in the Tory Government) were thinking in the backdrop of 1857–58 of furthering the British cause in India as best they could, Gladstone by putting the country romantically under a Liberal apprenticeship, and Disraeli by skilfully balancing in the colony 'the conservative and reforming elements and obtain[ing] the advantages of special Indian knowledge and of English progressive opinion'.[39]

Both Disraeli and Gladstone were convinced, as the majority of British law-makers and public seemed to have become, that the Indian tumult urgently called for an immediate change of guard, for the replacement of the Companyraj by a full-fledged British Raj. Gladstone saw in the Crown's taking over the administration of India from the East India Company a promise for India's 'true progress'.[40] Disraeli was less subtle than Gladstone and condemned the East India Company's Government as 'cumbrous . . . divided and deficient in that clear and complete responsibility which is the sole and essential source of all efficient Governments'.[41] He thought that 'every disaster [like that of the Revolt of 1857] is practicable if there be an inefficient and negligent Government'.[42] He even took Parliament to task for being indifferent to the Companyraj's callous incompetence and felt that if it did not take any interest, 'time is not far distant when they [the Britons] will lose India'.[43] This they could hardly afford to do, and apart from the great prestige and the military and political advantage they enjoyed for being the rulers of India (and no one was aware of it more than the master strategist Disraeli himself), Disraeli knew that a considerable number of Britons had 'an instant and immediate [economic] interest' in India, to whom the safeguarding of India 'was an object of first necessity'.[44] The immediacy and primacy of British interest in India (and in such clarity for a Conservative leader!) was an economic one: 'the ample supplies of raw materials' that the manufacturers in Britain received from India and the large number of 'good customers' that the British manufactures succeeded in getting there. India as the massive source of raw materials, as well as an enormous market for manufactured goods, would not work at all 'unless they [the Indians] are well-governed'.[45]

The way out was to transfer as soon as possible the reins of governance from the East India Company's hands to the hands of the Crown. This was exactly what political stalwarts and policy-makers like Disraeli wanted, namely, to take away the power of administering India from the Court of Directors and the Board of Control and to give it to a Minister of the Crown (Secretary of State) assisted by a Council of specialists, and responsible to Parliament.[46] But in what manner would the Secretary of State in Council run the government of the Indian subcontinent to suit the overall British interest, and in which directions? Here also one could find the necessary clues in what Disraeli stood for, not because of his status as the sole author or the promulgator of a post-Revolt blueprint of work for British India, but because of his being a true precursor of 20th-century colonial interests and strategies. (It has not been possible in this study to pinpoint any single person or a group of persons, among the public men and ideologues of the time in Britain, who propounded a new colonial policy for India with the 1857–58 Revolt in view.) According to Disraeli, the British occupation of the Indian territories had invariably been backed up with solemn treaties by which they promised 'to respect the rights and privileges, the laws and customs, the property and religion of the people'.[47] He was opposed to the Companyraj flouting any of its treaty obligations to the Indian princes and rulers, and particularly disapproved of its negation of their practices of adoption and the doctrine of 'lapse'.[48] But what Disraeli disliked most was the Companyraj's obsession for bringing about 'change' in India, for imposing, in his view, Western principles and systems unqualifiedly[49] on a heterogeneous 'great country' of diverse population — different in race, religion and language. He famously announced that he would 'never seek to confer the greatest happiness upon the greatest numbers'.[50] 'If you select in your Indian Government', he asserted, 'Englishmen animated by exclusively English feelings, you expose yourselves to the danger of finding reckless innovations, introduced in ignorance of the manners, habits and laws of the various nations in India, then you must be prepared to meet disturbances and disaffection in that country'.[51] This Government policy of 'change', according to Disraeli, had altered and interfered with all aspects of life in India:

> laws, manners, customs and usages, political organization, the tenure of property, the religion of the people — everything in India has either been changed, or attempted to be changed, or there is a suspicion among the population that a desire for change exists on the part of the Government.[52]

Irrespective of the damages it had done to the British, Disraeli looked upon the Revolt of 1857 as an opportunity to inaugurate 'a new policy' in India — a typical neo-Toryist (termed sometimes as left-Toryist or popular-Toryist) policy of balance, continuity and moderation, balancing agriculture with manufacturing, stability with reformism, aristocracy with bourgeoisie and feudalism with imperialism (or, in sugarcoated terms, the political economy of the ruler and the ruled).

Feudalism, howsoever revised, and imperialism, however modernized, had an immense attraction for any Tory, even if he or she wished to be a popular left-winging one like Disraeli. Disraeli was known to have a sentimental attachment to feudalism, 'a hierarchical society based on mutual responsibility and mellowed by tradition'.[53] He also shared the conventional Tory belief in landed interests being 'the guarantee of the stability and greatness of a nation'.[54] Further, he had faith in the aristocracy's capability to be 'conscious of its social duties' and 'to unite the classes' separated by irresponsible self-interests.[55] As with the British aristocracy, Disraeli was appreciative of the leading role the Indian nobility had played as 'a traditional institution in conformity with the history of India'. He was clearly of the opinion that the landed aristocracy 'could provide the natural leadership to India, much better than the foreign-educated middleclass'.[56] The feudal elements in India, according to Disraeli and other Disraelians, therefore, deserved more kindly treatment than they had received from the anti-feudalists till 1857. It was time, in the opinion of the Disraelians, 'for reassuring the native princes . . . [that] their rights would be respected', and that they would have 'a prospect of better government from a responsible Minister of the Crown'.[57] It ought to be foregrounded, they felt, that 'the Queen of England is not a sovereign who will countenance the violation of treaties . . . disturb the settlement of property', and disrespect 'their laws, their usages, customs, and above all, their religions'.[58]

Simultaneously, with attempts at assuaging the feelings of the outraged feudal chiefs, the Disraelians had to commit themselves to strengthening the imperialist hold on India — to reinforcing Britain's commercial and manufacturing ties with India. The pattern seemed to have emerged from Disraeli's overall strategy in Britain, i.e., the Tory Party's efforts towards the ascendancy of the landed classes as well as coming nearer to business and commercial interests. His effort to fashion a successful practical Conservative policy was 'to give satisfaction to the claims of agricultural interest without alienating the commercial and manufacturing interest' that had already assumed economic, and in due course, political preponderance.[59] Over and above continuing with the buyers' monopoly of agricultural products and purchase of Indian handicrafts (a straightforward way of appropriating social surplus), Disraeli was aware, as has been previously noted, that industrialized Britain had to utilize the empire as its major source of raw materials as well as an ever-expanding market for its finished products. To enhance its resource producing capacity, and to increase its people's purchasing power, the Indian economy had to become regenerative and sustainable to fulfil the long-term needs of the industrial and commercial bourgeoisie of Britain. This in commonplace Disraelian style was to acknowledge that Britons had 'a positive and instant interest in the good government in India, because they can not have the people of India as good customers unless they are well-governed'.[60] Establishing 'good government' in India and ensuring the 'well-being of Indians'[61] had to be effected for taking good care of the goose that was laying golden eggs, even if it meant some concessions in terms of modernizing the governance, of course, in homeopathic doses. A balance must be maintained between 'the happiness of India' and 'the welfare, power and glory of Britain',[62] by catering to the needs of British industrialism and by bringing Indian feudalism closer to the authorities in India.

The urgency of mollifying the *rajah*s, chiefs, *jagirdar*s, *zamindar*s and *talukdar*s, or of making up with them as soon as the Rising was over, might not exactly have been felt by Disraeli and the Disraelians wholly out of their love for British justice, for righting any previous wrong, or for an innate Tory liking for aristocracy, its tradition and culture. It was also felt by the British — more strongly perhaps than they ever explicitly expressed — out of a dire sense of insecurity, an overwhelming fear of the recurrence of a similar disaster and a frantic desire for some insurance against it, preferably from within Indian society. British imperialism in India had little reason to feel insecure or threatened till 1857–58 by internal enemies and inimical conspiracies. They had gathered enough confidence, ability and experience to deal with such eventualities and to emerge successfully from them. What they had not faced before 1857–58 was, however, the rising of an inflamed people, the rush of menacing crowds, the fear of aggressive numbers — the confrontation with the hydra-headed monster. The terrifying images of the tumult of a people constantly haunted them, led them to suffer through daily nightmares and forced them to live in the psychosis of further popular outburst, of 'another revolt' or 'another mutiny' — in 'anxieties of colonial existence and the sense of its fragility'.[63] It was not Bahadur Shah 'Jafar', Nana Saheb, Rani Lakshmi Bai, Khan Bahadur Khan, Babu Kunwar Singh and company that the British were mortally afraid of, but the humble innumerables in march — it was the people in arms, the masses in action, that they shuddered to think of confronting. They had often observed such furious mobilizations of the mob to have been spearheaded by the local respectables and landed magnates, the chiefs and princes, the elites and aristocrats — spontaneously, or by persuasion. Those like Disraeli who considered the feudal elements to be the 'natural leaders' of Indian society would obviously have looked to them as the ones who could influence their followings, restrain and perhaps control them. Their surmise was more or less true, because the people, especially the peasantry, had hardly any other alternative — in the absence of their own ideology and ideologue — than to accept the guidance of their exploitative, expropriating social superiors. That the peasantry and the rebels followed the feudal superiors' lead, unreservedly or reservedly, was an important point for the British to take note of, and an incentive for winning over the leaders and using their influence to stem the tide of popular unrest in the future. This is precisely what the British thought they must do, and went about doing it in a decisive manner.

Post-Revolt British attempts at reconciliation with the feudal elements did not, however, make an impressive start, and the initiative that Governor General Lord Canning tried to take at the time of the Companyraj's recovery of Lucknow was far from satisfactory. Missing the policy implication in full, and therefore only feebly conciliatory, Canning's overture through the Oude Proclamation (drafted on 3 March and published on 14 March 1858) hardly contained the generous expression of British goodwill that was essential for winning over a hostile landed aristocracy and a disaffected Oudh people. It attempted to lay down the mode in which the British Government would 'deal with the Talookdars, Chiefs and Landowners of Oude and their followers', first by rewarding those who firmly stood by the authorities at their hour of crisis, confirming their sole, hereditary proprietorship over the lands they held under 'moderate assessment'; and then, by conferring 'a proportionate measure of reward and honour' on those loyalists whose proprietorship over holdings could be established 'to the satisfaction of the Government'; and lastly, and ominously, by confiscating all others' 'proprietary right in the soil' to the Government for disposal in a fitting manner.[64] This 'confiscation' decree relating to landlords of all kinds, and landlordism in general, was not only unprecedented but also thoroughly destructive of all intentions to restore peace and order and to win over landlords as a class. All the conquerors, when they succeeded in overcoming a resistance, usually excepted a small number of people as still deserving punishment, and graciously forgave all others. 'Clemence' Canning (acclaimed later for his mercifulness towards the 1857 rebels!) seemed to have opted for altogether a different principle, reserving a few as deserving of special favour, and condemning the great majority to the severest of punishment. The Oude Proclamation, as it stood in April and May 1857, was not acceptable to anyone who wanted normalcy to return to post-rebellion India — not to Indians, nor to the public men in Britain, nor the freshly chastened (at the public forums and in Parliament for mismanaging India in the recent past) Court of Directors, and not even to such subordinates as the outgoing Chief Commissioner of Oudh (Sir James Outram).[65] 'We can not but express to you our apprehension', stated the Court of Directors to the Governor General, 'that this degree of disinherison of a people will throw difficulties almost insurmountable on the way of re-establishment of peace'.[66] The Court felt that the British authority in India should rest upon the willing obedience of a 'contented' people, 'but there can not be contentment where there is general confiscation'. They, therefore, asked the Indian Government 'to mitigate in practice the stringent severity of the decree of confiscation you have issued against the landowners of Oude'.[67] The directive against 'indiscriminate dispossession' was reaffirmed by the Court on 18 May 1858, resulting in the Canning Government's relenting and modifying the Oude Proclamation to assure 'that any proprietor who now comes in and supports the Government, none of his lands will be confiscated and that his claims to the lands which he held before annexation [of Oudh] will be re-heard'.[68] Eventually the *talukdar*s got back some 22,543 villages in Oudh, and twenty-two of them were given the power of magistracy to exercise.[69]

The British policy of befriending feudal India had thus narrowly escaped an early disruption in Oudh, but fortunately for its advocates, there was no further occasion for looking back on it thereafter. Soon the *entente* between British imperialism and Indian feudalism was ceremoniously consummated on 1 November 1858 with the British Queen Victoria's Proclamation to the princes, chiefs and the people of India. The dominant pro-feudal nature of the Proclamation is borne out by the fact that, barring a few references to reassure the people of India in such matters as religious non-interference, equal treatment, and impartiality in Government appointments, irrespective of race and creed, it laid most of its emphasis on the favourable manner in which the chiefs, aristocrats and landed magnates must always be treated. The Proclamation addressed the princes, *rajah*s and other chieftains separately from the *zamindar*s, *talukdar*s and the large estate-holders. It promised the former group that 'all treaties and engagements made with them, by and under the authority of the Honourable East India Company are by us [the Crown] accepted and scrupulously maintained and we look for the like observance on their part'. The Proclamation went further by committing the Crown to respect 'the rights, dignity and honour of the native princes as our own', to desire that 'they, as well as our own subjects should enjoy that prosperity and that social advancement which can only be secured by internal peace and good government'.[70] The latter group had simultaneously been assured in the Proclamation of the fact that the Crown's Government 'know and respect the feelings of attachment with which the natives of India regard the lands inherited by them from their ancestors', and that they therefore 'desire to protect them in all rights connected therewith, subject to the equitable demands of the State'. Further, the Crown's Government agreed to ensure that 'generally in framing and administering the law, due regard be paid to the ancient rights, usages and customs of India'.[71] The Proclamation evidently sanctified and charted out the future British policy of ruling over India from 1858–59 onwards in partnership with the feudal elements, and allowed the feudal system to survive and get co-opted within the structure of British-Indian political economy. The same Governor General (now also the Viceroy) Lord Canning, who, while rewarding a few loyal landed dignitaries, had wanted to punish mercilessly the rest or the large majority of them, lost little time in changing his stance to fall in line with the proclaimed British-Indian policy, and started supporting enthusiastically the lords and overlords. 'It was against all reasons', he conceded, 'to attempt to govern a conquered country in which, under all changes of dynasty, feudalism had remained rooted, by obliterating the aristocracy or by maintaining it shorn of all authority'.[72]

## IV

The whimpering feudal order's return to the Indian political scenario with a bang, and that too, within one year of its defeat in the civil war of 1857–58, was one of the greatest ironies of the world's 19th-century history. The irony was multi-dimensional: at one level it was due to the bourgeoized British officials' alienating the very peasants whom they wanted to benefit through their campaign against feudalism; at another, it was due to the feudal exploiters' assumption of the leadership of the rising of exploited peasants; and at yet another level it was the result of the victorious imperialist rulers' making up with the vanquished feudal order, and laying the foundation of a long-standing partnership of the imperial and feudal exploiters of the Indian people. Obviously the partnership was bound to be unequal: it entailed that the imperialist rulers took the role of senior partners by having the subservient feudal elements as their juniors.

The partnership nevertheless appears to have been exposed to two handicaps, both because of the weakness of the junior partners' position. The first was that they, or the feudal elements, were considered by the British as the 'natural leaders' of Indian society — a standing that was gradually to be challenged by an emerging English-educated Indian middle class. Armed with Western learning, and drunk with the liberalist nationalist flow of ideas, its members were certain to force the feudal political and socio-cultural value system into a corner, and in due course to threaten it in the eyes of their countrymen. The second was what the British seemed to have overlooked, or thought it politic not to over-emphasize in the heat of the hour, namely, the nobility's and the aristocracy's lacking in inherent strength: their inability to protect themselves, not to speak of even feigning to protect the British, from their class enemies — the peasantry and the rural masses aroused in the course of time and in another situation. It would then be the turn of the senior partners to come to the rescue of their juniors, and nobody could have the foreboding of it better perhaps than the British authorities themselves. And yet they had no alternative to reclining on their rent-receiving aristocratic ally, for despite its vulnerabilities, it was in regular touch through land with the rural society, which their nebulous English-educated middle-class liberalists had not yet attempted to do. The liberalists — 'the microscopic minority'[73] — still had no intimate connections with the people, with the commonfolk, especially in the countryside. The post-rebellion British authorities needed confidence-boosting support from those who demonstrated some inkling of being in a position to influence and guide the people, in the rural sector in particular, and India's feudal order apparently was more suitably placed to provide this support than anybody else. In hindsight, the British Raj seemed to have decided wisely in 1858 to cultivate a feudal alliance; it stood them in good stead, through ups and downs, and served their imperial interests for about a century. Contrarily, of course, the alliance adversely affected not only the destiny of the various agrarian categories in India, but also the fortunes of all Indians in general — by wilfully allowing the feudal system to continue unabated, and consequently by obstructing, retarding and distorting the country's bourgeoizing process, or its commercial and industrial progress. India was thus pushed to pilot a hybrid colonial economy, or to emerge from the age of imperialism to inaugurate the age of 19th-century colonialism.

## Notes

1. Rajat Kanta Ray, *The Felt Community: Commonalty and Mentality before the Emergence of Indian Nationalism*, Oxford University Press, New Delhi, 2003, p. 358, fn. 28.
2. A youthful Eurasian teacher at Hindu College in Calcutta, Henry Louis Vivian Derozio (1809–31) generated by the early 1830s among the Indian youth a spirit of materialistic, patriotic rebellion against irrationalities, orthodoxies and social injustices. Known as the idol-breaking Young Bengal, his brilliant crop of students (the Derozians) caused consternation among the local conservatives and left a rich tradition of radicalism unparalleled in 19th-century India.
3. Rosselli, *Lord William Bentinck*, pp. 206–7.
4. Percival Spear, *A History of India*, Vol. 2, Penguin Books, 1968, p. 143.
5. Stokes, *The Peasant Armed*; C. A. Bayly, 'Eric Stokes and the Uprising of 1857', in Biswamoy Pati (ed.), *The 1857 Rebellion*, Oxford University Press, New Delhi, 2008, p. 211. Stokes, however, qualifies himself by using the term 'peasant' sociologically rather than by class categorization (meaning that the status, function and culture of a cultivating people could very well be different in various parts — anti-Government in one place and not so anti-Government in another). His position does not, however, invalidate the point that is being discussed in this study, namely, that all who till the land are peasants, and while some till land owned by themselves and pay land tax, a good number till land owned by others and do not pay land tax. In the event of an intolerably high increase in land tax, it must not only cause hardship directly to the tax-paying peasants, but also wholly expose the non-tax-paying peasants' acute vulnerability (for not owning land) under the cumulative economic pressure.

6 Following in Stokes's footsteps, some, not minding 'village mud on their academic boots' (Bayly, 'Eric Stokes and the Uprising of 1857', p. 211), showed an urgency for over-emphasizing the role of the *bhaicharas* (village-controlling caste/clan brotherhoods) in swinging peasant mobilization between loyalism and hostility, such as the Rajput and the Jat *beradaris*' opposition to the Companyraj at one locale and friendliness towards it at another, not because of what it had or had not done to them, but on account of their inter-caste/clan jealousies *vis-à-vis* each other. Does this elaboration of the rebellious peasantry's fragmentary and contradictory standing deserve more historical attention than their desperate bid for forging unity against the common opponent, building up solidarity among themselves, and trying hard to come out of the mire of age-old disparities, diversities and divergences?

7 Proclamation issued by Prince Mirza Muhammad Feroze Shah, 17 February 1858, in Iqbal Hussain (ed.), 'Proclamations of the Rebels of 1857', mimeograph, Indian Council of Historical Research, New Delhi, 2008, p. 6.

8 Delhi Proclamation, 11 May 1857, in *ibid.*, p. 21.

9 Proclamation al-Hilmullah wal Mulkuallah etc., 30 April 1858, and also Proclamation of Rani of Jhansi, in *ibid.*, pp. 25 and 131.

10 *Ibid.*, p. 150.

11 *Ibid.*, p. 29.

12 Proclamation of the Chief Commander of the Army, 28 July 1857, in *ibid.*, p. 19.

13 S. A. A. Rizvi and M. L. Bhargava (eds.), *Freedom Struggle in Uttar Pradesh, Source Material*, Vol. 1: *Eastern and Adjoining Districts, 1857–9*, Publications Bureau, Information Department, Lucknow, 1957, pp. 451–52, Plate No. 19 (translated).

14 Court of Administration, Delhi, original document in Urdu at N.A.I., Mutiny Papers, No. 57, serial Nos. 539–41, Rizvi and Bhargava, *Freedom Struggle in Uttar Pradesh*, pp. 419–21. The document is undated, but in all probability it was issued in July 1857.

15 Order of Prince Birjis Qadr, 4 July 1857, in Hussain, 'Proclamations of the Rebels of 1857', p. 2.

16 Proclamation by Hurdeo Sharma, given near Bheema Sunker, dated Bhadrapud, Shud 13, Suke 1779/1857, in *ibid.*, p. 104.

17 Proclamation of Birjis Qadr, found in Foreign Political Proc., 27 May 1859, Cons. No. 81, pp. 57–60, N.A.I., in *ibid.*, p. 153.

18 Proclamation of Birjis Qadr, Lucknow, 25 June 1858, in *ibid.*, p. 53. They had no doubt that the inferiority of the downgraded people (*mehtar*, *chamar*, *dhanuk* and *passi*) was religiously ordained and that they 'can not claim equality with others'. *Ibid.*, p. 52.
19 Proclamation of Prince Mirza Muhammad Feroze Shah, 25 August 1857, in *ibid.*, p. 87.
20 Azamgarh Proclamation, 8 October 1858, in *ibid.*, p. 109.
21 *The Friend of India*, 7 October 1858, cited in Rizvi and Bhargava, *Freedom Struggle in Uttar Pradesh*, p. 455.
22 Parwana addressed to the Tehsildars, 16 January 1858, in Hussain, 'Proclamations of the Rebels of 1857', p. 12.
23 Hukum Nama of General Bakht Khan, 12 July 1857, in *ibid.*, p. 24.
24 Proclamation, Prince Mirza Muhammad Feroze Shah, 28 August 1857, in *ibid.*, p. 88.
25 Proclamation issued by Sreemant Peshwa Bahadur (n.d.), in *ibid.*, p. 120.
26 Proclamation dated 11th Rajab 1274#/25 February 1858, in *ibid.*, p. 154.
27 Public notice of the Cutchery of the Civil Court of Nasifabad (Muhammad Ahmadullah Khan Sahib), March 1858, in *ibid.*, p. 13.
28 Proclamation of Birjis Qadr, May 1859, in *ibid.*, p. 153.
29 Circular letter addressed to the Chiefs of Bundelkhand on behalf of Maharaja Sreemant Peishwa, 2 January 1858, in *ibid.*, p. 56.
30 Proclamation of Prince Mirza Muhammad Feroze Shah, 28 August 1857, in *ibid.*, p. 87.
31 Proclamation, Al-Hilmuallah Dharam ki Fath ka Khut, 30 April 1858, in *ibid.*, p. 25.
32 Courtesy Mohammed Ashfaque Ali Khan, Mutiny Papers, Collection No. 60 in Urdu, Serial No. 760, undated, N.A.I.
33 Speech of Jawaharlal Nehru, Prime Minister of India, Delhi, 10 May 1957, in Jawaharlal Nehru, *Selected Works of Jawaharlal Nehru*, ed. Mushirul Hasan, second series, Vol. 39, Jawaharlal Nehru Memorial Fund, New Delhi, 2007, p. 7.
34 The masses were too uneducated to have known or understood what the *Delhi Urdu Akhbar* of 21 June 1857 blurted out in style for the educated — the 'Seize the Opportunity' slogan-mongering — without, of course, offering in actuality even the far cry of any political programme.
35 Habib, 'Understanding 1857', p. 637.
36 *Ibid.*, p. 64.
37 Disraeli's speech, House of Commons, 29 June 1857, *Hansard Parliamentary Debates*, third series, Vol. 146, pp. 533–40.

38 Gladstone Papers, Add. MSS. 44747, folio 180ff., British History, cited in Gopal, 'Gladstone and India', pp. 3–4.
39 Disraeli's speech as Chancellor of the Exchequer, House of Commons, 26 April 1858, *Hansard Parliamentary Debates*, third series, Vol. 149, p. 1666.
40 Gopal, 'Gladstone and India', p. 4.
41 Francis Edwin Fenner, 'Disraeli's Indian Policy', Ph.D. thesis, St. John's University, New York, 1966, p. 6.
42 Disraeli's speech, Questions and Answers, House of Commons, 29 June 1857, *Hansard Parliamentary Debates*, third series, Vol. 146, p. 540.
43 Fenner, 'Disraeli's Indian Policy', p. 70.
44 Disraeli's speech as Chancellor of the Exchequer, House of Commons, 26 April 1858, *Hansard Parliamentary Debates*, third series, Vol. 149, p. 1666.
45 *Ibid.*
46 The Council was to consist of fifteen members, of whom at least nine must have served in India for no less than ten years, and have left India not more than ten years before their appointment. The scheme in its entirety was incorporated into the Government of India Act (21 and 22 Vict. C. 106) that the British Parliament enacted on 2 August 1858.
47 Disraeli's speech in the House of Commons, cited in Fenner, 'Disraeli's Indian Policy', p. 73.
48 *Ibid.*, p. 33–34.
49 Disraeli did not think it was possible to force the institutions and standards of one society wholly upon another of totally different roots. *Ibid.*, p. 176.
50 *Ibid.*, p. 19.
51 Disraeli's speech as Chancellor of the Exchequer, House of Commons, 26 April 1858, *Hansard Parliamentary Debates*, Vol. 149, p. 1666.
52 Cited from *Hansard Parliamentary Debates*, Vol. 47, in Fenner, 'Disraeli's Indian Policy', p. 73–74.
53 *Ibid.*, p. 18.
54 Paul Smith, *Disraeli: A Brief Life*, Cambridge University Press, Cambridge, 1996, p. 5.
55 *Ibid.*, p. 113.
56 Fenner, 'Disraeli's Indian Policy', p. 169.
57 Speech of the Earl of Albermarle, House of Lords, 21 April 1858, *Hansard Parliamentary Debates*, Vol. 149, p. 1921–22.

58 *Hansard Parliamentary Debates*, Vol. 147, p. 478–79, cited in Fenner, 'Disraeli's Indian Policy', p. 75.
59 Smith, *Disraeli*, p. 118.
60 Disraeli's speech as Chancellor of the Exchequer, House of Commons, 26 April 1858, *Hansard Parliamentary Debates*, Vol. 149, p. 1667.
61 *Ibid.*
62 Fenner, 'Disraeli's Indian Policy', p. 89.
63 Indrani Sen, 'Memsahib's Madness', *Social Scientist*, Vol. 33, Nos. 5–6, May–June 2005, p. 37–38.
64 Oude Proclamation, 3 March 1858, Allahabad, House of Lords, P.P., 1858, Vol. 4, papers 101 and 104, p. 4–5.
65 Minute by Major General Sir James Outram, 17 August 1858, House of Commons, P.P., 1859, Vol. 18, paper 237.
66 Secret Committee, Court of Directors to the Gov. Gen. in Council, 19 April 1858, House of Lords, P.P., 1858, Vol. 4, papers 101 and 104.
67 *Ibid.*
68 Minute by Major General Sir James Outram, 17 August 1858, House of Commons, P.P., 1859, Vol. 18, paper 237.
69 S. Gopal, *British Policy in India, 1858–1905*, Cambridge University Press, Cambridge, 1965, p. 7.
70 House of Commons, P.P., 1859, paper 10, Session I, cited in Desika Char, *Readings in the Constitutional History of India*, p. 299.
71 *Ibid.*, p. 300.
72 Gopal, *British Policy in India*, p. 14.
73 Gov. Gen. Lord Dufferin's epithet, attributed to the participants in the Indian National Congress, and uttered at St. Andrew's Dinner in Calcutta in 1886. See Majumdar et al., *An Advanced History of India*, p. 894.

# POSTSCRIPT

The inauguration of a distinct phase of colonialism in India from 1857 to 1858, and the *entente* established between British imperial capitalism and Indian indigenous feudalism after being opposed in a bitter armed struggle, was perhaps unprecedented in the history of the modern world. No one had imagined that the domineering forces in any society might wilfully compromise with the declining, especially after the capitalist Industrial Revolution in Britain and the cataclysmic bourgeois revolution in France. The joint venture, or the partnership, that the foreign and native exploiters of Indians had brought about was so marvellous and ingenious that one would very necessarily look for some serious strategic calculations leading up to it — some theoretical justification for its being put into effect. The author of the present study has been aware, to some degree, of the significance of this mid–19th-century development in India for a while, and has tried to locate the ideological foundation of the *entente* — the lines of thinking on both the warring sides which enabled a hurried understanding and a consequent partnership of mutual benefit. However, his modest searches into some of the socio-economic and political literature of the time, and attempts at following the leads of speculative discourses thereafter, did not throw much light. He has tried to present the results of his labours here, articulated more or less on the lines of realpolitik — accounting for security, practicability and profitability considerations — under the polish and platitudes of good old Toryism, at best the neo-Toryism of Disraelian brand.

## POSTSCRIPT

Beneath their newly found fondness for industrialism and the ways of the English middle class, and a growing paternalist concern for workmen and the poor, the Tories remained as before devotees of the British royalty and faithful to the British aristocracy. Following their grasping of governmental power in Britain, crucially between February 1858 and June 1859, they could neither be wholly unsympathetic to the Indian feudal order, nor unmindful of its suitability to play any assigned role. Tory softness towards the aristocracy and landed magnates of India was encouraged by their suspicion that the tumultuous Indian Revolt was largely the product of the East India Company's mismanagement of Indian affairs, obsession with Westernizing Indian society, unnecessary tinkering with Indian values and systems of governance, and, above all, uncalled-for flouting of the prerogatives of Indian princes and chiefs. If the humiliated, neglected and cornered feudal elements felt like empathizing with the mutinous sepoys and other rebels, and even joining and leading them, it could hardly be considered incomprehensible. Moreover, these Indian aristocrats had themselves also suffered personal setbacks in the rebellion and were on the verge of losing their all in the civil war. For the British home authorities and their Tory helmsmen, an act of forgiving the Indian aristocracy and forgetting recent estrangement was apt to rebound to the credit of British pluck and chivalry.

Aristocratic chivalry, however, had little to do with the calculations of 19th-century imperialists, and highly seasoned British ones at that — they were anxious to retain Britain's hold over India, and to ensure the safety, security and exploitability of the British-Indian empire, especially after its re-conquest at great cost. Britain could not afford to conquer India again and again and live in perpetual fear of further rebellions and massive risings of the people. Apart from taking remedial governmental measures to deal with popular outbursts, tightening the security networks and reforming and reinforcing the armies, the British felt that they must simultaneously have some allies within Indian society in the vast countryside — from among those who seemed to enjoy social pre-eminence, and could make their voices heard and rally others if required. In the light of the Revolt's accentuation and waning in the rural areas surrounding the urban centres, no category of the Indian public appeared to be more worthy of a British offer of hands than the combination of princes, chiefs, landed magnates and landlords of various denominations. As had been witnessed by the British during the numerous popular risings against them in 1857–58, the feudal elements in India looked to be in a better position than all others to influence and exercise some control over common men and women in the localities where they held sway. It was the hostile commonalty that started scaring the authorities and the non-official Europeans most in 1858 — the foreboding that a rising of the frenzied, blood-thirsty mob may spread from one place to another.[1] The mob, or the mobilized rustic masses of people that spilled from villages to towns, was essentially rural-centred and likely therefore to be amenable to landlordist overtures. Consequently, the Indian aristocrats and landlords seemed to the British to be usefully available as social allies, and the best watch and ward to take care of any troubles brewing in the country's immense interior. Along with the advantages of a feudal alliance, the authorities must also have been aware of its disadvantages — the liability of having continually to stand by these allies and cover up the grave socio-economic contradiction between exploitative aristocratic landlordism and the exploited peasant masses. This contradiction, which had been known to anti-feudal British high-ups but was overshadowed by the impendency of a conflict of the rulers and the ruled, was bound to come to the forefront in due course after the Revolt. It was also likely to plague the Government and make it incumbent upon it to come to the rescue of its alliance partners in uncomfortable circumstances, and often for upholding unjust causes.

The real beneficiary from an unequal alliance with the victorious British imperialism was feudal India, consisting in those vanquished in the civil war. Its representatives were not only spared from the pre-1857 interference of the Companyraj into their affairs, but also felt relieved at the prospect of getting British support in dealing with peasant unrest and popular outcries. All the post-1857 years of British-Indian history were replete with occurrences in which the authorities had to impose themselves in favour of landed magnates and against agitating peasants by bending the laws, resorting to the use of force, and thrusting disagreeable settlements upon the aggrieved. The story was the same whenever the inhabitants in a prince's or chief's domain, including its peasantry, wanted redress for the wrongs they suffered, pleaded for relief from oppressive governance, and demanded — most audaciously, indeed — civil rights. They had invariably to face the unrelenting *durbar*, the unresponsive Resident or Political Agent, and the unsparing coercive machineries of both. With British backing following the formation of the *entente* in 1858, feudal economic and social exploitation as well as aristocratic contempt for the lesser humanity continued unabated, if not considerably boosted.

Having won the war, British imperialism naturally became the biggest gainer in 1858–59, and therefore able to be indulgent to its junior partner by allowing some part in the massive squeezing of the Indian people. Imperialist expropriation of social surplus in India continued through the rigorous collection of land tax and other forms of public revenue, as well as through unequal trading arrangements for the exportation of raw materials — agricultural, minerals and plantations (in much of which British capital was being invested) — and the monopolistic importation of finished metropolitan manufactures. Since the British liberalist initiative for bourgeoizing India, and linking it as a satellite of Britain in the world capitalist system, ran into difficulty in 1857–58, the imperialist keenness for industrializing India took a nose-dive. It gave way by sparing British capital from any future competition with emerging Indian capital, or the national bourgeoisie. Such avoidance of any healthy rivalry and competition was bound to affect adversely the growth of the Indian bourgeoisie and result in slowing down the process of capitalist development in India. Besides, if the safety and security of the Indian empire was believed in 1858–59 to be dependent on the *entente* with the landed aristocracy and landlords, then the feudal economic mechanism of the earlier times had to be safeguarded, even anachronistically sustained. It had to be allowed to function to the detriment of modern industrial capitalism, thus holding back the country's path of progress.

Once the socio-economic forward movement gets stunted, and its return to backwardness becomes both unnatural and untenable, some retardation and distortion are likely to set in. That is exactly what happened to India, and the effects showed up in the country's economic report-card of the mid-19th century. The growth of its total national income was believed to be slow, and the income per capita tended to be stagnant,[2] and that, too, despite a low rate (0.04 per cent) of population increase.[3] The industrial development of the country was half-hearted and halting, and capital formation, or internal savings for reinvestment in the economy, abysmally poor for a nation of India's potential surplus. The trend of the share of industry at such a low level of capital formation was so negligible that its proportion in non-agricultural machinery turned out to be minimal — only 1.92 per cent of the gross national product during 1901–13, and 1.78 per cent in 1914–16.[4] It is worth recalling here that a large part of India's total social surplus was being controlled in the latter half of the 19th century by the money-lenders and landlords,[5] and that the princes, big *zamindar*s, landlords and other intermediaries, including tenants-in-chief, appropriated nearly 20 per cent of the national income.[6] Indians' standard of living and facilities for life (health and education) were reported to be dwindling to their worst, and the overwhelming majority had no alternative but to depend upon inadequately productive and technologically archaic feudal agriculture. India's bane throughout turned out thereafter to be the hybridity of its economy — the perverse mix of capitalism and feudalism — to the comfort and convenience of the *entente*.

The economic stagnancy and underdevelopment which were thus being thrust upon India since 1858–59 seemed to foreshadow the evolvement of a distinct societal formation or sub-formation in the world, namely, colonialism. Colonialism did not come into operation the world over as a mode of production, but as a mechanism for appropriating social surplus which was produced in a colony under various modes. Several such methods of production and relations of production, as under feudalism, slavery and bondage, petty commodity manufacture, financial and commercial capital, as well as technologically advanced industrial capital, can somehow function together. Their co-existence, naturally grounded in subterranean tensions, may continue in a colonial country (like India) if the basic control of its political economy stays in the hands of metropolitan capital, exercised through colonial governance and worked out with the help of dependent and subservient social forces. The plurality would in effect mark the celebration of the multiple modes' social surplus absorptions in a colony, presided over by the dominant colonialist one.

Colonialism in India saw in the main the operation of two systems of production and social surplus accumulation: the commanding capitalist one and the persisting feudal other. Functioning together did curtail their scope and effectiveness, and brought some amount of distortion and retardation in both — heavily hampering the advancement of capitalism and slowly slackening the hold of feudalism. Whatever was the pace of progress or regress, the Indian people continued to suffer simultaneously from the two exploitative modes, and were subjected in consequence to seemingly never-ending handicap and underdevelopment. Since the co-existence of and co-ordination between the capitalist system and the feudal one was agreed upon and put into effect by the British Raj itself after the great Revolt, the author of the present study feels that the years 1858–59 should be recognized as the beginning of 19th-century colonialism in India. Not only India, this juncture also marked the very point to which the beginning, diversification and spread of colonialism throughout the world can be traced, wherever the Western powers were able to set up their colonies — in Asia and Africa in the main.

The Indian people eventually succeeded in attaining freedom from the British rule on 15 August 1947, but were unable to pull out of the crippling effects of colonialism. British capital was crucially in control of the Indian economy in the first decade after independence, and apparently remained so for some more years. In the very extensive agricultural sector, the situation was infinitely

# POSTSCRIPT

worse, and most Indians had to bear the heavy burden of landlordist exploitation practically through the rest of the 20th century.

Howsoever much it tried, as perhaps Sindbad the sailor did in *Tales from the Arabian Nights*, India could not shake off the unyielding 'old man' holding tightly on to its back.

## Notes

1. The typical British middle-class disdain for the violent mob, such as the 'Parisian mob' of Revolutionary France, has been reflected in Charles Dickens's famous novel, *A Tale of Two Cities*.
2. Raymond W. Goldsmith, *The Financial Development of India, 1860–1977*, Yale University Press, New Haven, 1983, p. 4.
3. N. Sinha, 'Demographic Trends', in V. B. Singh (ed.), *Economic History of India, 1857–1956*, Allied Publishers, Bombay, 1965, p. 104.
4. Goldsmith, *The Financial Development of India*, pp. 20 and 80.
5. Angus Maddison, *Class Structure and Economic Growth: India and Pakistan since the Moghuls*, George Allen & Unwin, London, 1971, p. 69.
6. Surendra J. Patel, 'Distribution of National Income in India', *Indian Economic Review*, Vol. 3, No. 1, 1956, cited in Chandra, *Essays on Colonialism*, p. 86.

# GLOSSARY

| | |
|---|---|
| *abwab* | irregular cesses on land |
| *amil* | a collector or farmer of revenue |
| *anna* | a unit of currency equivalent to 1/16th of a rupee |
| *atta* | wheat flour |
| *babu* | a term of respect and a usual title of a *zamindar* |
| *bandobast* | settlement or arrangement |
| *bania* | trader/shopkeeper, money-changer and money-lender |
| Baquar Eid | Muslim festival of sacrifices |
| *batta* | discount or premium |
| *bazaar* | a fixed marketplace |
| *begar* | forced and unpaid labour |
| *beradari* | of common descent, literally, brothers |
| *bhaichara* | brotherhood |
| *biswahdar* | under-proprietor |
| *chamar* | 'untouchable' caste, leather-tanners who handle dead animals |
| *corvée* | forced labour |
| *cutcherry* | a court or a public office |
| *dalal* | brokers, agents between buyers and sellers |
| *dhanuk* | a downtrodden community of bamboo basket-makers |

## GLOSSARY

| | |
|---|---|
| *diwani* | the office, jurisdiction and emoluments of a *diwan* — a minister or a chief officer of the State |
| *durbar* | princely court/authority |
| *faujdar* | the chief of police or magistrate in charge of a city or *taluk* under the Moghuls |
| *feringhee* | a European/a white man |
| *gadi* | a king's cushion or throne |
| *hat* | a market held on a fixed day |
| *havildar* | a sepoy non-commissioned officer |
| *hukumat* | a government or a region |
| *ijaradar* | undertaker of land tax collection/land revenue farmers |
| *inam* | rent-free lands |
| *istimrari* | a small feudal estate |
| *jagir/jagirdar* | assigned estate or village/revenue assignee or holder of villages or *jagir*s |
| *jama/jamma* | assessment |
| *jamadar* | a subaltern Indian officer in the army next in rank below the *subedar* |
| *jihad* | a holy war against infidels |
| *kafir* | the unbelievers, who do not accept the teachings of Muhammad |
| *kalapani* | the seas, transportation beyond the seas |
| *karbari* | an Indian ruler's minister or agent |
| *khas* | an estate directly under the Government's or the landed magnate's own management |
| *khetmajdoor* | agricultural labourer |
| *kisan* | a small farmer who tills land |
| *kulin* | a sub-division of Brahmins of the highest purity in their caste, and most covetable as sons-in-law |
| *lakhirajdar* | owners of rent-free land |
| *lambardari* | village controlled by powerful landholders (*lambardar*s) |

## GLOSSARY

| | |
|---|---|
| *madrasa* | Islamic schools or colleges teaching various subjects |
| *mahajans/mahajani* | money-lenders–cum–traders/money-lending |
| *mahal* | a unit of revenue assessment |
| *majdoor* | agricultural and industrial labour |
| *malguzar* | a person who pays revenue either to the Government or a *zamindar* as representatives of others |
| *mamlatdar* | revenue officer at the head of a *taluk*, subordinate to the Assistant Collector, who helps in revenue collection, receives and keeps the accounts of the *taluk*, and also enjoys lower magisterial powers |
| *maufidar* | holder of rent-free lands |
| *mauja* | village |
| *maulavi* | learned Muslims, well-versed in Islamic law |
| *mehtar* | 'untouchable' caste, sweepers or scavengers |
| *mohalla* | a ward of a town |
| *muafi* | land grant free of revenue |
| *musahib* | sycophants-cum-confidants |
| *nawab* | a person of high rank and formerly a governor of a province under the Moghul government |
| *nazrana* | a present or an offering from an inferior to a superior, from a tenant to a landlord |
| *pandit* | a learned man and a teacher |
| *pargana* | sub-division of a district |
| *passi* | 'untouchable' caste, pig rearers and toddy tappers |
| Patel | headman of a village, hereditary |
| *pathsala* | petty indigenous schools |
| *pattah* | lease deeds |
| *patwari* | village registrars and accountants |
| peon | foot soldier |
| *poligar* | subordinate feudal chiefs, or petty chieftains in south India, especially in the Carnatic, paying tribute or service to the paramount authority |

# GLOSSARY

| | |
|---|---|
| *praja mandal* | people's committee |
| *purbia* | persons from the eastern part of Bengal Presidency or from eastern Uttar Pradesh |
| purdah | veil, a custom for women to keep their faces and bodies covered from public observation |
| *raja/rajah* | king or prince |
| *rayat* | cultivator |
| *rayatwari* | system of direct settlement with *rayat*s |
| *salami* | a quit-rent or an amount paid by a freeholder to the landlord in lieu of services expected of him |
| *sanad* | documentary proof of rights conferred by the Government |
| *sans-culotte* | literally, 'without silk breeches', the proletariat in 18th-century France who joined the French Revolution of 1789 |
| *sati/suttee* | a Hindu wife who burns herself along with the corpse of her husband on the funeral pyre |
| sepoy | a solider (Indian) |
| *sir* | a name applied to the lands which are cultivated by the hereditary proprietors or *zamindar*s themselves, as their personal share, by employing in the main labourers on payment, or tenants-at-will |
| *sowar* | cavalryman |
| *subedar* | the chief Indian officer of a company of infantry |
| *taluk/talukdar* | an estate of several villages/the holders of estates with land revenue rights |
| *tehsil* | revenue district; local self-government centre between a district and villages |
| *tehsildar* | a revenue collector |
| *thakur* | Rajput estate-holders |
| *thuggee* | the practice of highway robbery after strangling the victims |
| *tol* | colleges for the study of Sanskrit under *pandit*s |
| *toofeer* | surplus |

# GLOSSARY

*tota*                  cartridge

*Vidhava Vivah*      *Marriage of Hindu Windows* (a work by Ishwar Chandra Vidyasagar)

*zamindar*           a landholder and a collector of revenue, removable under the Moghuls; the collector of revenue turned landed proprietor, holding land in return for payment of a fixed revenue to the Government

# BIBLIOGRAPHY

## Primary sources

### Government records

1. Land Revenue Records, 1830–37 and 1838–59
2. Proceedings, Home Department, Judicial, 1833–35 and 1857–67
3. Proceedings, Home Department, Revenue, 1857–67
4. Letters from the Court of Directors to the Governors General, 1837–58, and from the Governors General to the Court of Directors, 1852–53 and 1858–60
   — *National Archives of India, New Delhi*

5. Revenue Despatches, Court of Directors to the Governors General, 1830–58
6. Revenue Letters from the Governor General to the Court of Directors, 1830–58
7. Revenue Reports, North-Western Provinces, 1822–23, 1840 and 1850
8. Selections from the Revenue Records of the Government of North-Western Provinces, Vols. 1 and 2 of 1856, Calcutta; and 1873, Allahabad
9. Selections from the Educational Records of the Government of India, eds. H. Sharp and J. A. Richey, 1920–21, Vol. 2, Calcutta
   — *India Office Records, British Library, London*

# BIBLIOGRAPHY

## Private papers

1. Melville, Rolls 10 and 14
2. Dalhousie, Rolls 1645, 1672–76 and 1717
3. Wood, Rolls 2059–62
4. Trevelyan, Roll 1242
5. Bentinck, Rolls 1729, 1734–37 and 1739
    — Microfilms, Private Archives, National Archives of India, New Delhi

6. Mackenzie, MSS EUR F 140/142–43 and IOR/J/1/33–37 (1806)
7. Wingate, IOR/L/MIL/12/76–83/103
8. Campbell, MSS EUR 349/10
9. Wilson, MSS EUR 301/9
10. Auckland, MSS EUR 470/1
11. Elliot, MSS EUR D 310 and D 314
    — India Office Records, British Library, London

12. Bentham, 114/125–27, 131/448, 169/121, 002/307 and 017/202–6
    — Manuscript Section, University College London Library, London

## Parliamentary papers relating to the East Indies

1. 1837–38, House of Commons, Vol. 4
2. 1840, House of Commons, Vol. 37
3. 1852, House of Commons, Vol. 11
4. 1852–53, House of Commons, Vol. 75
5. 1856, House of Commons, Vol. 45
6. 1857, House of Commons, Vol. 29
7. 1857–58, House of Commons, Vol. 2
    — Library, National Archives of India, New Delhi

8. 1857–58, House of Commons, Vol. 43
9. 1852–53, House of Commons, Vol. 75
10. 1852, House of Lords, Vol. 11
11. 1859, House of Commons, Vol. 18

BIBLIOGRAPHY

12. 1857–58, House of Lords, Vol. 11
13. 1852–53, House of Commons, Vol. 27
— *India Office Records, British Library, London*

*Hansard parliamentary debates, third series*

1. 1857, Vols. 155 and 156 (Commons and Lords)
2. 1858, Vols. 154, 158 and 159 (Commons and Lords)
3. 1859, Vols. 152 and 154 (Commons and Lords)
4. 1860, Vol. 159 (Commons and Lords)
 — *Sarvepalli Gopal Room, National Archives of India, New Delhi*

5. 1860, Vols. 156, 157 and 158 (Commons and Lords)
 — *Parliament Library, New Delhi*

*Contemporaneous tracts and treatises*

Mill, J. S., *Memorandum of the Improvements in the Administration of India during the Last Thirty Years*, 1858, published anon.
— *India Office Records, Tract No. 790, British Library, London*

*Notes on the North-Western Provinces of India*, by a District Officer, W. H. Allen and Company, London, 1869 (2 copies).

Shakespeare, A., *Memoir on the Statistics of the North-Western Provinces of Bengal*, compiled from official documents, Baptist Mission, Calcutta, 1858.
— *National Library, Calcutta*

*Report on the Census of the North-Western Provinces*, 1853 (title page missing).
— *Asiatic Society Library, Calcutta*

Grant, Charles, *Observations on the State of Society among the Asiatic Subjects of Great Britain, Particularly with Respect to Morals; and on* the *Means of Improving It*, chiefly in 1792, London, privately printed in 1797.

— India Office Records, British Library, London

## Secondary sources

Ambirajan, S., *Classical Political Economy and British Policy in India*, Cambridge University Press, Cambridge, 1978.

Bayly, C. A., 'Eric Stokes and the Uprising of 1857', in Biswamoy Pati (ed.), *The 1857 Rebellion*, Oxford University Press, New Delhi, 2008.

Beaglehole, T. H., *Sir Thomas Munro and the Development of Administrative Policy in Madras, 1772–1818*, Cambridge University Press, London, 1966.

Bharti, Braham Datt, *Christians, Conversions and Abuse of Religions Freedom in India*, Erabooks, Vellore, 1980.

Bhattacharya, Sabyasachi (ed.), *Rethinking 1857*, Orient Longman, New Delhi, 2007.

Brown, Judith, *Modern India: Origins of an Indian Democracy*, Oxford University Press, Oxford, 1984.

Campbell, George, 'Essay on the Tenure of Land in India', in John Webb Probyn (ed.), *Systems of Land Tenure in Various Countries*, Cassell, Peter, Galpin and Co., London, 1876.

Capper, John, *The Three Presidencies of India: A History of the Rise and Progress of the British Indian Possessions*, Ingram, Cooke and Company, London, 1853 (reprinted in 1997 by Asian Educational Services, New Delhi).

Chandra, Bipan, *Essays on Colonialism*, Orient Blackswan, New Delhi, 2009.

Chaudhuri, S. B., *Civil Rebellion in the Indian Mutinies, 1857–59*, The World Press, Calcutta, 1957.

Checkland, S. G., *The Rise of Industrial Society in England, 1815–1885*, Longman, London, 1971.

Choudhury, Deepkanta Lahiri, '"1857" and the Communication Crisis', in Sabyasachi Bhattacharya (ed.), *Rethinking 1857*, Orient Longman, New Delhi, 2007.

Dalrymple, William, *The Last Moghul: The Fall of a Dynasty, Delhi, 1857*, Penguin/Viking, New Delhi, 2006.

Das, B. N., *History of Education in India*, Vol. 2, Dominant Publishers and Distributors, New Delhi, 2003.

Datta, K. K., *Reflections on the Mutiny*, University Press, Calcutta, 1967.
Datta, K. K., and V. A. Narain eds., *A Comprehensive History of India*, Vol. 11, People's Publishing House, New Delhi, 1985.
Daunton, M. J., *Progress and Poverty: An Economic and Social History of Britain, 1700–1850*, Oxford University Press, Oxford, 1995.
Desika Char, S. V. (ed.), *Readings in the Constitutional History of India, 1757–1947*, Oxford University Press, New Delhi, 1983.
Fenner, F. E., 'Disraeli's Indian Policy', Ph.D. thesis, St. John's University, New York, 1966.
Ghosh, Suresh Chandra, *Dalhousie in India, 1848–1856*, Munshiram Manoharlal, New Delhi, 1975.
——, *History of Education in Modern India, 1757–1986*, Orient Longman, New Delhi, 1995.
Godase, Vishnubhatta, *1857: The Real Story of the Great Uprising*, Harper Perennial, New Delhi, 2011.
Goldsmith, Raymond W., *The Financial Development of India, 1860–1977*, Yale University Press, New Haven, 1983.
Gopal, S., *British Policy in India, 1858–1905*, Cambridge University Press, Cambridge, 1965.
——, 'Gladstone and India', in Donovan Williams and E. Daniel Potts (eds.), *Essays in Indian History: In Honour of Cuthbert Collin Davis*, Asia Publishing House, Bombay, 1973.
Grossman, Henryk, 'The Evolutionist Revolt against Classical Economists in England — James Steuart, Richard Jones, Karl Marx', part II, *Journal of Political Economy*, Vol. 51, No. 6, December 1943.
Gupta, Maya, *Lord William Bentinck in Madras and the Vellore Mutiny, 1803–7*, Capital Publishers, New Delhi, 1986.
——, 'Vellore Mutiny, July 1806', in Maya Gupta and Amit Kumar Gupta (eds.), *Defying Death: Struggles against Imperialism and Feudalism*, Tulika, New Delhi, 2001.
Gupta, Sulekh Chandra, 'Agrarian Background and the 1857 Rebellion', *Enquiry*, No. 1, February 1959.
——. *Agrarian Relations and Early British Rule in India: A Case Study of Ceded and Conquered Provinces (Uttar Pradesh, 1801–1833)*, Asia Publishing House, New Delhi, 1963.
Habib, Irfan, *Essays in Indian History: Towards a Marxist Perception*, Tulika, New Delhi, 1995.
——, 'Understanding 1857', in Sabyasachi Bhattacharya (ed.), *Rethinking 1857*, Orient Longman, New Delhi, 2007.

——, 'Rashtriya Vidroha ki Kahani', Special Issue on 1857, *Naya Path*, No. 21, May 2007.

——, 'The Coming of 1857', in SAHMAT, *Red the Earth That Year, That Year . . .*, New Delhi, 2007.

Hibbert, Christopher, *The Great Mutiny: India, 1857*, Penguin Books, Allen Lane, London, 1980.

Hill, Christopher, *The Century of Revolution, 1603–1714*, Routledge, London and New York, 1980.

Hilton, Boyd, *A Mad, Bad and Dangerous People? England, 1783–1846*, Oxford University Press, New York, 2006.

Hobsbawm, E. J., *Industry and Empire: An Economic History of Britan since 1750*, Weidenfield and Nicolson, London, 1968.

Husain, Iqbal, Irfan Habib and Prabhat Patnaik, *Karl Marx on India*, Tulika, New Delhi, 2006.

Hussain, Iqbal (ed.), 'Proclamations of the Rebels of 1857', mimeograph, Indian Council of Historical Research, New Delhi, 2008.

Innes, Arthur D., *A Short History of the British in India*, Inter-India Publications, New Delhi, 1985.

Jones, Richard, *Literary Remains, Consisting of Lectures and Tracts on Political Economy of the Late Rev. Richard Jones*, ed. William Whewell, 1859 (reprinted by J. Murray, New York, 1964).

Joshi, P. C., *Rebellion: 1857*, National Book Trust, New Delhi, 2007.

Lefebvre, Georges, *The French Revolution*, Columbia University Press, New York, 1962.

Lucas, James Joseph, *History of the North India Christian Tract and Book Society, 1848–1934*, North India Christian Tract and Book Society, Allahabad, 1935.

Maddison, Angus, *Class Structures and Economic Growth: India and Pakistan since the Moghuls*, George Allen & Unwin, London, 1971.

Majumdar, R. C., *The Sepoy Mutiny and the Revolt of 1857*, Firma K. L. Mukhopadhyay, Calcutta, 1963.

Majumdar, R. C., H. C. Raychaudhuri and K. K. Datta, *An Advanced History of India*, Macmillan, London, 1950.

Majumdar, Shaswati (ed.), *Insurgent Sepoys: Europe Views the Revolt of 1857*, Routledge, New Delhi, 2011.

Malthus, T. R., *Principles of Political Economy Considered with a View to Their Practical Application*, Basil Blackwell, Oxford, 1951 [1836].

March, N. C., and R. P. Sturges, 'Malthus and Ricardo's Inductivist Critics', *Economica*, new series, Vol. 40, No. 160, November 1973.

## BIBLIOGRAPHY

Marshall, Alfred, *Principles of Economics*, Vol. 1, Macmillan and Co., London, 1890.

McCulloch, J. R., 'Revenue and Commerce in India', *Edinburgh Review*, March 1827.

Mill, J. S., *Principles of Political Economy*, ed. W. J. Ashley, Longmans, Green and Co., London, 1909.

Mill, James, *The History of British India*, 2nd edn, Vol. 2, London, 1820.

Miller, W. L., 'Richard Jones: A Case Study in Methodology', in Mark Blaugh (ed.), *Pioneers in Economics (18): Thomas Tooke (1774–1858), Montford Langfield (1802–1884) and Richard Jones (1790–1855)*, Edward Elgar, Aldershot, 1991.

———, 'Richard Jones's Contribution to the Theory of Rent', in Mark Blaugh (ed.), *Pioneers in Economics (18): Thomas Tooke (1774–1858), Montford Langfield (1802–1884) and Richard Jones (1790–1855)*, Edward Elgar, Aldershot, 1991.

Mishra, P. S., *The Revolt of 1857: Saugor and Nerbudda Territories*, Sharada Publishing House, New Delhi, 2001.

Moore, R. J., 'Composition of Wood's Education Despatch', *English Historical Review*, Vol. 80, 1965.

———, *Sir Charles Wood's Indian Policy, 1853–66*, Manchester University Press, Manchester, 1966.

Mukherjee, Rudrangshu, 'The Revolt of 1857 in the North-Western Provinces', in Barun De (ed.), *Essays in Honour of Professor S.C. Sarkar*, People's Publishing House, New Delhi, 1976.

———. *Awadh in Revolt, 1857–58*, Oxford University Press, New Delhi, 1984.

———, 'Awadh in Revolt', in Biswamoy Pati (ed.), *The 1857 Rebellion*, Oxford University Press, New Delhi, 2008.

Mukherji, Radhakumud, and R. C. Majumdar, 'Social Condition', in R. C. Majumdar (ed.), *The History and Culture of the Indian People*, Vol. 2: *The Age of Imperial Unity*, Bharatiya Vidya Bhavan, Bombay, 1968.

Mukherji, S. N., 'Educational Policy', in K. K. Datta and V. A. Narain (eds.), *A Comprehensive History of India*, Vol. 11, People's Publishing House, New Delhi, 1985.

Nehru, Jawaharlal, *Selected Works of Jawaharlal Nehru*, ed. Mushirul Hasan, 2nd series, Vol. 39, Jawaharlal Nehru Memorial Fund, New Delhi, 2006.

O'Gorman, Frank, *British Conservatism: Conservative Thought from Burke to Thatcher*, Addison-Wesley Lingman Limited, Boston, 1986.

## BIBLIOGRAPHY

Panigrahi, D. N., *Charles Metcalfe in India: Ideas and Administration, 1806–1835*, Munshiram Manoharlal, New Delhi, 1968.

Patel, Surendra J., 'Distribution of National Income in India', *Indian Economic Review*, Vol. 3, No. 1, 1956.

Pati, Biswamoy (ed.), *The Great Rebellion of 1857: Exploring Transgressions, Contests and Diversities*, Routledge, London, 2010.

Penner, Peter, and Dale Maclean (eds.), *The Rebel Bureaucrat: Frederick John Shore (1799–1837) as Critic of William Bentinck's India*, Chanakya Publications, New Delhi, 1983.

Price, Ralph B., 'The "New Political Economy" and British Economic Policy for India', *American Journal of Economics and Sociology*, Vol. 35, No. 4, October 1976.

Punjabi, K. L., *Bombay Land Revenue System*, Praja Bandhu Press, Ahmedabad, Broach, 1938.

Rahim, M. A., *Lord Dalhousie's Administration of the Conquered and Annexed States*, S. Chand, New Delhi, 1963.

Rag, Pankaj, and Geeta Sabherwal, *The First War of Independence: Documents of Jabalpur and Mandla*, Directorate of Archaeology, Archives and Museum, Madhya Pradesh, Bhopal, 2007.

Ray, Rajat Kanta, *The Felt Community: Commonalty and Mentality before the Emergence of Indian Nationalism*, Oxford University Press, New Delhi, 2003.

Ricardo, David, *An Essay on Profits*, John Murray, London, 1815.

——, *Principles of Political Economy and Taxation*, Everyman's Library Edition, London, 1949.

Rizvi, S. A. A., and M. L. Bhargava (eds.), *Freedom Struggle in Uttar Pradesh, Source Material*, Vol. I: *Eastern and Adjoining Districts, 1857–9*, Publications Bureau, Information Department, Lucknow, 1957.

Robertson, H. D., *District Duties during the Revolt in the North-Western Provinces of India in 1857*, London, 1859.

Rosselli, John, *Lord William Bentinck: The Making of a Liberal Imperialist, 1774–1839*, Thomson Press, New Delhi, 1974.

Roy, Kaushik, 'Structural Anatomy of Rebel Forces during the Great Mutiny of 1857–58: Equipment, Logistics and Recruitment Reconsidered', in Sabyasachi Bhattacharya (ed.), *Rethinking 1857*, Orient Longman, New Delhi, 2007.

Roy, Tapti, *The Politics of a Popular Uprising: Bundelkhand in 1857*, Oxford University Press, New Delhi, 1994.

——, *Raj of the Rani*, Penguin, New Delhi, 2006.

# BIBLIOGRAPHY

Rude, George, *The French Revolution*, Weidenfeld and Nicolson, London, 1988.

Saha, Panchanan, *1857 Revolt: British Response*, Biswabiksha, Calcutta, 2008.

Sen, Indrani, 'Memsahib's Madness', *Social Scientist*, Vol. 33, Nos. 5–6, May–June 2005.

Sen, Surendranath, *Eighteen Fifty Seven*, Publications Division, Government of India, New Delhi, 1957.

Sengupta, K. P., *Christian Missionaries in Bengal (1793–1833)*, Firma K. L. Mukhopadhyay, Calcutta, 1971.

Sengupta, Subodh Chandra (ch. ed.), *Samsad Bangali Charitrabhidhan*, Vol. 2, Sahitya Samsad, Calcutta, 1988.

Sharma, Raj Bahadur, *Christian Missions in North India, 1813–1913: A Case Study of Meerut Division and Dehra Dun District*, Mittal Publishers, New Delhi, 1988.

Sharp, H., and J. A. Richey (eds.), *Selections from the Educational Records of the Government of India*, Vol. 2, Government of India, Calcutta, 1920–22.

Sinha, N., 'Demographic Trends', in V. B. Singh (ed.), *Economic History of India, 1857–1956*, Allied Publishers, Bombay, 1965.

Smith, Paul, *Disraeli: A Brief Life*, Cambridge University Press, Cambridge, 1966.

Snell, K. D. M., *Annals of Labouring Poor: Social Change and Agrarian England, 1660–1900*, Cambridge University, Leicester, 1985.

Spear, Percival, *A History of India*, Vol. 2, Penguin Books, London, 1968.

Stokes, Eric, *The English Utilitarians and India*, Clarendon Press, Oxford, 1959.

———, 'Traditional Elites in the Great Rebellion of 1857: Some Aspects of Rural Revolt in the Upper and Central Doab', in Edmund Leach and S. N. Mukherjee (eds.), *Elites in South Asia*, Cambridge University Press, Cambridge, 1970.

———, *The Peasant and the Raj: Studies in Agrarian Society and Peasant Rebellion in Colonial India*, Cambridge University Press, Cambridge, 1978.

———, *The Peasant Armed: The Indian Revolt of 1857*, Clarendon Press, Oxford, 1986.

Thapar, Romila, 'In History', in Andrea Major (ed.), *Sati: A Historical Anthology*, Oxford University Press, New Delhi, 2007.

Thompson, F. M. L., *English Landed Society in the Nineteenth Century*, Routledge and Kegan Paul, London, 1963.

## BIBLIOGRAPHY

Verelst, Harry, *A View of the Rise, Progress and Present State of the English Government in Bengal*, Nourse, London, 1772.

Ward, J. T. (ed.), *Popular Movements, c. 1830–1850*, Macmillan, London, 1970.

Webster, John C. B., *Christian Community and Change in 19th Century North India*, Macmillan, New Delhi, 1976.

Wood, Ellen Meiksins, *The Origin of Capitalism: A Longer View*, Verso, London, 2002.

Yadav, K. C. *The Revolt of 1857 in Haryana*, Manohar, New Delhi, 1977.

—— (ed.), *Delhi in 1857*, Vol. I: *The Trial of Bahadur Shah*, Academic Press, Gurgaon, 1980.

Yechuri, Sitaram (ed.), *The Great Revolt: A Left Appraisal*, Peoples Democracy, New Delhi, 2008.

# INDEX

absolute rule 46, 149
absolutism 12
Anglicist system of education 20
anti-British camp 128
anti-Britishism 142
anti-feudalism 46, 144
anti-feudal policy-makers 111
anti-imperialism 144
anti-*thuggee* campaign 32

*badshahi lakhirajdar*s' 61
Badshahi regime 149, 150
Benthamite doctrine of jurisprudence 15
Bentinck, Lord William 13–15, 19–20, 24, 28–9, 32–5, 39–45, 49–50, 58, 60, 68–9, 84–7, 91, 93, 112, 137, 142, 162, 182, 185, 188
*beradari*s 144, 163
'Black Act' of 1836 15
'Bloodless' or 'Glorious' Revolution 47
bourgeois empowerment, Revolutionary France 78
bourgeoisie 3–5, 7–9, 11, 46–9, 80, 154, 156, 170
bourgeoization: Benthamite intellectual movement 10; bourgeois development in India 10; Evangelicals and the Utilitarians 11; feudal social structure 10; ideologues 10; legal codes, Macaulay 14; reforms 14
Brahmo Samaj 31
British revenue assessments 104
British victory 135

Canning, Lord 24, 32, 157–60
capitalist farmers, development of 81, 102–3, 110
capitalization of agriculture, process of 98
'change,' policy of 154
Charter Act of 1813 18, 24
Charter Act of 1833 15, 18, 24
child widows 31
Christianity: and Christianizing 141; missionaries, proselytizing 127
Christian nation 127
Civil War (1642), Britain 47
'Clemence' Canning 158
commercialization 52
Companyraj 13; beginning of 103; courts 148; and rebels, disparities 134; supporters 125; taxation policy 99
co-ordinated system (Wood) 23
Cornwallis, Charles 15, 28, 48–50, 54, 75

# INDEX

Dalhousie, Lord 13–14, 16, 21–2, 24–6, 29–33, 35–40, 63–5, 119, 142
decree of confiscation 159
'Deen and Dharma,' defence of 141
despotism 10, 49, 50
Dharma Sabha 31
Diamond Harbour 37

education: Anglicist system of 20; co-ordinated system (Wood) 23; disadvantages 27; English medium 17; English-vernacular school system 22; female 23, 26–7; filtration theory 20; girls' schools 26–7; medium of instruction 18–19; missionary activities 25; reorientation, Macaulay 16; secular 23; Utilitarians 11; vernacular education 21; Western medical learning 39
electric telegraph 37–9
Enfield rifles, greasing on cartridges 120
English education 20; and educational institutions 128; English-educated people 142; vernacular school system 22
European Christian Reformation 11

farmers' rents 101
farms: assessment 81; 'gross produce' principle 82; 'net produce' criterion 82
female education 23, 26–7
female infanticide 29–30, 33, 128
feudal alliance 161, 169
feudalism: agricultural improvements 52; bourgeoisie 46–9; Civil War (1642), Britain 47; commercialization 52; despotism 49–50; Industrial Revolution 47–8; Industrial Revolution in Britain 47; nobility and church, domination 46;

nobility, military character 47; permanent *zamindari* settlement 50–1; *rayatwari* settlement 51; Whig line 50; *zamindar*s' quasi-legal powers 50
filtration theory 20
French Revolution of 1789 46
funds, allocation of 118

General Criminal Law of India Act XLV 16
girls' schools 26
governance: absolute authority 12; absolutism 12; Bentham's view 12
Great India Peninsula Railway Company 36
'gross produce' principle 82

Hardinge, Lord 13, 20, 32
Hindu–Muslim unity 146–7
Hindu Widows Remarriage Act 32

ideology 146
*ijaradar*s 53–4
India's 'true progress' 152; befriending feudal India, policy of 159; buyers' monopoly of agricultural products 156; 'Clemence' Canning 158; decree of confiscation 159; feudal alliance 161; good government, establishing 156; India, source of raw materials 153, 156; natural leaders' of Indian society 157, 161; neo-Toryist policy 154; Oude Proclamation 157–8; partnership 160; policy of 'change' 154; post-Revolt work, British India 153
Indo-Western intellectual fusion 27
industrial capitalism 3, 7, 48, 171
Industrial Revolution 7–9; bourgeoisie in Britain 9; in Britain 47; chemical and engineering 8; economic

192

# INDEX

relationship 8; impact 7–9; mass production 8; technological inventions 7

Jafar, Bahadur Shah 121, 124, 157
*jagirdar*s 53–5
*jagir*s 53, 64, 144
Jhansi, annexation of 64
jingoism 140
jingoist extremities 140

*kisan*-cum-sepoy outbreak 150
*kulin*s 31

Ladies' Society for Native Female Education 26
*lakhirajdari* claims 61
*lakhiraj*, issue of 60–1
land administration 74, 77; free labour or *begar* 74; *jagirdari-zamindari-talukdari* intermediaries 77; land tax 77; Permanent Settlement (Cornwallis) 75, 77–8; tenants and cultivators 74
land alienation, rise in 106, 127
land grants 55
land settlements, annexation of Jhansi 64
land transfers 106–7
'lawless' Gujars 129
law of rent in 1815 (Malthus) 78
leaders' of Indian society 157, 161
legal codes, Macaulay 14
liberalists 161

Macaulay's Penal Code 15–16
Mackenziean settlement 84
Madras Railway Company 36
*mahajani karbari*s 144
*mahal*, rental value 86
marriage: child 31; widow remarriage 31, 33, 128
Meriah rite 32, 33
Metcalfe, Charles 51

Minto, Lord 28
missionary activities 25

Napoleonic Code Penale 15
*Narrative of the Escape from Nowgong to Banda and Nagode* 130
neo-Toryist policy 154–5
'net produce' criterion 82, 84, 90; intermediaries, elimination of 87; Mackenziean settlement 84; *mahal*, rental value 86–7; Pringle's principles 85; proprietorship, NWP 88; Regulation IX of 1833 86; Regulation VII of 1822 83, 85, 86; soil, classifying 91; Wingate-Goldsmid, survey and settlement 91
nobility and church, domination 46

Orientalists 17, 18, 19
Oude Proclamation 157–9

*Parashara Samhita* 31
'parmonium' 12
patriotism 141, 145
peasantry: anti-feudal policy-makers 111; capitalization of agriculture, process of 98; Classical Rent Theory (*see* Ricardian Rent Theory); collection of land revenue 95; immobility of labour 99; land transfers 106–7; money-lenders and businessmen 107; from murder to suicide 109; peasant indebtedness 106; peasant protest 109; in pre-capitalist India 111; *rayat*s and peasants 111; refusal to cultivate land 109; rise in land alienation 106; settlement officers', determination of assessment 97; settling tax arrears 95; suicide, rate of 110; survey and settlement operation 96; system

# INDEX

of 'rewards' 96; taxation policy, Companyraj's 99; tendencies of over-assessment 98; *zamindari* exactions 108
peasants' rents 101
pensions 2, 30, 57, 60, 64, 118, 123, 126
Permanent Settlement (Cornwallis), Bengal 49–52, 62, 75, 77–8
*poligar* opposition 125
political economy, notions of 99
postage, uniformity of 38–9
post-Industrial Revolution phase 77
Post Office Act 38
post-Revolt work, British India 153
poverty 82
preaching in chapels 25
Pringle's principles 85

racial discrimination: anti-Britishism 142; Christianity and Christianizing 141; defence of 'Deen and Dharma' 141; English-educated people 142; harassment and ridicule 140; patriotism 145; Rising of 1857–58 143; social superiors 150
'railway mania' in Britain 35
railways, introduction of 128
Rani Lakshmi Bai 64, 131, 145, 157
*rayat*s and peasants 111
*rayatwari*: principles, tenants and cultivators 76; settlement 51, 75–6, 78
Regulation IX of 1833 86
Regulation VII of 1822 83, 85, 86
rent, definition 78
rent-free tenures, settlement of 59
Rent Theory: direct revenue settlement, Bombay 76; free labour or *begar* 74; *jagirdari-zamindari-talukdari* intermediaries 77; land administration 74, 77; land tax 77; law of rent in 1815 (Malthus) 78; Permanent Settlement (Cornwallis) 75, 77–8; *rayatwari* principles, tenants and cultivators 76; Ricardian theory (*see* Ricardian Rent Theory); scientific land taxation system 80; tenants and cultivators 74; wage labour 80; yeomen-cum-capitalist farmers 81; *zamindari* 'injustice' 77
retaliation, acts of 135
Revolt of 1857 64; acts of retaliation 135; aftermath 136; allocation of funds 118; assaults and retaliatory actions 135; Bahadur Shah 'Jafar' 121, 124, 157; British victory 135; Companyraj's supporters 125; declarations and proclamations the rebels 151; disparities, Companyraj and the rebels 134; Enfield rifles, greasing on cartridges 123–4, 134; greasing on the cartridges 120; hesitation in joining 131, 141; hym nodies and folklores 146; *kisan*-cum-sepoy outbreak 150; *kisan*s-turned-sepoys 132; in Meerut 129; participation 151; peasantry's hierarchical order 123; peasants's opposition 129–31; pledge of religious non-interference 120; racial divide in the army 118; recovery of Delhi 133; reinforcement of 60,000 British soldiers 133; sepoy's grievances 118; setback 123; superstitious religiosity 119, 123; towns 132
reward and honours 149
rewards, system of 96
Ricardian Rent Theory 99, 127, 143; beginning of Companyraj 103; British revenue assessments

# INDEX

104; competition among tenants for land 101–2; decline in prices of grains 104; development of capitalist farmers 103; in England and European countries 99; farmers' rents and peasants' rents 100; and India 103, 111; land revenue settlements, comparison 105–6; mechanism of 'transfer' 100; objections, methodological/analytical/epistemic 100–1; political economy, notions of 99; pre-Revolt with post-Revolt revenue, comparison 104–5; 'ryot' tenure 101; taxation strategy 102; theory-based assessments 103
Rising of 1857–58 143
Roy, Raja Ram Mohan 28
'ryot' tenure 101

Sale Law 60, 95
*sati*: banning of 29; Indian women 27; practice of 28; threat of force 29
scientific land taxation system 80
settlements, land: annexation of Jhansi 64; *badshahi lakhirajdars*' 61; issue of *lakhiraj* 61; *jagirdar*s and *zamindar*s 55–5; *lakhirajdari* claims 61; land grants 55; 'lapsing' of succession 63–4; pensions 57; rent-free tenures, settlement of 59; Revolt (1857) 64–7; Sale Law 60; *talukdari* issue 56–7; *talukdari* rights, loss of 58–9; *talukdar*s and *ijaradar*s 54
slavery: abolition 33; and bondage 172; and superstition 14
social abuses 128
social superiors 150, 157

soil, classifying 91
*subedar* 118, 134
Suez Canal project 34
suicide, rate of 109–10
superstitious religiosity 119, 123

*talukdari*: issue 56–7; rights, loss of 58–9
*talukdar*s 54
Tattva Bodhini Sabha 31
taxation strategy 102
telegraph 33, 37–9, 133
*thuggee*s, cult of 32
traditionalism and modernism 150
'transfer,' mechanism of 100
transport, system of 35; Grand Trunk Road 34, 35, 37; lines of communication 37; 'railway mania' 35; railways 33, 35–7, 39; roadways 33–5; sea-borne steam navigation 34; steamer transport 34; telegraph 37

Vellore mutiny of July 1806 123–4
vernacular education 21
Vidyasagar, Pandit Ishwar Chandra 27

wage labour 80
Wellesley, Lord 28, 50
Western medical learning 39
Whig line 50
widow remarriage 31, 33, 128
Wingate-Goldsmid, survey and settlement 91
Wood's Despatch 22

yeomen-cum-capitalist farmers 81

*zamindari*: exactions 108; injustice 77; quasi-legal powers 50; settlement 49